Science and the Paranormal

Science and the Paranormal

Altered States of Reality

Arthur J. Ellison

Foreword by David Fontana

Floris Books

First published in 2002 by Floris Books

© 2002 Estate of Arthur J. Ellison

British Library CIP Data available

ISBN 0-86315-368-2

Printed in Great Britain
by J W Arrowsmith, Bristol

Contents

Foreword

This is a truly remarkable book by a truly remarkable man. It is a remarkable book because it succeeds in doing four things, rarely attempted in any previous publication on the paranormal (to use the popular term). Firstly it gives a review of the evidence for the existence of paranormal abilities across a wide range of fields. Secondly it draws upon the author's personal experience in studying these abilities in himself instead of relying only upon observing others. Thirdly it gives practical guidance on how the reader can attempt to develop similar abilities for him or herself. And fourthly it presents a coherent model to explain the paranormal and to set it within the context of what we know of science and of the human mind.

And its author, the late Arthur Ellison, was a remarkable man by virtue both of his scholarship and distinction as a leading electrical and electronic engineer (he was Emeritus Professor and Head of Department at the City University in London) and his extraordinary courage and integrity in lecturing and writing on the paranormal. At a time when most orthodox scientists still regard the existence of paranormal abilities with extreme scepticism and view those who champion them with deep suspicion, Arthur Ellison spoke our fearlessly for what he knew to be true. For Arthur, after half a century and more of detailed investigation — much of it carried out alongside but without prejudice to his heavy commitments as an internationally respected and influential engineer — was in no doubt not only that paranormal abilities exist, but that they can be demonstrated and observed using the strict protocols of modern science.

Thus *Science and the Paranormal* is a book that deserves to be read by scientists as well as by interested laymen and women. It challenges many of the basic assumptions that for too long have been allowed to underpin modern science and the materialist-reductionist philosophy with which it is associated, and makes clear that the world is a much more mysterious — and exciting — place than materialism would have us believe. I use the word 'exciting' advisedly, for Arthur was in that tradition of scientists — among them many of the greatest names in their respective fields such as Albert Einstein, Sir James Jeans, Niels Bohr, David Bohm, Sir John Eccles, Lord Rayleigh, Sir Arthur

Eddington, Alfred North Whitehead and Erwin Schrödinger — who have been as enthused by the fundamental questions that remain unanswered by science as by those to which answers have been found. And Arthur's enthusiasm, his over-arching desire to know, gave him a youthful eagerness which, allied to the gravitas of a mature and cautious intellect, made him an ideal researcher, whether the subject was an abstruse problem in modern electronics or the workings of telepathy, precognition and other paranormal abilities.

I first made Arthur's acquaintance many years ago, when I was doing a programme on the psychology of personality for BBC radio, and one of the people we interviewed (from another studio, so we were not face-to-face at the time) was Arthur Ellison, who had been invited to talk about the paranormal. Imagine my fascination when I heard a distinguished professor of engineering not only express his belief in paranormal abilities, but back up this belief with telling examples from his own experience. Shortly afterwards we met at a conference in Oxford, and from that time onwards we remained firm friends. My own interest in the paranormal went back to boyhood, and as a postgraduate at Cambridge I had at idle moments read enough of the research literature to convince me there were indeed good grounds for a scientific interest in the subject. But it was not until I had the first of many long conversations with Arthur that I realized just how extensive these grounds were. Shortly afterwards I joined the Society for Psychical Research (SPR), of which Arthur had twice served as President, and from then on he and I met regularly and had many opportunities to work together, of which more shortly.

Arthur's work for the SPR spanned nearly half a century (he joined in 1955), and he rightly regarded its foundation back in 1882 as the beginning of the scientific investigation of the paranormal. As a prodigious student of the subject, he was an expert on the history of this investigation. He was working on *Science and the Paranormal* at the time of his death in September 2000, and although the book was virtually finished I feel he would have wished to add a short introductory chapter detailing something of this history. He would have wished to emphasise that the experiments and the findings with which he deals in the book grew out of this history, and are part of an ongoing development in research into the paranormal which consistently not only confirms many earlier findings, but adds new material to them and opens up stimulating possibilities for future research. He would also, I feel sure, have wished to pay tribute to the men and women who pioneered the scientific examination of the subject, for he had an abiding respect — one might well say an affection — for these giants from the past.

And well he might. For psychical research — research into the paranormal — has attracted some of the finest intellects in the sciences and the arts over the years since the founding of the SPR. What is more, many of these men and women, though starting off sceptically, became convinced — through direct experience — of the reality of paranormal phenomena. One thinks of scientists in the early years like Sir William Barrett, Sir William Crookes, Sir Oliver Lodge and Lord Rayleigh, psychologists such as William James, Robert McDougall, Sigmund Freud and Carl Jung, writers of the calibre of Sir Arthur Conan Doyle, Mark Twain, Walt Whitman, Victor Hugo and Robert Louis Stevenson, British Prime Ministers William Gladstone and Arthur Balfour, and philosophers of the stature of Henri Bergson, Ferdinand Schiller and Gilbert Murray. The SPR alone has had 12 Nobel Prizewinners as members, and many Fellows of the Royal Society. Thus, as Arthur Ellison was well aware, the charge that psychical research only attracts the foolish and gullible could not be further from the truth. It would be more accurate to say that it attracts those with minds open to the unanswered questions of science, and those who take the time and the trouble to read the vast, carefully argued writings on psychical research produced by the luminaries I have mentioned and by many others of equal standing.

The laboratory-based research into the paranormal (usually known as parapsychology) can be said to have started as long ago as 1930, when under the guidance of William McDougall as head of the psychology department, Joseph and Louisa Rhine set up the first ever parapsychology laboratory at Duke University in North Carolina. Beginning with simple card-guessing routines as a test for telepathy between a sender (who looked at the cards) and a receiver (who did not), the Rhines and their colleagues proceeded over a period of years to amass impressive evidence not only for telepathy but for clairvoyance, precognition and even psycho-kinesis (the ability to move objects with the power of the mind). Sceptics tried resolutely to discredit the Rhines' findings on the basis of sensory leakage (the ability of recipients to get to know the identity of cards by normal means), deliberate fraud on the part of some senders and recipients, and mistakes in the statistical analysis which showed the odds against results being due to chance alone. However, the era of scientific investigation into the paranormal was well and truly launched.

Since the time of the Rhines, a number of laboratories in Europe and in the USA have continued — often using more rigorous methods of control than those used by the Rhines or employed in other areas of science — to produce results supporting the existence of paranormal abilities. Hal Putoff and Russell Targ at the Stanford Research Institute (now SRI International), Ed May and his team at the Laboratory for Fundamental Research at Palo Alto, the late Chuck Honorton in various laboratories and at the University of Edinburgh, Marilyn Schlitz at the Institute of Noetic Science, Charles Tart at the University of California, William Braud at the Institute of Transpersonal Psychology, Gary Schwartz and Linda Russek at the University of Nevada, Dean Radin at the University of Las Vegas, Ian Stevenson at the University of Virginia, Erlundur Haraldsson at the University of Iceland, Robert Morris and his team at the University of Edinburgh, Peter Fenwick at the Institute of Psychiatry in London, Adrian Parker at the University of Göteborg, Robert Jahn and his team at the University of Princeton, and many others have made and are continuing to make major discoveries in the field. The remote viewing experiments conducted initially by Putoff and Targ and later by May and his team over the years 1970 to 1994 — and funded by the US military, the US Defence Intelligence Agency, the CIA and NASA to the tune of some \$20 million — produced positive results in favour of paranormal abilities (or anomalous cognition as those involved preferred to call it) with odds against chance of a hundred billion billion to one.

Thus the experiments discussed by Arthur Ellison in this book have an impressive pedigree. Never a one to rely just on the published literature, Arthur knew many of the people I've just mentioned personally, travelling many thousands of miles at his own expense to visit their laboratories and see their work at first-hand. As I have already mentioned he went even further, spending countless hours successfully developing his own abilities and experimenting upon himself in a number of areas of the paranormal. He expressed constant frustration at the failure of sceptical scientists not only to study the published research literature but to attempt such development for themselves. It was not scepticism that irked Arthur, it was ignorant scepticism, the scepticism of those who 'know' in advance, and without troubling to study the subject, that paranormal abilities are impossible.

As I said earlier, Arthur and I had many opportunities to work together. We served alongside each other on the SPR Council for many years, and he and I, with colleagues, founded the Society's Survival

Research Committee in order to develop even further the work done by the Society to document evidence for the survival of consciousness after physical death. But it was during the two years of the Scole investigation (which Arthur describes in some detail in the book) that we spent most time together, working in harness with Montague Keen, the Secretary of the Survival Research Committee, who led the investigation. As an engineer, Arthur had a particular interest in physical phenomena — the claimed ability of certain mediums to work with so-called spirits in order to produce materializations, the paranormal movement of objects, paranormal lights — in fact the full range of phenomena so enthusiastically studied by many of the early members of the SPR. As Arthur makes clear, many of the extraordinary things we witnessed during our investigation defied explanation by normal means, and the experience of working alongside him while the work went on was a privilege for which I shall always be profoundly grateful. Montague Keen and I could not have wished for a wiser companion or a truer friend.

By virtue of the number of first-hand examples of paranormal phenomena that Arthur gives, there is a sense in which *Science and the Paranormal* is autobiographical, an account of the life of one gifted man who pushed forward the boundaries of our knowledge of ourselves and the world. In doing so, he never lost his scientific objectivity. As is clear from the book, he was as consistently (though always gently, for he was that kind of man) critical of those who believe in the paranormal on the strength of flimsy or misunderstood evidence as of those who refuse to believe on the strength of findings from properly conducted research. But he also never lost his willingness to speculate on the implications of paranormal abilities for the mind and for the various levels of consciousness contained within it, and for what we might call the higher or spiritual side of our nature. The final chapter of his book, in which he advances a model designed to tackle these issues, is ground-breaking and exciting in its scope. It is not the easiest chapter in the book by any means, but it is one that repays careful study. Some may disagree with what Arthur says in it, and with the philosophical idealism and the extensive knowledge of the Western and Eastern psycho-spiritual systems such as Theosophy and Buddhism which underpins much of this thinking. Arthur would not mind. It was his firm belief that no-one has a monopoly of the truth, and it was this belief that made him not only so impatient of fellow scientists who claimed to know it all, but so ready to subject his own ideas to debate and critical scrutiny.

All I can say is that, although he and I did not always agree on the details, I regard his ideas as forming one of the most comprehensive, well-founded and well-considered attempts to make sense of the paranormal currently available to us.

It will I think be clear from these ideas and from much else that he says during the book that Arthur's experiences of the paranormal convinced him of the reality of survival after physical death. These experiences, as I've made clear, took in not only the field work about which he writes in such detail, but his own inner life. His out-of-body experiences indicated to him that consciousness can exist outside the brain and the physical body, and his lucid dreams (the development of which became one of his major research interests in the last years of his life) helped to further this understanding. He was a committed and highly experienced meditator, able as he says elsewhere to hold his mind like a still pool, and this ability undoubtedly helped him to experience the altered states of consciousness that took him beyond the narrow conventions of our 'normal' way of encountering the world and ourselves within the world. Equally helpful was his conviction that the outer world, the world of apparently hard and objective experience, is not 'real' in any final sense, and is in part shaped by our beliefs about it and the action of our minds upon it.

With Arthur's death, at the age of 80 but in full intellectual and creative vigour, we have lost one of the finest researchers into and thinkers about the paranormal of the last many decades. Happily, his influence will live on. He touched the lives of innumerable people by his writings, by his lectures at home and abroad, by his frequent appearances in the media, and by the summer courses in the paranormal that he ran for many years at the University of Loughborough. Together with the results of all these endeavours, his book stands as a tribute to a fine scholar, to a true gentleman, and to a rare and precious spirit.

Professor David Fontana
Cardiff, 2002

Preface and Acknowledgments

In welcoming the hopeful reader to this book may I say the following. All my life I have been interested in the nature and purpose of life. After these many years of reading, thinking, researching and discussing with friends the perennial problems of life and consciousness, some of them answerable and others probably not, I decided to write this book which is, to a great extent, autobiographical. My preferred way to truth is via open-minded science rather than belief or faith and, in what follows, my tentative conclusions are based on much experimentation — both in my own consciousness and of the practices of others in healing, meditation and in psychical research. I have attended seances of all kinds over many years. I have attended courses in self-development and have lectured on that subject myself. I have given courses with demonstrations on hypnosis. One result of all this somewhat unusual spare time activity, in parallel with a busy life as head of a large university engineering department, is that I have made many friends all over the world who have assisted and advised me. The arrival of the Internet has greatly helped me in that I have been able to discuss with, and get information from, some of the best-known names in research into consciousness.

My background is professional engineering — electrical and mechanical. This has taught me a great deal and friends have kindly suggested that my feet are firmly on the ground — even if my head is occasionally in the clouds.

I am extremely grateful to a number of most helpful friends and would like to express my thanks to Eleanor O'Keeffe, formerly the Secretary for the Society for Psychical Research (SPR), and to Willys Poynton, SPR Librarian, for much help with references; to Peter Johnson, current SPR Secretary, for other help; to my friend Montague Keen for kindly reading, commenting upon and suggesting corrections and improvements to the MS; and to the SPR Council for permission to publish extracts from the Society's Journal and Proceedings. I am grateful to my many colleagues on the Council over the years for helpful discussions. Colleagues in The Scientific and Medical Network have always been helpful in discussions after lectures and I thank them. I am grateful also to many 'mature' students on my Loughborough University summer courses, many of them medical doctors, psychologists and psychiatrists, for confirming that my understanding of their subjects was not too far astray. Wryly, I sometimes think that I have an advantage over experts in these other professions in not having been subjected to the conditioning by distinguished people in their universities which goes with an 'education' in those subjects. I am especially grateful to the mature student — a very successful businessman I called John — for his passing over to me all the correspondence and other records relating to his unusual cases of multiple personality disorder. My editor Christopher Moore has been a great help and encouragement and his patience has been exemplary. To him I am deeply grateful. I also thank the publishers and copyright holders of the books from which I have quoted, for permissions where obtainable (see Reading List).

Finally, I am more grateful than I can express to my wife Marian for her help and encouragement over the years. Without this the book would probably never have been finished.

Professor Arthur J. Ellison
June 1999

CHAPTER 1

Normal Western Science and Reality

In the following pages, we shall be considering a quite different and perhaps more fruitful way of looking at our normal daily consciousness. It is therefore clear that we should start by reviewing the way in which we have all been conditioned to 'normal reality' in our twentieth century Western culture. All cultures do not look at the world in the same way. We must consider also the almost unconscious psychological defences we have to any suggestions that our present view might not be the most helpful or the 'truest' way of considering our experiences of the physical world. And we must see how this can be made obvious. In other words, we must analyse exactly what we are doing when we examine the world around us and how we use normal science to 'describe reality.'

In doing this we shall find some disagreements with many 'normal scientists' — including those whose job is particularly to help the public understand science. I beg leave to suggest that they hardly know what they are themselves doing! But readers must make up their own minds whether they agree with me or not. All I can do is present the evidence for open-minded consideration.

Let us start then by considering our experiences when we first entered the physical world at birth. A baby is born and opens its eyes for the first time. What does it see? The answer is — it may be obvious to some readers — nothing. It has presumably experiences going on in its mind and it does not 'understand' any of these. One might say that it is not separate from the rest of the universe. We shall return to this concept when we consider — in Chapter 18 — mystical experience. The baby's parents then almost at once start to condition it by telling it the cause, in their Western culture's opinion, of those experiences going on in its mind. They point to objects and give them names. They indicate that that object waving about just there is part of itself — its toe — and they show it that other objects are separate from itself. Gradually it is conditioned to the idea that it is surrounded by objects separate from itself. It is itself an electrochemical machine having a little computer at the top and five 'sensory channels' providing inputs to that computer. It learns of that separate physical world through those five sensory channels, which provide the only ways of doing so. And any other experiences going on in its mind are either useless fantasies or elaborations of the facts gleaned from out there. One vitally important fact is always missed — and by many of the philosophers too: *that the physical body itself is one of those 'objects out there.'* This renders completely fallacious any reasoning based on the idea that the physical body *is* the human being and is separate from the other objects around and receives information from them.

Many children have experiences of things which the adults around them do not. They are considered by the already normally conditioned adults to have over-active imaginations and those adults *'know'* that the things they experience are not 'true.' Some children have imaginary playmates; others have out-of-body experiences and describe floating around the house at night. Sometimes their parents become angry and scold the children, who then stop talking of the experiences they have. Such adults have a heavy responsibility for destroying the possible flowering of what might be looked upon as an extra window on the universe they do not themselves have. We shall discuss this sort of experience later, with the evidence.

So all of us tend to grow up in our culture with the idea that we are an electrochemical machine surrounded by objects we perceive via the five senses. This is our *metaparadigm,* our big model or paradigm on which our understanding of all our experience is based. The very language with which we discuss these matters is based on that paradigm. It is founded on *dualism:* that we (the subject) are here, the objects are there, and there is a relationship between them. A philosopher would call this a philosophy of classical realism and. for most of us in our Western science-based culture it is, we would say, obviously true.

What, then, *is* science? This is an enormously important topic to understand clearly as we shall be using the scientific method throughout this book and because our educational system is supposedly based on it. It is considered of great value by most people in our culture and indeed often as the only possible and reasonable way to understand the universe after thousands of years of superstition.

Modern western science started some three or four hundred years ago with Galileo, Newton, and others. Up until that time, if one wanted to know something about the physical world and the things in it one often looked up the writings of Aristotle. The scientific method involved referring to the physical world for facts about it. For example — perhaps oversimplifying a little — if you wanted to know the number of teeth in a horse's mouth you would, many centuries ago, have referred to Aristotle; the modern scientist would find a horse and look in its mouth.

The scientific method involves first observation, and then the devising of theories. These might truly be described as mental models, in terms of which the perceived world and the objects in it can be understood, explained. Those theories are then, if possible, tested to destruction. If they cannot be falsified then they are used for predicting future relevant occurrences. It is important to understand that the scientific method is not a way of proving anything. The theories devised are used until they prove unable to make appropriate predictions. When this occurs for a theory, then further facts of experience are, as a result, available, with which to devise a new theory. This also is used until it breaks down.

Much of scientific knowledge deals with matters of which no one has any direct experience. No one has ever directly seen an electron, for example, but according to the theory it is a stream of electrons which causes chemicals on the back of the screen of a cathode ray tube to fluoresce, and so paint the television or computer picture. The theory is very useful. The theory of matter in the form of different particles — electrons, protons and neutrons — enables all sorts of useful things to be done. Experiments in large machines, smashing streams of particles together, have shown that they can be considered as made up of smaller components, and much of modern physics is devoted to the study of these particles.

We are all aware of the story of Newton and the falling apple. The genius of Newton devised from this simple fact, which everyone had often observed, the theory of gravitation, hypothesising that it did not apply only to objects falling to earth: *all* objects attracted *all* other objects. The force between any two varied directly, he suggested, as the product of the masses and inversely as the distance between them. At the present time this might be considered almost common sense. This idea of a force through empty space was considered by Newton's great German contemporary Leibniz as a ridiculous metaphysical idea; but it worked. With that theory we can understand and model the workings of the solar system, and indeed of the whole universe. It is today used to predict and control the movements of space shots.

Later work showed that when objects were moving at speeds

approaching that of light then Newton's gravitational law broke down. Another great genius, Einstein, devised another theory, even more outlandish, which suggested that the presence of objects distorted the space around them (more accurately, the space-time). Einstein's theory suggested, then, that objects distorted the space around them and other objects just travelled freely through this warped space. There is no idea of an attraction between them. Einstein's theory reduces to Newton's theory at velocities much below that of light but at speeds approaching that of light it is essential to use Einstein's for accurate results. The important point I am making here is that the theories of science give us ways of predicting what we shall *observe* to occur under certain circumstances. And I shall often be emphasising that, despite the apparently normal descriptions I shall necessarily use, and have just been using, *all these observations occur in the mind.*

Let us first examine what most scientists, indeed, most non-scientists, consider science to be. Most people think science's business is to describe in ever greater detail the world in which we find ourselves. In this understanding, we shall in time have a complete and accurate description of everything, and science will come to an end. It is often said that scientists have 'discovered' something or other, i.e. it was 'out there' all the time and now we know about it. Very often newspapers speak of science itself *discovering* something instead of an individual scientist or group of them.

All this is what was termed 'normal science' by the American philosopher of science Thomas Kuhn, in his book, *The Nature of Scientific Revolutions.* The reader will remember that it is based on this paradigm we have just considered, called realism. Kuhn defines the work of 'normal scientists' as 'puzzle solving within an unquestioned paradigm.' All the problems which are said to be paranormal, to which I have referred, are the results of that paradigm (realism) being inadequate to the job of accounting for many of our most important human experiences — and many other experiences too. Scientific theories are paradigms (models) within that metaparadigm and take it for granted.

I suggest that science actually is: *a process of building mental representational models patterning and ordering our mental experiences.* As we have seen, we have nothing for certain other than mental experiences. It was Descartes who started from the only position he felt was certain — that he was thinking and therefore he existed. *Cogito ergo sum:* I think therefore I am: we have nothing for certain but our thoughts. We considered this earlier and it will be appreciated that our normal scientific model of perception ends with electrochemical pulses arriving at the cortices of the little computer in our head. We pointed out at that time how our parents and others conditioned us to 'understand' all this in terms of a 'world out there,' taken as the source of that information. It was never considered, at school or university or elsewhere, and this was pointed out earlier, what a circular argument this is, our own body being one of those objects 'out there.' Nor was it ever suggested to us that there are other perfectly respectable ways of modelling our experiences. We shall consider this later. For most of the matters of ordinary daily life it is of little or no importance; a somewhat naïve realism is perfectly adequate. The reason we have to consider it here is because we shall later be trying to understand, that is to model, those unusual experiences called paranormal.

One very important result of having an 'unquestioned mental model' which represents all our experiences, as the 'normal scientists' have realism, is that it decides for us to a considerable degree what we are likely to accept as 'possible' and what is 'impossible.' The spoon-bending phenomena associated with Uri Geller provide a good example. If a spoon is a normal metal object out there in physical space and independent of ourselves and governed in its behaviour by the laws of metallurgy, crystallography and strength of materials, then it is 'obviously' ridiculous to consider that it can be bent by gentle stroking. Such phenomena *must* be the result of conjuring. I shall be giving later evidence that metal bending in this paranormal way is most certainly not always the result of conjuring and should not so readily be dismissed.. It has enormously important implications for science.

Any human experience which can be neither explained nor described within the terms of the current scientific paradigm of realism (and there are many such) is therefore called paranormal. These experiences — and many will be considered later — show clearly to any scientist with an open mind that realism is inadequate as a complete way of modelling all our human experiences. There is another and possibly better way of modelling them, as we shall see. To dismiss quite common paranormal experiences as trivial or unimportant because they do not fit realism is surely the height of bigotry and unworthy of the name of science. Yet it is done often and by otherwise quite distinguished scientists.

You will remember Dr Johnson's stone-kicking by which he attempted refutation of idealism (that it is all in the mind). An equally vacuous suggestion is sometimes made that if you think that everything is in the mind just go and jump in front of the next big red bus to come along. If one did that, of course, and did not act as though the world we are in was real, one would immediately have one's consciousness changed to a different level, which will be also in the mind — but that will come later.

The likelihood is that our language also — based on realism/dualism — is very likely to mislead us. It is important to keep this in mind. We may — in fact I think we shall — find later that a different philosophical basis has a wider and more encompassing scope. We shall consider the claims of monistic idealism ('it's all in the mind' — but nonetheless 'real') when we have looked at the scientific evidence that appears to require it.

It is important also for the reader to realize that when I am suggesting that all we can be certain of, when we say that our experiences of the world, considered to be real and 'out there,' are actually in the mind, I am not embracing the philosophy of solipsism. This is the theory that the self is the only thing that can be known to exist and that the world we appear to be perceiving exists only for us. Of course the experiences of other people are much the same as ours. The relatively slight differences are well accounted for in the philosophy of realism by variations in the working of the senses, or by optical illusions and the like.

Scientific views of quantum physicists

We shall also consider the views of those scientists who are, most people would agree, at the forefront of science. I refer to the quantum physicists. As we shall see, those who agree with the Copenhagen interpretation of quantum mechanics enunciated by Niels Bohr and his colleagues at Copenhagen (probably a majority of the leading quantum physicists), would say that the universe depends on us, its 'observers,' for its meaning and reality. To use an expression of John Wheeler, we are in a 'participative' universe. Objects — and usually they consider small particles of which every larger object is considered to be composed — objects do not exist until they are 'observed,' i.e. measured. The 'observation' is said to 'collapse the wave function,' which is, in effect, a set of probabilities or potentialities. This is mentioned briefly now, in this introductory chapter, because it indicates that even some 'normal scientists' appear to be compelled, by open-minded reason and logic and the results of ingenious experiments which we shall be considering, to move towards what appears to me to be a position of idealism (although many do not go all the way). It seems most encouraging to observe that the prosecution of the normal scientific method, if done with open-mindedness and clear thinking, shows the major difficulty at the heart of realism.

Are we all in a 'trance'?

Hindu philosophers believe that our observations through our aware-ness of the physical world lead to a *maya* or illusion and not to reality — that things are not at all as they seem. The American psychologist and parapsychologist Charles Tart calls this the 'consensus trance' which we nearly all share almost all the time. Many of the practices of raja yoga, meditation, are designed to awaken us to reality. We shall refer to this again when we have examined the multifarious evidence that it must be true. It will arise when we consider lucid dreaming in Chapter 4. We shall also have a few suggestions to make as to the pos-sible purpose of our illusory state. Many of the paranormal experiences being reported by ordinary people appear strongly to indicate that the universe is by no means a fortuitous concourse of atoms hurrying aim-lessly to a pointless end. We shall mention later some of the various statistical surveys which show this. All the great religions of the world are undoubtedly the results of the founders having such paranormal experiences — and interpreting them in various ways, i.e. modelling and categorizing them, usually later much elaborated and not always to the advantage of Truth, over the centuries.

Defence reactions to evidence

Another important matter we shall be looking at in more detail later, with examples, is the psychological defence reaction all of us usually experience when our favourite models appear to be under attack. The reader may already have observed this in themselves! This is particu-larly evident in two areas: the first is religion (and often politics, which has certain rather similar characteristics), and the second arises among those scientists whose very naïve realism is threatened by good evi-dence that it is not wholly true. We shall have several examples of the latter in Chapter 15. It has always surprised me to see the virulence which appears in some distinguished scientists when confronted with that evidence. Their scientific objectivity rapidly disappears and their normal reason and logic are replaced by anger, and escape from the anomalous evidence. They do not find to their taste a state of 'cognitive dissonance,' i.e. apparently knowing two things at the same time which cannot both be true. Most of the rest of us are not nearly so worried.

Later we shall see a few examples of this behaviour of orthodox scientists, and the usually more reasonable attitude of others, which I have come across in connection with work on the paranormal.

As I said at the start, my preferred way to truth is through open-minded science, and I hope the reader will find acceptable evidence in what follows for all the views that are put forward for consideration.

CHAPTER 2

The Near Death Experience (NDE)

Probably the nearest anyone comes to death without actually permanently dying is in the near death experience, when the physical body is 'clinically dead.' In true clinical death there is no heart beat, no breathing, no detectable brain activity. This is the condition when there is a 'cardiac arrest' and many such cases occur in hospital cardiology departments. Many years ago a doctor would have been willing to sign a death certificate for many patients in this state. However, for the past twenty years or more it has been found possible in a high proportion of cases of clinical death and by injections or electric shocks, to get the heart and breathing going again so that the patient regains consciousness.

Most doctors have been taught in medical school that a human being is an electrochemical machine and therefore, when all vital signs of consciousness are absent, they would not expect the patient to have any consciousness. However, something like over half of those NDE patients describe a wide-ranging and fascinating set of experiences which have been the subjects of many papers, books and lectures in the past score of years. I propose now to describe briefly a typical near death experience, before we consider in detail what it appears to imply about the true nature of human beings. We shall then be able later to make comparisons with certain other altered states of consciousness (ASCs) and hopefully then be able to move some way towards a better understanding of them all. In other words, we shall have some of the data required to model a human being. We shall see that the model will need to incorporate many more features than would be required for an electrochemical machine.

As so many books have been written about the NDE I do not propose to make this a long chapter but to give only a brief account of a typical 'full' experience and mention a few facts which are closely relevant to our study of human beings and consciousness. These facts can then be included in the total of those we shall have later from many other experiences of ASCs of various kinds.

The five stages of a complete NDE

Some of the following descriptions and terms were used by Raymond Moody, who wrote the first book outlining the stages of a complete NDE. We must bear in mind that not every NDE is complete: the experience can end without extending to the full five stages.

First, if the cause of the experience was a severe accident or a cardiac arrest, extreme pain would probably have been experienced. When the NDE starts the subject finds that all pain has ceased and there is a state of complete peace and tranquillity.

The second stage is an experience of being separated from the body. Sometimes, not always, there is a loud buzzing or roaring noise experienced by the subject as the separation takes place. The subjects find they are apparently floating in the air above or near their body, which they can see, and they are able to watch the nurses and doctors, or others in the case of an accident in the open air, working on their body. But if they try they are unable to make their presence felt. They usually feel a sense of supreme detachment and unconcern. Often they think that they must have died and begin to wonder what is to come next. At this second stage many experiencers have described a wide-ranging extra-sensory perception (ESP) and later describe, often with complete accuracy, what has been going on elsewhere. For example, a relative has been described hurrying into the hospital entrance wearing exactly what the unconscious patient later described. If the relative talked to someone else then the words they used can often be remembered later and repeated to them.

A fascinating feature of the experience at this stage has been frequently mentioned. The subjects say sometimes that they observed the doctors and nurses working on their body and could see and hear what they were doing and saying. However, they sometimes say that they knew what they were going to say or do just before they did it. (How they could see and hear when their senses were closed in clinical death will be considered a little more fully in Chapter 3 on the out-of-body experience.) The subjects appear to be experiencing telepathy which is, as it were, automatically changed into what seems like the operation of the normal senses. Some of them describe the experience as 'just knowing.'

A most important feature of this stage of the experience is sometimes described using words like: 'I was not a wife (or husband) or somebody's secretary, or an engineer or accountant: I was myself.' One might describe it as realizing oneself as the actor who had been playing a particular part in the life that is apparently just ending. Sometimes at this stage subjects find themselves able to 'see' what is going on in distant places or in places quite inaccessible to ordinary sight.

The third stage of a complete NDE has been called 'entering the darkness.' Here the subjects find themselves apparently moving out into a vast dark space or sometimes entering a dark tunnel travelling, by the feel and sounds, at considerable speed. Sometimes there is a 'dual consciousness' at this stage with the experience of both moving along rapidly but also being stationary as before.

The fourth stage has been described as 'entering the Light.' The subjects often observe first a tiny pin point of light in the far distance. It enlarges rapidly as they move towards it until it appears as the lighted entrance to a tunnel. They move out of that entrance into that light, and experience an overwhelming feeling of love, joy and acceptance, with all their faults overlooked. Experiencers sometimes use expressions like 'I rushed into the arms of the Light.' They say 'I was so familiar with him. He was related to me as total love, total understanding, total acceptance ... beyond words.'

What occurs here is very interesting, significant and illuminating. The large sphere of brilliant yet not dazzling light appears often to have within it a figure. If the experiencer is a believing Christian then the figure appears as the traditional Christ, just as the experiencer imagines Him. The figure holds out his arms in welcome and acceptance. Sometimes the experiencer feels that the sphere of light is God. If the experiencer is a believing Buddhist than the figure may appear as the Buddha, seated in the traditional lotus posture. Presumably for a Jew the figure would be of Abraham but I have not yet come across a case of this.

At about the stage of moving towards the Being of Light, there is an interesting event called the 'review.' In this there is a sort of playback of the events of the life that has just ended. But it is not like running a filmed record again. It not only takes place all at once (yet with complete clarity) but the subjects say that they were able to observe the effects of their actions on others from the point of view of those others. I remember one subject who said that he had a fight in a bar with someone. Not only did he relive the blow he gave to the jaw of the opponent but he also experienced receiving that blow as though he were the other person and experienced the feeling of hatred and resentment felt by that other. All this is at the same time observed and 'judged' by the individual from the standpoint of the 'higher level' which was mentioned earlier. A psychologist might describe this as 'depersonalization.' Those subjects who have the experience never afterwards judge people on appearances only. Having escaped the personal ego perspective they are then honest in their assessment of themselves and honest and sympathetic to other people. The Being of Light often accompanies the life review and makes comments like: 'You have to go through more experiences. There are still things for you to do.'

Following the review, a complete NDE goes on into what we can only call the 'next world.' Here the subject often describes seeing, amid the beauty and colour and sometimes music of a glorious world rather like the earth at its best, deceased near-relatives looking young and happy who appear ready to welcome them into the world where they now are. Sometimes they hear glorious music and smell gorgeous perfumes. Always there seems to be some sort of 'symbolic barrier' separating them from that world. That barrier might be a river — they would see the relatives on the other side of the river — or it might be a closed gate in a fence or a door in a wall. (The river reminds one of the ancient Roman belief concerning the River Styx and the boatman who had to be paid to row the passenger across.)

At some time during all these experiences — and there are all sorts of varieties of them — the dying subject sometimes hears a voice saying something like: 'It is not yet your time: you have to go back.' The state is so delightful that this is often the last thing they want to do. Or perhaps they themselves feel that they must go back — perhaps to look after a baby or someone else who really needs them. And they find themselves rushing back down the tunnel; or perhaps they just 'wake up' in their hospital bed, racked with pain, finding that the doctors and nurses had finally managed to resuscitate them.

There are some comments and clarifications we should make of this experience before we consider it in more detail. The first is certainly this. If a 'normal scientist' or doctor says that it was all a fantasy, the result of the side effects of drugs or the results of anoxia (shortage of oxygen to the brain) the experiencer is almost tempted to laugh out loud. They would say: 'This was the clearest most meaningful experience of my life. I have never been thinking more clearly than I was during that experience.' Any neuropsychiatrist would confirm that the results of anoxia or drugs are muddle and confusion, not the crystal clarity which the subjects describe.

The second comment is the appearance so often of symbols. The NDE is in some respects very like a dream. Dreams will be briefly considered in Chapter 4 but they also are often replete with symbols. It is as though the non-normally-conscious parts of us (and by 'us' I mean the mind) are trying to tell us things about our lives in dreams. This is perhaps because the only images in the memory store are experiences of the physical world and the unconscious mind has nothing else to use. As we shall see when we consider other ASCs, the meaning of symbols is often of great importance. Freud and Jung both emphasised this and wrote much about it.

If one wanted to indicate that for some reason a subject was unable to proceed further, what better symbol could be used than a closed gate or door? This symbol is often to be found in NDEs.

The third comment to be made is this. The life of someone who has had a full NDE is usually completely changed for the better. By 'better' I mean 'spiritually better' in the sense of caring about the well-being of others more than about their own. Some NDEers have said that life is evolution but until they confronted death they did not really start to live. I believe without exception NDEers have not the slightest doubt about survival of bodily death.

In our Western culture we like to think that we are normally in charge — except in death, when we certainly are not. The 'final battle' is lost. People are often afraid of dying — but never after they have had an NDE. It is interesting that atheists and agnostics often believe in God after an NDE.

Not every NDE is a delightful experience like the description above. Some NDEs are what might be called 'hellish' and involve an experience of going down rather than up (symbols again) and perhaps finding oneself in a dank gloomy cave rather than a welcoming Light. The physically or mentally ill produce similar imagery. It is as if part of the self is all-wise and all-loving and knows that the experiencer needs to be woken up to this state of the psyche. A therapist who had herself had an NDE told me that. I do not know what proportion of NDEs are unpleasant but I believe — and hope! — that it is quite small.

evidence of his ESP, so I had only his word for it. However, he seemed trustworthy and reliable.

Several true stories I heard about the NDE I thought delightful. One, told by Kenneth Ring (the author of valuable books on the NDE and its significance) concerned a Southern US 'Bible puncher.' He had an NDE, and a little later, when he was feeling better and surrounded by his theological friends, was telling them about it, very excitedly. He said that he had had a talk with God and, he said, God was not interested in theology.

Another story was told by a British experiencer who died and whose body was put on a slab in the hospital mortuary. The following morning he had partially recovered to find himself on the slab as the mortuary attendant was walking nearby. He sat up. The attendant promptly fainted and so the NDEer got up off the slab and went to get him a glass of water.

Here is an experience typical of several I particularly noted because of its evidential value. One NDEer in the final stage of the experience was being welcomed by her young and happy deceased parents. They were at the other side of a garden gate. She could see along the garden path into the cottage where they apparently lived and there was a table laid for tea with three settings. 'You were expecting me?' she said. 'No,' they replied, 'it is not yet your time: your Aunt is expected.' When she had recovered from her NDE and was sitting up in bed with a few visitors, one of them said that they had a piece of sad news to impart. While she had been ill her aunt had died. What did they think when she said that she already knew!

A final word at the end of this account of the NDE: Remember that the above is not science fiction or fantasy. This sort of experience, in many detailed variations but in principle the same, has been shared by literally many millions of our fellow human beings. It is important for us all to realize that these are highly significant human experiences and each of us should consider what impact they have on our personal views of human beings and the world. We should think carefully about them and see how they fit with other experiences to be described in later chapters.

A postscript

Since writing the above, a new book by Dr Sabom has added useful additions to knowledge of the 'normal' NDE and I append a brief description.

Dr Michael Sabom, a cardiologist, described the following experience in his book *Light and Death,* which throws considerable extra

light on the NDE, especially on suggestions that even though the brain
during an NDE was apparently not being used, activity was still going
on in it, perhaps at a deeper level, and that therefore the body was not
really clinically dead.

Dr Sabom describes a daring operation for the removal of an
aneurism in the wall of the large (basilar) artery at the base of the
patient's brain. In this operation the body temperature is lowered to
60^0 F, the heartbeat and breathing are stopped and the blood drained
from the patient's head. Just about everything relevant was measured
including temperatures at many points in her body and brain, with the
brain rhythms at both the cortex and the brain stem. Loud clicks put
into her ears led to evoked potentials at the brain stem, where the
auditory cortices are. As the body temperature fell, the heart began to
malfunction and finally stopped. At this point her brain waves ceased
entirely and the evoked potentials were no longer able to be elicited.

When the surgeon opened her skull she felt that the buzzing of the
saw was pulling her out of her body and she had a crystal-clear view
of everything going on, including several very unusual things, confirmed afterwards. She could also clearly hear the conversation.
During this period she had a feeling like going up in a tunnel at high
speed. She heard her grandmother calling her and recognized many
of her relatives; they appeared to be made of light. They stopped her
from going into the light. She had children to bring up and wanted to
come back.

When the aneurism had collapsed, on the blood being drained
from her body, it was clipped and excised. Warmed blood was then
allowed to circulate back into the patient's body. The loud clicks in
the patient's ears had continued and at this point evoked potentials
returned indicating revival of brain stem activity. Likewise, the brain
waves on the electro-encephalograph (EEG) reappeared corresponding to activity in the cerebral cortex. Initial problems meant that the
heart had to be started again with defibrillator paddles.

The patient was taken back to the tunnel by her uncle. When she
saw her body she felt repelled by it. She said that it looked like what
it was: 'dead.' The uncle pushed her and she dived back into her
body. It was painful. She was taken to the recovery room almost
seven hours after the start of the operation.

Dr Sabom, in his book, refers to his earlier opinion that the body
in the near death experience was not really dead but near death.
Death had to be redefined from the state of 'no breathing and no heart

beat' to one of loss of 'brain function.' During the operation the patient was 'dead' by all three of the latest criteria for death: no EEG activity, no brain stem response and no blood flow through the brain. However, it is agreed that there is no event definitely indicating death. Once again we have to make up our own minds!

Chapter 3

The Out-of-Body Experience (OBE)

There have been accounts from antiquity, and occasionally over the centuries since, of human beings 'leaving their physical bodies' and travelling elsewhere. Many readers of such accounts living in our western science-based culture would say that the subjects were dreaming and that the accounts had no basis in reality. They meant nothing, despite what the ancients thought. We live in more enlightened times. But what if, as a result of travelling in that way to another place, it was possible to make observations and bring back verifiable facts? What then? It is possible to bring science to bear on this experience, as we shall see.

Some forty or so years ago I thought that if one could have an experience of existing apart from the physical body and actually observe that body at the same time, then that would surely settle for me, once and for all, whether the death of the physical body meant the end of a human being. It seemed to me that if, during that separation, the physical body was destroyed, clearly I should continue to exist in that other body. Sadly, I have discovered since, the problem of the human survival of bodily death is not so easily solved. I had a lot to learn.

Since that time so many years ago, when I managed to have two such OBEs, I have had other experiences of apparently existing apart from the physical body. We also now have much more data of other kinds bearing on this same problem. Some of this was considered in the preceding chapter when we noted that many millions of subjects had had the out-of-body experience as an early stage of a near death experience.

I propose now to describe and evaluate my own OBEs. They well illustrate various experiential facts and conceptual and philosophical difficulties — and also I can reassure the reader that the facts I shall give them are as accurate as I am able to make them.

My own experiences

Normally when starting research one reads as much as possible of what has already been written on a subject. In the case of my OBEs of so long ago I was able to read everything on it that had been published in English. I selected a particular book to follow. This was *The Projection of the Astral Body* written jointly by S.J. Muldoon, who had many such experiences, and H. Carrington, a well-known psychical researcher. This seemed an ideal partnership.

It seemed clear that if one is attempting to project the 'astral body,' as producing an out-of-body experience was traditionally described, then it is necessary to 'believe' that it exists. I had no problem with this as I had read the 'classical' Theosophical literature many years earlier and had talked to psychics who claimed to be able to observe it. Their observations indicated that it was made of 'subtle material unknown to science,' and interpenetrated and projected all around the physical body. We shall see later that this is by no means a correct description but it is certainly what they appear to observe.

Muldoon gave various suggestions about how to project the astral body, so I followed a number of these in turn. Mental exercises, as I remember, involved imagining that the astral body was rather bigger than the physical and that one's consciousness was 'filling' it. They also involved imagining that the astral body could 'revolve' within the physical body. This was quite difficult to do but I managed to lie on my back (on my bed, in pyjamas) and imagine myself looking at the ceiling first, and then a side wall of the room, then the floor underneath the bed on which I was lying, the other side wall, and then the ceiling. I can even today do this with very little difficulty. Strangely, I have more difficulty doing it anti-clockwise than I do clockwise. These various mental exercises are designed to loosen the grip of the physical body on the astral body. I carried them out for one hour each night for about a month and then found myself to be cataleptic: in other words I was lying on my back unable to move a muscle. Splendid, I thought, that is stage one completed. Muldoon had said that the cataleptic state pre-ceded a projection. Now for stage two! I then 'willed' and imagined myself in the astral body floating upwards. The important factor seemed to be much more imagining than willing.

It was as though I was embedded in the mud at the bottom of a river and the water was gradually reducing the viscosity of that mud. Slowly I seemed to free myself from the physical body and floated gently upwards towards the ceiling. The light was on and I could clearly see the ceiling approaching; as I got nearer I could also clearly see the small cracks in the plaster. I was still cataleptic (in the 'other body' as well as the normal physical body) as I gently floated through the ceiling into the darkness of the roof space. I then continued through the tiles of the roof, and the speed gradually increased as I got further away from the physical body. I could see the moon and a few dark clouds. Never shall I forget that experience of shooting up into the sky, lying on my back cataleptic, dressed in pyjamas, my hair flying in the wind. I can still hear the 'whoosh' as I shot up into the sky.

Writing my notes after that first successful experiment I pondered on what I had done. First, I realized that as I needed scientific evidence this experience was clearly a waste of time. Every sensible person with their feet 'on the ground' would say that I had dreamed the whole incident. And how could I prove, or indeed myself know, otherwise? Clearly I had to do better than that if the experience was to be of any scientific value. I resolved next time to try to go further afield and attempt to acquire some physical evidence. It seemed that a good first step would be to try to go into the town centre (I lived in Rugby, Warwickshire at that time) and look into a few shop windows in streets where I did not normally go and observe the details, writing all this down when I returned to the body. I could then go in the normal way the following day and check whether my observations had been correct or had been fictitious. The personal unconscious mind has a great deal of practice in dramatizing scenery, as it does it very effectively and persuasively every night when it produces our dreams.

So I continued with the method which had apparently been so successful and in two more nights found myself cataleptic again. This time when I had floated up to ceiling height I changed the direction of imagining/willing and floated horizontally feet first towards the window. I had remembered that Muldoon had stated that if one travelled a few metres away from the body then the catalepsy would disappear and the 'projector' would be free to move about in the ordinary way. Muldoon called that few metres 'cord activity range.' It will perhaps be remembered that in Ecclesiastes reference is made to death in terms of 'or ever the silver cord be loosed, or the golden bowl be broken.' (Eccles. 12:6) Many projectors have described to me observing a sort of hose pipe joining the back (usually) of the 'subtle body' to the front of the physical body and this pipe can stretch indefinitely, they say, and is the link between the two bodies, enabling rapid return to the physical body in emergency or whenever it is desired. Sometimes that return occurs spontaneously anyhow. Muldoon then explained that when the silver cord is stretched beyond 'cord activity range' it has thinned to a silvery line, and the 'vital forces' flowing between the two bodies will be reduced to a low ebb allowing the catalepsy to disappear. What exactly 'vital forces' means is not clear, but engineers will recognize a kind of electrical Ohm's Law analogy where the electric current for a given difference of potential is reduced when the resistance is increased. Anyhow, it is not safe to stretch analogies too far. Would it work? Was it true what Muldoon had himself found? I should mention that I did myself not notice any 'silver cord' but I did not remember to look.

My intention then was to float through the top of the window frame and describe an arc on my way to the lawn at the rear of the house, where I hoped that I would be free to walk into the town and acquire the evidence I felt was needed. I floated through the window and was about to make the descent when I had a most interesting experience. I felt two hands grab my head between them, pull me back into the room and push me downwards into the physical body. I can feel those strong fingers to this day! That is all. That was the end of the experience. I heard no voice and had no idea of the 'correct' explanation — but I can easily imagine how a Spiritualist or, indeed, how a psychiatrist would explain it, each using their own mental models. I am content to say that at present (all these years later) I have no explanation that I am confident is reasonably correct.

At that stage of the experiment, having been losing an hour's sleep a night for a month, I was becoming somewhat inefficient at my work during the day, so I discontinued. I became ever busier and it is only lately, in the last several years, that I have continued this work on my own consciousness and that of others.

The experiences of others

Having had my own experiences I was in a much better position to evaluate the experiences of others. The first one I considered was that of a friend who was a fellow member of the Society for Psychical Research. He told me that whenever he accidentally fell asleep lying on his back he had a spontaneous OBE and found himself floating about a metre or two above his body. Incidentally he said that he was 'absolutely terrified' and immediately struggled to get back. I greatly envied his easy ability! He then said that on one occasion when this occurred to him he glanced down (not being in a cataleptic state, as I had been) and observed that his soiled linen was to be seen in a bag near his dressing table waiting to be sent to the laundry. When to his great relief he was back to normal, he looked again and the linen bag was no longer to be seen: it had been sent to the laundry earlier in the day. Clearly what he had been observing from his up-in-the-air position had been not his room but *a dramatized reconstruction of a memory of his room.* Perhaps my picture of seeing the normal physical world from 'another body' was a gross over-simplification. And the apparently inoperative physical senses did not create a problem: perhaps the OBE is a little like dreaming. Incidentally, I now believe that my own cataleptic state during my projections was the result of Muldoon's saying it would be so: in other words, his 'suggestion' to me. Maybe I had drifted into a light autohypnotic trance as a result of that hour's concentration. In these subtler areas of the mind what one *believes* tends to be true. We shall have many other examples of this phenomenon later. Incidentally, my friend took to tying round his waist when he went to bed a large bath towel with a knot at the back. This effectively prevented him, he said, from falling asleep on his back.

I talked to others and re-read some of the books. I discovered that the 'view' of the room where the projection had taken place showed sometimes not only the apparently normal physical features but the physical features plus some symbolic additions. How could one 'see' one's room without one's normal physical eyes anyhow? This difficulty arises, of course, equally with the near death experience and was briefly mentioned in Chapter 2. It provides a significant pointer to an alternative view of how we perceive the normal physical world. Regarding the symbolic additions, I heard of one case where the apparently normal room had bars on the windows which prevented the experiencer from getting out. Also it is often mentioned that everything appears to be clearly visible even though the experience may be taking place in pitch darkness. No, our normal scientific ideas regarding seeing and hearing do not seem to apply; and we shall be using these facts when we consider the philosophical implications of these and other experiences.

The reader may remember from Chapter 1 that there is no way of conclusively proving that there is anything at all 'out there' in this rather illusory physical world. In fact 'out there' does not, as we have suggested earlier, make a lot of sense, since our own body with its senses is simply another of those 'objects out there.' As also suggested earlier, we just assume this as rather naïve realists, never having thought about it and having been educated along the customary lines of our Western culture, where everyone else appears to be having much the same experiences as ourselves and they too never question them. 'Normal scientists' are, of course, by definition, dogmatic believers in realism and therefore they never look at the evidence that it is too simplistic a belief.

There are some other experiences which must be discussed here in view of their importance. First, some months ago I was put into contact with a lady in Glasgow who had had spontaneous OBEs several times a week for many years. Every time she was terrified. Her life was becoming a hell: she was afraid to go to sleep. She was a patient of one of the biggest general medical practices in Glasgow, and none of the doctors there had ever heard of the OBE. She was referred to a large hospital in Glasgow: nor had any psychiatrist there, she told me, ever heard of an OBE. All these doctors could do was to prescribe tranquillizers — which made very little difference to her although occasionally there were a few unpleasant side-effects. The first real help and reassurance she got that she was not becoming mentally ill was from me — an engineer. I congratulated her on having an extra window on the universe which most of us do not have. The large reduction in her stress and fear happily appeared to reduce greatly the experiences which she had previously dreaded. I have come across many cases in various areas of this subject of altered states of consciousness which have led to great worry and disquiet on the part of their experiencers, who have almost invariably been unable to get any real help or reassurance from their Western scientifically-educated doctors. Psychic experiences apparently indicated to them that the patient had mental illness. If I as an engineer/psychical researcher have come across so many cases then does this not mean that there are many hundreds of thousands of others 'out there' who are not getting the help they desperately need and deserve? It really is vital that we get to know with a little more certainty the facts of ASCs and that scientific papers are published in medical journals so that doctors also may have better ways of dealing with their patients who are by no means mentally ill but might be described as a little unusual.

Our leading scientific journals rightly have quality control exerted by a rigorous refereeing system. They really must learn to have on their refereeing boards a few scientists who are not 'distinguished normal scientists' but have open minds and, hopefully, some of the experiences of the kind we are discussing in this book. Sadly, Thomas Kuhn said that this will never happen and we shall have to wait for the 'normal scientists' who blindly believe in the current paradigm of realism to die, before they are replaced by younger more open-minded scientists ready to embrace a different and wider paradigm when the evidence demands it. As the 'paranormal' evidence becomes ever stronger I hope and pray for the sake of the many suffering patients whom I have discussed above that he is wrong!

Some experiments on the OBE

During this last two or three years I have been carrying out more experiments endeavouring to throw light on the OBE. When I was President of the Society for Psychical Research I met most of the leading researchers in the subject from all over the world. Many of them attended the Centennial Conference which we held at Trinity College, Cambridge, in 1982, where a number of the founders were Fellows, to celebrate a century of good quality scientific research into the 'paranormal.' (It was not called that until fairly recently.) Part of the result of that conference was that subjects frequently write to me and I often hear from people who have OBEs. Always, if I am convinced of their honesty and genuineness, I ask them to assist me with experiments. Usually they agree, and I ask them if they think that they might be able to read and inform me of a 3-digit random number I have on my book-case. They say that they will try. Then I usually never hear from them again! However, that is not always the result. I propose now to describe the results obtained by my best subject to date in endeavouring to carry out that task.

Before that I might mention that most psychics tell me that they have difficulty in 'reading' numbers and letters (so-called alpha-numeric data). I thought that I would try this first, however, as I hardly believe anything I read in this subject unless I have personal experience of it! The use of three objects, each standing for a digit, would of course be just as good as digits. It looks as though, when they have psychic experiences, a psychic is functioning in the right hemisphere; trying to read alpha-numeric data pushes them into the left hemisphere where such data are normally processed. We are of course here using the ordinary realism model to describe what is happening since we must start scientific investigations where current science is.[1]

I got to know my best subject (so far!) in the following way. I had read several of the books written by her husband and wrote to tell him that I liked them. I told him of the experiments I was doing or planned to do and he told me that his wife was psychic, could have OBEs when he helped her by hypnosis, and that they were willing to collaborate with me.

This is what we did. I took out my old five-figure logarithmic tables from a bookcase, opened the book at random and put my finger on a page at random. I then read off the five-figure number at which I was pointing and selected the three least-significant digits, namely the three on the right of the five digits. (A statistician friend confirmed that that number was near-enough random for anyone.) I wrote down the number in large figures on a piece of paper and put it on the top of my bookcase.

I had no idea how my new OBE volunteer from Ireland would find her way to my house and study so I thought that directions might be a good idea. I made a map from a well-known part of London to my house via railway lines and parks and added a more detailed local map. I imagined her coming across the Irish Sea to London and using the map from there. However, she needed none of this. She just 'came.' (We shall have more detail of this sort of 'psychic travelling' when we come later to discuss the US 'distant viewing' experiments in connection with their intelligence work.) When her husband wrote to me after the first 'visit' (in the days before we both had email) he gave me her description of my study in addition to what she had read of the 3-digit number. Some parts of this description were roughly correct and some wrong. Incidentally, this is the reason why I wanted, if possible, to use random numbers. Every study has books in it and usually pictures. And the pictures would probably include country or sea scenes of various kinds. It would be very difficult to evaluate these data meaningfully.

So I was given the three digits and — to my delight — two of them were correct. I changed the digits for three more produced in the same way and informed them of the encouraging result. We did the experiment again three more times and, to my growing delight, each time she got two of the three digits correctly — but not in the correct order. I began to wonder why she could not get all three. Still, getting two out of three random digits four times in a row (disregarding the order) was very encouraging. The chance expectation i.e. the chances of getting two out of three four times in a row was, my statistician friend informed me, one chance in about 2000. So this was very highly significant: she did seem to be getting information about those numbers and it did not seem to be just good luck. The fifth trial was rather different. Her husband said that they had an artist friend who could also have OBEs if he helped her by hypnosis and he would send her with his wife to see whether they could help each other. His letter telling me that they were doing this crossed with my letter to him telling him the result of the fourth experiment. The result was most interesting. His wife, who did not know that the numbers had been changed, got exactly the same result as she got in the immediately preceding experiment but, the numbers having been changed, got them all wrong. However, their friend the artist got two out of the three correct!

Since then the experiments have involved only the usual subject and not the artist friend, and scarcely anything has been right. We really do not know why this is so. It looked as though (to use a very unscientific term) Mother Nature discovered that we were getting too close to the truth about the universe and rapidly drew the curtains! I suppose the real reason is something to do with the psychology i.e. the 'belief systems,' of us all, especially of the psychic. Experiments in the paranormal seem to depend on the 'gestalt' i.e. the whole set-up including everyone involved. Dr Sabom found that when he compared what the NDE patients had observed from their elevated position in the hospital ward while their bodies were being resuscitated with the facts in their medical files they were accurate. When we come to consider the 'distant viewing' experiments in the US, we shall see that the more expert 'distant viewers' were able to get accurate detailed information time after time. So it does not look as though there is any other reason for failure except our own psychological characteristics, beliefs and methods.

I have rarely had a subject as good as this first one in my recent series of experiments. All my other OBEers, as I said earlier, have rarely got three or even two digits correct. But usually I never hear from the volunteers again, which perhaps indicates that they were unable to carry out the experiment.

Before I leave experiments on the OBE state I must describe a most significant set of experiments I carried out some years ago with one naïve hypnosis volunteer and two distinguished psychics. A former fellow SPR Council member, Simeon Edmunds, had written a book concerning hypnosis and the paranormal and he had there asked for volunteers for experiments. Simeon had sadly died but we had at the SPR a list of some twenty or thirty volunteers. Another member (Maxwell Cade) and I resolved to continue and to concentrate first on the OBE. We found that in every ten volunteers about two or three were able to have an OBE when it was suggested to them under hypnosis. I invited one of the best of these to visit the University one evening for some experiments. This is what I did.

I intended to study whether and to what extent it was possible in the OBE to observe accurately the normal physical world. It was not enough, I knew, to observe something which others also knew because a correct result could have been explained by telepathy from someone else. The scientific evidence for the existence of telepathy was very strong and I was in no more doubt about it than I am about almost any 'normal' fact. Also it would not be good enough to produce a fact (say a random number on a computer screen) which no one looked at until after the subject had stated what it was. This could simply have been explained as the result of 'precognitive telepathy' or 'foreknowledge of a later state of someone's mind.' The evidence that this sometimes occurs is very strong too. So I had to test for what is called in the jargon 'pure clairvoyance' i.e. knowledge of something physical (a random number) via the OBE, which no one knows or will ever know. Many people have said to me that that is not possible, so may I explain how I did this (in the middle 1950s) when computers were not common.

I asked a final-year electrical engineering student to build as his degree project a gadget to do the following: when a button on the front of a box was pressed a 3-digit random number was to appear in a window at the back. Then when three digits were put into the box from dials at the front and another random number was obtained at the back by pressing the appropriate button, the electronic equipment inside the box automatically compared the random number previously at the back with the number which had been inserted at the front. The equipment then scored 1 on a 'correct' counter or on an 'incorrect' counter, depending on whether the numbers put in agreed or disagreed with the numbers that had been showing at the back. The actual number that had been at the back was irretrievably lost and no one would ever know it. But it would be known whether the number put in at the front was correct or incorrect.

The experiment was then as follows. The lady volunteer sat in my armchair and was put into a hypnotic trance. My secretary (to take notes and act as a chaperone) sat with me and the subject at the front of the box, which was on a large table a little way back so that there was no danger of any of us seeing the numbers at the back. There were also no reflecting surfaces which might have shown any of us, perhaps even without our conscious knowledge, the three-figure number at the back. I pressed the button at the front of the box and the 3-digit number appeared at the back (assuming that the equipment was working correctly — and it had been when tested immediately before the subject arrived). I then asked the subject to 'leave her body' (as she had been taught before), go round in her 'other body' to the back of the box, read the numbers. and tell me what they were. This she did with no apparent difficulty. As this was the first time, I thought that I should consider this a 'pilot guess' and go round to the back of the box and see how she had done. We could then start the experiment proper. To my enormous delight she had correctly given me all three digits, and in the right order. The chances of doing that if pure chance was all that had been operating was, of course, about 1 chance in 1000. (I say 'about' because I felt it most unlikely that she would ever give me 000, for example, which was just as likely as any other numbers to come up. Human beings have such preferences.) Anyhow, that was enormously significant.

I then resolved that I would not now look at the back but would do a run of 20 'guesses.' I gave her another OBE and asked her again to tell me what the numbers were. This time, immediately, she had difficulty. She said: 'The numbers are very small: I am having great difficulty in reading them.' She made one or two desultory tries but eventually admitted that she could not clearly see the numbers and we had to end the experiment. I taught her how to use auto-hypnosis to produce her OBE and she promised to go away and practise reading small numbers, to be set up by her boy friend in the next room at home. As often happens in such experiments she got married, moved to another part of the country and I never saw her again!

There were two interesting sequels to this experiment. Some months later I had a telephone call from the distinguished American psychic Ingo Swann to say that he was in London and would like to invite me out to dinner. I invited him to the University for drinks beforehand and told him about that experiment. His immediate reply was: 'Let's try an experiment now!' I explained that I had not checked the equipment lately and it might not work correctly, but he said that it probably would. So I pulled it out from a cupboard, switched it on and did a few trials. All seemed to be well so I said: 'Let's do a run of twenty before we go to dinner.' Ingo said to me: 'I don't need an out-of-body experience: I'll just tell you what the numbers are.' He then sat at the table (in front of the box) and I pressed the button which produced the 3-digit number at the back. Ingo said that the numbers would be presented to him on a little internal screen 'in his head.' He gave me a 3-digit number and I put it in at the front of the box and pressed the button for the next one. We did that for 20 'guesses.' At the end I set up the dials to tell me how many he had got right. To my extreme surprise and delight the box indicated eight. Getting correctly eight 3-digit numbers out of twenty by chance must have odds against it of astronomical proportions! So, very satisfied, we went to dinner. During dinner I suggested to Ingo that we could do an experiment like that across the Atlantic by telephone with distinguished witnesses observing both in London and in New York City.

The following morning I had been thinking that the result was too good to be true and when I arrived at the office I switched on the box and did a run myself. The box told me that I also had eight correct! Clearly there was something wrong! My Chief Technician had a look and told me that the chip switching the seven bars of the liquid crystal numbers had dirty contacts and it would always indicate eight — which was the condition when all the seven luminous bars were lit. So we never did that transatlantic experiment!

The second sequel occurred when I had another well-known psychic in the laboratory. Matthew Manning, the distinguished British psychic, had very kindly agreed to do a week's experiments during one August vacation and he agreed to try that experiment with the random number box. This time I resolved that there would be no trouble with dirty electrical contacts. The box was switched on early in the morning so that it would be at a steady temperature and the Chief Technician did several runs with it and got the correct results. He scored correctly only when he looked at the back and put in the right number. I also did several runs with the same results. So, every precaution having been taken, I said to Matthew that we were ready. As with Ingo, Matthew said that he did not need an OBE to do an experiment like that. He also said that the numbers would appear on an internal screen in his head. So we did a run of twenty 'guesses.' With baited breath I set the dials to see how many he had got right. Eight! Sadly, it seemed, the same trouble had recurred. The technician took the box away and again cleaned the contacts so that it worked perfectly. Each of us again did several runs with no problems. Then we did another run with Matthew. Again he got eight!

Considering this afterwards it seemed to me, and to experienced SPR colleagues with whom I discussed these results (and that adds up to a great many years of hands-on experience), that the personal unconscious minds of both Ingo and Matthew discovered for some reason unknown to us that the discovery of those numbers by pure clairvoyance was impossible. The personal unconscious mind is both amoral and very obliging and helpful, as I well know from much experience with hypnosis, in which one is in communication with that part of the mind. So, Ingo's and Matthew's unconscious minds both knew that we wanted a high score and as they could not produce it for us by pure clairvoyance they did it by psychokinesis (PK), in effect spoiling the contacts to give us the highest score it could — eight. But no 'normal scientist,' having no experience at all of the operation of the psychic faculties and of the unconscious mind, would ever accept that as an 'explanation' and would say that it was just coincidence — even though it occurred only with the two gifted and 'trained' psychics and with no one else.

It should perhaps be mentioned at this point — and we shall discuss it further later when we have more and stronger evidence — that some quantum physicists would say that as the 'physical world' is a function of the consciousness of us 'observers,' the unseen numbers 'do not exist' until they are observed and no one ever observes them in the first and original version of the experiment with the naïve volunteer (on 'pure clairvoyance'). In their jargon, consciousness 'collapses the wave function' and causes the digits to be something 'real' rather than potentialities having a certain probability (measured by the wave function). I have checked this statement with professors of physics and they confirm that some of their number (those who agree with the so-called Copenhagen interpretation of quantum mechanics of Niels Bohr and his colleagues) do indeed interpret the world in this way. But this will be dealt with more fully later.

The reader will appreciate how enormously important experiments of this kind in psychical research potentially are. They include the possibility that we might be able to throw extra light on quantum physics from a quite different area of science, intimately concerned with consciousness.

I would like to finish this section with another experience of mine throwing a little more light on the psychology of the 'normal scientist.'

A year or two ago I heard an after-dinner talk by a distinguished brain chemist/neurologist about the brain and consciousness. I asked him this question: Could he please explain to me how it is that psychiatrists are not exceedingly interested in normal rational healthy people who have some of the experiences of their psychotic patients — namely, psychics? His answer? 'Lot of nonsense ... next question please!' The reader will perhaps agree with me that comment is hardly necessary!

How to have your own OBE

I cannot finish this chapter without saying a little about how the reader may share with me the experiences I have been having. They will then know at first hand exactly what we are discussing and will develop their own views about it, which will be an infinitely better situation than just reading my own.

In Chapter 5 on near-sleep imagery I describe the way I recommend that a reader may try to experience the hypnagogic state. This is probably easier to achieve than the out-of-body experience, and the adventurous reader might with advantage try this first. However, learning to become very relaxed is also probably the best way into the OBE too, just as it is the best way into normal refreshing sleep. Having done this as described there, the next stage to the OBE might well be to develop the cataleptic state I also describe there. The experimenter/reader might then do exactly what I described earlier in this present chapter which was successful for me. However, if it is not successful then there are alternatives to try in turn. One is to imagine oneself 'lifting off' from the physical body without being cataleptic but when in an exceedingly relaxed state. This may lead to success: as I suggested earlier, we are all different and by no means everyone who has an OBE does it from the state of catalepsy as I did. Yet another method is to project when 'the vibrations' start. Robert Monroe found, and described in his book *Travels Out of the Body,* that his OBEs started from his body being in a state of what he describes as 'vibration.' I do not imagine that he was speaking literally. The body probably *felt* as though it was vibrating. I suggest that a reader who would like to try Monroe's method should get his book and read it carefully. He describes in some detail just what was successful for himself and worked over many years. He had a great deal more experience of it than I did but he was not a 'scientist,' and his approach was a little different from my own.

Remote viewing

In the past few years there have been a number of television programmes about the American remote viewing programme, which was
started during the Cold War. A group of psychics used their powers
to discover facts about the covert operations of the USSR, and various other matters, a story told in the excellent book by Jim Schnabel:
Remote Viewers: the Secret History of America's Psychic Spies. I
attended a course given by David Morehouse, one of that very successful group, and learned a great deal.

It became clear to me that successful remote viewing involves one
of two methods of obtaining psychically information remote in time
and space. Dave Morehouse told us that no psychic in the programme
got all his perceptions accurate but the best, after a long training lasting several years, got about 60 per cent right. So several psychics
were used and what appeared in common in their data seemed to be
fairly reliable.

The first method we were taught seemed to have certain similari-
ties with the use of an 'internal screen' which I have already mentioned earlier in connection with Ingo Swann and Matthew Manning.
The 'tyro percipients' tried to become very relaxed and allow images
to appear before their 'internal eye,' having first been given a target.
Other kinds of information such as feelings, were also of interest.
The target used in the course was a photograph inside a sealed envelope selected at random from a pile and identified by a random number written on the envelope when the experiment began. In the case
of the real thing, the target may have been something like the inside
of a building in a remote part of the USSR, and believed to be concerned with something like war preparations. We were given training
(the course lasted only one week) in teasing out very subtle intima-
tions of information appearing in the relaxed conscious mind without
altering it by the operation on it of the conscious critical analytical
mind.

When all our 'perceptions' were written down and the envelope
then opened it appeared to me remarkable how relevant to the target
some of the perceptions were. We did not know which at the time, of
course. However, we were all very new and most of us were not psychics. It became quite clear to me that good visualization was a necessary concomitant to success and Dave Morehouse told me that this
would come in time. (I suspect that, in my own case, it might be a

long time!) Many of his own perceptions — and he gave us several packets of his own real data — were virtually fully accurate.

There was reference in the course to a more advanced method of remote viewing and this seemed to involve out-of-body 'travelling' and 'observation,' not unlike my own long-time experiments, described earlier, to observe random numbers or corresponding objects.

The reader who is particularly interested in the methods and results of this very covert US programme (now courageously blown wide-open by Dave Morehouse) will find much detail in the book by Jim Schnabel. Dave Morehouse's own story is to be found in his book *Psychic Warrior*. A number of courses on remote viewing are frequently available.

CHAPTER 4

The Lucid Dreaming Experience (LDE)

Normal dreaming

Everyone dreams — whether they remember doing so or not. During dreaming there are swift movements of the eyes from side to side, the so-called rapid eye movements. The dreamer is then said to be in REM sleep. If they are awakened at that time, they will remember that they were dreaming. These are what I refer to as normal dreams. In normal dreams we are not aware that we are dreaming and accept everything that occurs without any question or analysis. Normal dreams appear to be created by the personal unconscious mind using material obtained from the memory store, and occasionally from some deeper part of the unconscious mind. The 'deeper' material appears to be occasionally precognitive — it foretells the future. Dreams are full of symbolism. They often appear to indicate that the unconscious mind is trying to give the conscious mind a message. These messages seem sometimes to be from a wiser deeper part of us. There are in various parts of the world, I think particularly of the USA, dream groups of people who meet regularly to discuss and try to analyse their dreams. What the dream is trying to say is sometimes very helpful. There are many excellent books about normal dreaming and dream analysis so I propose to leave normal dreaming at this point and turn to the rather less known lucid dreaming.

Lucid dreaming

It is not so well known that it is quite possible to be aware that one is dreaming and can be possessed of a full memory and one's full critical faculties. In the latter the dreamers are well aware of who they are and have their full normal memory including their name, address and telephone number, what they were doing yesterday and what they propose to do tomorrow. Lucid dreams are also highly symbolic. The dreamer

There are still, I am told, many sceptical doctors in cardiology wards who doubt the existence of the NDE, but they surely do not listen properly to their patients. In such hospitals nurses know of lots of cases.

Important experiences of NDEers

There are a number of experiences of NDEers which are important and significant in that they give us clues to the nature of human beings and indicate that there is much more to each of us than an electrochemical machine. Some of these have been recounted to me by subjects who have had one or more NDEs. As mentioned earlier, the first doctor to write a book describing the NDE was Raymond Moody. He then discovered that another doctor, Elizabeth Kübler-Ross, had also been collecting details of cases at the same time as he. I spent a weekend with Dr Moody and about thirty people who had had an NDE and I there learned a great deal about the experience. First, I would say that I have never met more fulfilled people. They were delightful to be with. All wanted to be helpful to others and several had attended classes since their NDE to improve their education because, they told me, they knew nothing, and how can one help people in that state!

The radical changes resulting from an NDE are not always welcomed by the spouse of the subject. A number of the people I met were sadly divorced or separated. I imagined a prestige-conscious couple where the husband was advancing in his business career and might soon be asked to join the Board of his company. His prestige-conscious wife was looking forward to a bigger car and a larger house. Then her husband had an NDE. Thereafter he lost all interest in 'getting on' in his career, refused to attend cocktail parties where he might meet the 'right' people, but was much more interested and concerned about whether the old widow in the corner house was being properly looked after and happy. He was a completely different man from the one his wife had married.

Several of those thirty NDEers I met told me that the wide-ranging extrasensory perception (ESP) which they had had during their NDE had persisted for some time afterwards. One of them told me that whenever the telephone rang he always knew who it was. The same applied to the front door bell. This began to worry him greatly. Some months later the door bell rang, and he did not know who it was. What a relief it was to know that he was back to normal! Regrettably he had kept no records as is well aware that their physical body is asleep in bed. They are therefore in a position to carry out good scientific experiments on the condition in which they find themselves.

It has been found that when a lucid dreamer makes rapid to-and-fro eye movements in the dream body these are duplicated in the physical body and this enables a dreamer to carry out pre-arranged experiments in the dream. The eyes are the only part of the body which is not cataleptic when one is dreaming. Without catalepsy the body would tend to carry out the actions taking place in a dream. I remember one experiment in a dream laboratory in which a dreamer had been asked to lift heavy weights in his dream. He signalled that he was about to do so by three such rapid eye movements. Afterwards he signalled again that the experiment was complete. Experimenters in the dream laboratory had earlier attached electrodes to the muscles of his arms and legs (as well as to his eye muscles) and, when he lifted the weights, observed muscle tensions appearing in the relevant arm and leg muscles — but rather smaller than would have been the case had he lifted the same weights in 'real life.' The muscle tensions are produced in the physical body by electrical signals from the brain and the record produced on a moving paper strip by a pen tracing these electrical signals is called an EMG, or electromyogram. The 'normal' rapid eye movements in a dream are duplicated in the physical body and, as mentioned earlier, signify that someone is dreaming; they are in the so-called 'REM sleep.' The other muscles of the body are cataleptic in that state, otherwise the body would tend to do just what the dreamer was experiencing in the dream.

I propose again to explain how I produced such lucid dreams for myself and describe some of the experiments I have so far carried out and what I hoped to learn, and have learned, from them. I found them to be highly illuminating — infinitely more so than reading about someone else's lucid dreams would have been. Once again I can only advise a researcher to learn to have such dreams themselves, if they are to carry out any research worthy of the name in this area of consciousness. Reading books is not enough.

Learning lucid dreaming

There are a number of ways of learning lucid dreaming but I decided in this book to concentrate especially on exactly what I can speak about from personal experience. The first thing I did was to learn to remember my normal dreams. Some years ago I wanted to study the symbology of dreams and discover whether they really were sometimes precognitive (as J.W. Dunne had found) so I put pencil and pad beside the bed and, as soon as I awoke, wrote down whatever I remembered of my dreams. I did this for some months. My personal unconscious mind rapidly understood what I wanted and began to wake me up every few minutes with a new dream. I was getting very little proper sleep! However, I was able often to see what my personal unconscious mind was telling me. It became clear to me as a result of this that a wiser deeper part of myself (I do not mean the personal unconscious mind) took the opportunity while dreaming of proffering advice and encouragement via the dream, which is created by the personal unconscious mind, and which will include that advice and encouragement through symbols. (If we attach no importance to our dreams and do not bother with them I feel fairly sure that the unconscious mind will no longer transmit this advice.) I continued this practice for some months but eventually abandoned it for the good night's sleep that I needed.

Having some years ago written down my dreams as I have described, and with the aim of discovering possible precognition, I learned rather more recently of lucid dreaming. I started off learning how to do it as I did before, but this time gave clearer instructions to 'George,' which is what I call my personal unconscious mind (see further below and Chapter 18). It is useful to understand how to ask George to do certain things like this. As a result of many years practice of meditation I was able to get into a very relaxed state very rapidly and in that state was able to give George the necessary instructions. It will be remembered that George — and I shall go on calling that part of me George for brevity — George is very naïve, very obliging and amoral. He believes and carries out the instructions of the conscious mind (or the instructions of a hypnotist) if they are sufficiently clear and it is possible to carry them out — and assuming that there is not a good reason why he should *not* carry them out, perhaps for reasons of honesty or morality. Writing down and re-reading one's dreams impresses him with the fact that you consider them of importance, so he naturally tries to assist in the way I have described.

Another and more psychologically respectable name for George is the personal unconscious mind or alternatively the lower unconscious. Assagioli, the founder of Psychosynthesis, defines and describes it in the following terms. Here we have:

the intelligent co-ordination of bodily functions; fundamental
drives and primitive urges, many complexes charged with
intense emotion; dreams and imaginings of an inferior kind,
lower uncontrolled parapsychological processes; various
pathological manifestations; phobias, obsessions, compulsive
urges, paranoid delusions.

I call this 'personal unconscious' George because it is a part of us
which seems to have a certain autonomy and is amoral, arational, and
very helpful but not highly intelligent. 'George' is what aircraft pilots
call their automatic pilot and he seems to have much in common with
that instrument, running many of our bodily operations and activities
when we are not paying attention to them. It is George who drives the
car home from the station when our conscious thoughts are on other
matters. George acts as though he is a separate part of us.

Using the steps outlined later (see Chapter 18), I told George that I
wanted to wake up only a few times during the night for some really
meaningful dreams and not every few minutes, as happened on the first
occasion. This began to occur quite soon and I was 'launched' on the
new research.

When I was successfully writing down several dreams each night I
got started on phase 2 of the 'training.' This involved doing a particular thing on a number of occasions during the day. The particular thing
was what the psychologists call a 'reality check.' Most if not all of
them consider the normal physical world to be 'real' and these other
experiences to be something else — fantasy, I presume. So a 'reality
check' is either a confirmation that one's consciousness is in the 'real
world' or discloses that one is in fact actually dreaming. A commonly
recommended reality check is to look at one's watch, look away and
then look at the watch again. If the time indicated is the same on both
occasions then one is, in fact, probably awake. If it is different one is
probably dreaming. I tried this but I discovered what seemed to me a
better reality check for me. (It may not be so for everyone.) What I do
is to try to levitate — float upwards. If I do in fact float upwards then
I am most certainly dreaming. If I do not I am probably awake. Serious
researchers in the field of consciousness will, as they gain experience,
work out their own favourite ways of doing these things.

It took me about a month before I had my first, very brief, lucid
dream. I found myself saying 'Am I dreaming now?' and found that I
clearly was. I hardly needed to carry out the test: it was obvious.

Unfortunately, I immediately awoke in my bed. It was some weeks later before I had my second period of lucidity. I again awoke almost immediately. This indicated the need for the second thing I had to learn: how to keep the lucid dream going and not just wake up. There are several often-mentioned ways of doing this. The one mentioned most often is to spin round like a top. I tried this but found it ineffective for me: perhaps because I did not spin fast enough, or something else was wrong. Another method of staying lucid is to examine one's hands. I did not find this very effective for me, either, but probably realized at that point the principle involved. The next time I was lucid I devised a method which worked beautifully for me and confirmed what I thought these various methods were really doing. I rapidly thought, as I realized that I was lucid, that the right thing to do was not to think, even for a split second, of even the possibility of awakening but to keep my attention on the level of consciousness I was in. I remembered that on the other occasions I had briefly thought 'Am I going to wake up?' and I did. So I picked up a stone from the ground on which I was standing when I became lucid and examined it in very great detail, admiring the various shades of brown in it and the tiny cracks that I could see. My years of meditation practice, following the learning of concentration, were useful here, and this worked beautifully.

Then I was able to look around properly and found myself standing in a cobbled street in a beautiful medieval village. The sun shone brightly from a brilliant blue sky and all the colours of the cottages around me were brighter than I ever remembered seeing before. I felt full of energy and happier than I have felt for a long time. It was almost like a mini-mystical experience. Then, fully aware of everything around, with a complete memory and critical faculty, I thought of what I had intended to do when I had my first fully-lucid dream. My idea was to see whether I could find a Wise Old Person — a Jungian archetypal figure — who might give me advice, first on effective lucid dreaming! Here was where I made my first silly mistake: I thought that I might find a wise old person in a university! So I continued walking and a little way out of the village came across three young men talking together. I asked one of them whether there was a university in the neighbourhood. He motioned over the hedge and I looked and saw a group of grey stone buildings at the other side of a large field. How I did this I do not understand because I had to levitate about three metres to clear the hedge. Then I floated across the field towards the buildings. I landed in a cloister on more cobble stones and walked along, looking for someone to ask for directions. Further round the cloister were three young men — presumably students — sitting at a table in conversation. I was just about to ask them where I might find a professor when I awoke.

That dream lasted just 48 minutes. I knew this because I had had two very brief lucid dreams immediately preceding that one and on awakening from each I had glanced at my luminous clock.

There were several things I noted, following that lucid dream. The first was that I now knew a method that worked to maintain the lucidity. Next time, I resolved, I would every half hour or so do what I had done at the beginning and examine some feature of the scenery in detail and see whether that would give me a longer period of lucidity. The second thing I noted was the brilliance of the scenery and the joyous feeling I had. The third thing was those two groups of three young men. Clearly lucid dreams as well as 'normal' dreams contain symbolism. Faint memories lingered that somewhere C.G. Jung had remarked that the unconscious seemed to like threes. What that actually meant I had no idea. Finally, I thought that if I am 'flying' somewhere when my half-hour 'maintenance task' arrived, then I should have to hope that examining my hands would be effective in keeping my consciousness there.

A final remark on that lucid dream: It had been noticed, and I certainly noticed it on that occasion, that dreams take place in 'real time.' In other words, experiments involving a lucid dreamer guessing time intervals and signalling by rapid eye movements to experimenters in the dream laboratory have indicated that the passing of time seems very much the same as it does in the waking state. I doubt that clocks and watches would remain synchronized with 'real' timekeepers; however, I have not done an experiment to check.

It was again a month or two before I had my next lucid dream of a reasonable length. This was quite different, for some reason. I became lucid in the middle of a field and there was a drizzling rain. Between the two dreams I had discussed the problem of how to find a Wise Old Person, and my wife had made a very perceptive suggestion. She said: 'Why don't you just go into a likely house and *expect* to find one there?' So this is what I did. Looking around I noticed a house at the edge of the field. It seemed to be the only one, so I levitated and shot horizontally across the field and (carrying out another experiment) shot straight through a window and into a room. There seemed to be no crashing of breaking glass. I landed on my feet and looked around. In a large armchair sat a bearded man wearing a Sufi-type conical turban and a yellow robe. Cross-legged on the carpet in a circle all around him were young men. They looked somewhat unkempt and I assumed that they were 'students.' I politely approached the older man and he asked me for my name and telephone number. I gave him these (wondering why he wanted the latter) and then looked for a piece of paper on which to write them down for him. All the bits of paper I could find were already fully covered with writing. I decided to press the pencil very hard on the paper so that the number would stand out on the top of other writing, so I looked around for a pencil. All the pencils I could find were broken. It occurred to me that I could write if I prised the wood away from the lead with my thumb nail, as I had no penknife. I did this, but in the meantime had been looking rather more closely at the WOP. He looked none too clean, in fact there appeared to be several weeks of soup stains on the front of his robe. I excused myself, feeling that he could hardly be a genuine wise person, and withdrew back through the window into the field — and promptly woke up. Since then I have wondered whether I was right. Should one necessarily expect a WOP to be clean? The perceptive reader will again notice the proliferation of symbols of various kinds. I have no idea what they mean — assuming they mean very much at all. That seems just to be the way the unconscious works.

I had one lucid dream which taught me a great deal and I must include that in this small collection. It did not last very long but was nearly as delightful as the first. I found myself standing on lush grass in the sunshine feeling that I was not very far from the sea and I did a different kind of experiment which I have thought deeply about since. It taught me a lot. I first looked very carefully at my body. It appeared to be in every way much the same as 'usual.' My heart was beating, apparently quite normally; I was breathing, also apparently normally. I felt very fit and energetic. I looked at, and felt, the ground: it was just as usual. *Nothing seemed, at least superficially, to be different in any way from my normal life.*

I thought of those scientists and philosophers who looked upon our normal daily life as 'real' and the dream life as fantasy and felt sure that they had never had a lucid dream. And I thought of those Tibetans who learn lucid dreaming so that they can have full 24-hour consciousness — and discover that the ordinary daily life is a 'dream' too. And I thought of Jung and his dream of entering a temple and finding a yogi in meditation — and the yogi had his own face. Was the yogi dreaming Jung, or was Jung dreaming the yogi? I wondered whether a pathologist would find all the internal workings of my 'dream body' just the same as usual — perhaps because he *expected* them to be like that. And I wondered what I should find if I were able appropriately to examine it, knowing only a little about the inner workings of the body. And I thought how wonderful it would be if we were able to teach the disabled to experience lucid dreaming so that, hopefully, they would feel as well and active as I did then. But perhaps they would have to be re-educated to feel that. Many more thoughts of this kind flitted through my mind as, I hope, they will flit through the mind of the reader.

Some normal symbolic dreams

Earlier I mentioned that wise help and advice sometimes seems to come to us through our dreams. I wanted to include some examples of this from my own experience.

Many years ago I used to have a fairly regular dream involving my wandering around a house. I had this dream — which had a quite different quality from all my more normal dreams — every ten or fifteen years at one time. In more recent years it has not been even that frequent. It is many years since I had the last one. It rapidly became clear to me that that house was a symbol of my life. When I was young I had in this dream a somewhat untidy room somewhere at the back of my house. I remember wandering around trying to find it and observing that the house seemed to be under continuous construction. There seemed to be carpenters and builders everywhere. Gradually over the years the house seemed to get tidier and my room was nearer the front entrance. I remember well a dream which seemed to mark a turning point in the series when I entered the house at the front entrance, turned left immediately up the stairs and found my room was the first one on the next floor up. This time it was neat and tidy with a tasteful decoration, pristine white lace curtains and a bed covered with a spotless white counterpane. An equally spotless white carpet covered the floor.

The next dream I had of my house, perhaps fifteen or twenty years later, involved my leaving my room and wandering about the passages of the house. I went down one dark passage I had not noticed before and discovered some steep curving wooden stairs going higher. Ha! I thought, this will be the way to the loft, which will be full of broken chairs, old tennis rackets, boxes and dust. I scrambled up the stairs, pushed up the trap door in the ceiling and entered the loft. To my amazement it was not at all as I had imagined. I found a long table running almost the full length of the loft and around it sat Indian ladies dressed in beautiful saris. They were making other beautiful Indian clothes together with slippers embroidered in gold and silver threads and other bright colours. The ends of this room formed the triangular gables ends of the house and they appeared to be made of clear glass. Through the clear glass at both ends I could see that we were level with snow-capped mountain peaks. No one said anything to me and I passed through the length of the room and went down through another trap door into the house below, where I awakened.

These 'big dreams' (as some Native American tribes call them) had a completely different quality from any of my more 'ordinary' dreams and gave me a great deal of encouragement.

As already observed, there are many 'dream groups' of people who meet regularly, especially in the United States, to discuss their dreams and find out what they are indicating to them from that deeper level of themselves. Concerning this, it is clear to me that, first, I am not qualified to discuss the symbolism of dreams and do not propose to do so further. (There are excellent books available.) Secondly, it is also clear that the only person who can 'interpret' your dreams is yourself. When you have puzzled out the correct meaning it has its own validity: you just suddenly realize that it is absolutely right.

CHAPTER 5

Daylight or Near-Sleep Imagery

Hypnagogic or hypnopompic states

There is a most interesting ASC which occurs just as one is falling asleep or waking up. The state of being almost asleep is called the hypnagogic state and that of starting to awaken is called the hypnopompic state. The word *hypnagogic* is derived from the Greek meaning 'leading into sleep' while *hypnopompic* means 'guiding out of sleep.' Probably a high proportion of people pass so quickly through these states that they do not notice anything unusual at all: they just change from waking to sleeping. However, many others have most interesting experiences as they fall asleep, including panoramic or kaleidoscopic scenes all around their room. Sometimes faces are seen and heard talking together. It is not difficult to learn how to remain in these states and, for those unaccustomed to them, this can lead to most interesting experiences. I well remember an early SPR paper (by a Mrs Leaning) in which a subject describes how she was lying watching two faces talking together when suddenly one of the faces looked her full in the face and said to the other: 'She can see us you know!'

My purpose here is to describe my own experiences of this imagery in different contexts and to give some views as to its possible value. The major problem to be considered is the origin and possible meaning of this imagery. From my experience it is to me quite obvious that sometimes there is a great deal more to it than just random meandering of the brain, as the inexperienced might suggest.

During the 1939–45 war I spent two days a week at classes in London and had to travel there by train from South Farnborough, Hampshire, where I worked (at the Royal Aircraft Establishment) to Waterloo station — a journey which took about one hour. A most significant experience took place on the train returning in the evening after a very tiring day which started very early. I was dozing in the corner of the carriage on a warm spring day and suddenly observed before my eyes a red brick wall. The wall extended right across my field of vision, was within a short distance of my eyes and was brightly illuminated, apparently by the sun. Every crack in the bricks and the mortar between them was brightly illuminated and in crystal clarity. I remember thinking at the time that this was some deeper part of me telling me that at that moment there were difficulties in going forward with my life. This thought was of the vaguest and I had no actual evidence at that time that this was the true interpretation. For all I knew there was no meaning at all in the vision. It was, however, followed by others and the whole series seemed to me to be significant.

The next hypnagogic image occurred when I was deeply relaxed in my study. My feet were up on a stool and I was lying in an armchair. (The aim was to see whether I could repeat the out-of-body experience I had had several years earlier.) When I had attained a deep state of relaxation in my darkened room suddenly there appeared in front of me what looked like a framed picture. It looked about a half-metre square and showed in bright colours a table beautifully laid for tea. The table was covered by a pristine white damask table cloth on which were laid delicate china. As I recall there were plate, cup, saucer, milk jug, sugar and teapot. The table was against a window with fresh white lace curtains drawn back by ties and through the window was visible a sylvan scene: fields in the foreground with trees, cows grazing peacefully and in the background snow-capped mountains. Again I had no idea what this meant, if anything, but it did give me a delightful feeling of tranquillity and a reassurance that all was well. I did notice that when I attempted to analyse such an image it immediately switched off. Analysis uses the left hemisphere of the rain and creative imagery uses the right side, so this might be expected.

The next image that occurred in this series was in the middle of the night when I awakened drowsily from sleep. This was not framed but occurred as a single object, as it were floating against the dark background of the night. That object was a slipper. It had a pointed curled-up Persian-style toe and was embroidered with gold and silver threads with other threads of bright colours: red, blue, green, yellow. For some reason that Eastern slipper gave me the impression that I was now on the right lines and walking forward and that I should look for useful guidance particularly to the East. It gave me a quite opposite message from that of the brick wall I saw earlier, and this image greatly encouraged me. I do emphasise that all the images in this whole series were bright and clear and I have not had that sort of experience before or since — except for the final image of the series and which I shall now describe. I also am not at all clear why I ascribed to them the meanings that I did. However, I felt quite sure at the time of each that I knew what I was being told. Who or what was telling me — some deeper part of myself or something outside myself — I had no idea.

The final hypnagogic image of the series also occurred in the middle of the night. (I suppose that strictly it was a hypnopompic image.) That night I again woke up into the blackness of my room and there, apparently floating in the air in front of me, was the most beautiful bowl of roses I have ever seen. The bowl was predominantly blue and had gold chasing on it. The roses were all a deep red and looked as though they had just been picked and arranged by an expert hand. Every one was perfect. I have difficulty in describing the deep joy that gave me before I again fell peacefully asleep. Again, I cannot give any reasons or logical arguments to justify why I should have felt as I did.

Those images are the sum total of my experiences (so far) of this sort of mental imagery. The roses were 'presented to me' as I awoke from sleep and therefore formed a hypnopompic image. The others were on my way into sleep (had I continued along the same route) and were therefore hypnagogic images.

The reader will see during the course of the book the many and varied ways in which that wider, deeper part of ourselves (or perhaps occasionally something outside ourselves?) sometimes takes a hand in encouraging and guiding us. Towards the end we shall examine just what I feel I mean by this and by then we shall already have considered a wide range of experiences of different kinds.

It should perhaps be mentioned for completeness that for some reason I have never had the fairly common experience of panoramic scenes around my bedroom walls as I have been falling asleep. Also, I have never experienced 'seeing' faces or people talking, which I also understand is quite common.

Guided imagery

I shall never forget my first experience of guided imagery, which I had as part of a week's introductory course in Psychosynthesis. Until then I had not realized the power of the 'imagination.' If you are asked to imagine something there are very good reasons why you imagine certain details of that 'something' rather than others. This will become clear as we proceed. We shall see later that at the subtler levels of the universe, that is, of the mind, the imagination is 'externalized' and becomes, as it were, the surrounding 'scenery.' One may learn how to alter it at will.

For the guided imagery experience I lay on my back on the carpet with a pillow under my head and relaxed with eyes closed. The guide then asked me to imagine that I was lying in a field and asked me to look around (in my imagination) and say what the grass was like (sparse or lush). Then she said that I should get up (in my imagination) and look around again, when I should find a path across the field. I did this and the path led to a stile in a fence at the edge of a wood. This I was asked to climb over and continue on the path through the wood. I should come out into a small clearing where I should find something. Here I found (imagined) a small deer-like animal. The guide then asked me what the animal was doing. It was looking at me rather warily from a safe distance. She asked me what kind of animal it was and I said a hart — not realizing until it was pointed out to me afterwards that there are two ways of spelling the word that sounds like that. In other words my unconscious was giving the conscious me a very clear message. We shall consider this at the end of the description. The guide pointed out to me that I could come back at any time I wished to see how my hart/heart was getting on.

I was then asked to walk further along the path in the wood and told that I should come across a house, which I should approach. She first asked me to describe the front door and then go inside. This I did and found myself in a pleasant downstairs room where I found a welcoming man. After a short conversation with him the guide told me to go along a passage where I should find a door leading to a cellar. Finding the door I was asked to descend the stairs behind it. Expecting that the cellar would be full of broken furniture, other unwanted articles and cobwebs, I descended the stairs. To my surprise I found a nicely whitewashed room containing a deal table in the middle, a quantity of logs on the floor neatly piled against one wall and a white-coated technician. At the other side of the cellar was a steam engine driving an electric generator. The supply of steam evidently came from a boiler fuelled by the logs. I noticed that the output from the generator passed through a large old-fashioned switch on the wall from which a cable travelled upwards and disappeared through the ceiling. I asked the technician what he did. He explained that his job was to supply the house with energy. I replied that I was myself an electrical power engineer and my job was once to design large electric machines. Could I give him any advice? He nodded, so I mentioned that I could hear a stream flowing past the wall of the house and that if he put the shaft of the generator through that wall a water turbine could be put on it and the generator would be driven by the power of the water. He would then not need to cut the wood and clean the boiler and could do other more useful things. He seemed pleased, asked me to arrange this and I said goodbye and ascended the stairs back to the house.

It still seems strange to me what was happening. I was clearly making up that story and yet it seemed more as though it was being presented to me by some other part of me. It had what I can only describe as a certain validity.

The guide then asked me to go upstairs. The reader will perhaps remember the last chapter in which I described one of my 'normal' symbolic dreams, especially the one where I found stairs leading to an attic and found a room full of Indian ladies making beautiful Indian clothes and slippers. I somehow knew that I was to go up to that room and not to my bedroom one floor below. I did this, pushing up the trap-door leading to the 'attic.' All the Indian ladies were still there and took no notice of me. The guide then said that I should find someone there to whom I could speak. I looked around and found another door at the side of the attic which I had not noticed on the last occasion. Tapping gently on it I entered and found a grey-haired and bearded old man (looking just like Roberto Assagioli, the founder of Psychosynthesis). He was sitting at a computer keyboard but looked up towards me, smiled and greeted me. I asked him politely what he did. He said: 'I send instructions down to the house below ... but ...' he added, shaking his head sadly, 'sometimes they take no notice of me.'

That was more or less the end of the creative visualization experience. I was then asked to go back to the field and come back to 'normal reality.' The whole experience impressed me more than I can say. We shall have much more to say about the significance of the various components of these experiences later when we have more data to consider.

The guide then pointed out to me the fact I mentioned earlier — that there are two ways of spelling hart/heart and the fact that my hart was so cautious and wary of approaching. I realized then that I was becoming far too intellectual and was neglecting my emotional side. Realizing this I changed my normal behaviour with the family and we now have a much more balanced and happier life. When I go imaginatively to that glade in the woods for my regular meditation my little hart is still there but now he comes and puts his chin on my foot while I am meditating!

Shamanic journeying

Shamanism involves probably the oldest system in which altered states of consciousness have been used for the benefit of human beings. It has been used in primitive and more advanced tribal communities the world over for probably some 20,000 or 30,000 years or more. It is the system used by 'medicine men' as far apart as Red Indian (native American) tribes and Siberian communities, to help cure the sick and obtain guidance for the tribe from what is considered to be a wiser source than living members.

I have had one experience of a shamanic 'journey' and so I propose to describe this. From the books I have read about shamanism it appears to be quite typical. First I lay down on a mattress and relaxed my muscles and mind. This is typical of most practices in regard to entering altered states of consciousness. The shaman then commenced his rapid drumming. I imagine that this helps to put the brain into the right state for the experience — a practice which will be noticed and referred to on more than one occasion in connection with other ASC entry methods.

The shaman then asked me to think of a suitable hole down into the ground such as a hollow tree or tube. I remembered a hollow oak tree in a park near my home. He then asked me to imagine that I was float-ing out of my body and diving down this hole into the ground. The hole, he said, would open out into a tunnel going steeply downwards. I walked down it in accordance with his instructions. Occasionally I informed him by slightly moving a designated finger that I had done what he asked. He told me that the tunnel would open out into a cave and so I imagined that it did this. I walked out through the entrance into a landscape rather like the countryside and he told me that an animal would come towards me from the north. This he referred to as my 'power animal.' He then said that if it came towards me also when I faced east, and then south, and then west, I could accept it as genuine. The animal was a small deer-like creature — a hart.

The reader will remember my hart appearing in the creative visual-ization experience which was part of my experience in Psychosynthesis described above. Creative imagery was considered of importance by C.G. Jung in his studies of the unconscious and this is, it seems to me, probably where Assagioli got it. Jung had probably read about, or had experience of, the very ancient shamanic journeying practices before he devised his own guided visualization procedure.

The shaman then asked me to follow my power animal and this I did. It led me across the countryside and up a mountain. The reader will appreciate that I was using my creative imagination in doing this. I have read in books on shamanism that for a shaman the countryside is real and objective to his 'open eyes.' I am myself not a good visualizer and had to imagine the scenery, which I then 'saw' as it were through closed eyes: in other words it was as though I looked at scenery and then closed my eyes, knowing that it was there to be seen. There is a good reason why the creative unconscious mind imagines one scene rather than another. I was assured that 'imagining' the scenery was just as good as apparently 'seeing' it.

The hart led me into a small temple near the top of the mountain where I found a Wise Old Man. I asked him a question and received an answer. As I understood from what I had earlier read that only one question should be asked per visit I then took my leave.[2]

The hart, bouncing ahead of me, then led me down the mountain to other scenes. I proceeded across the countryside, still to the continuous rapid drumming of the shaman, which I found a great help. The drum is considered to be the shaman's horse on which he rides — and I now understood why. When a shaman is himself journeying, his assistant provides the drum beat. The modern shaman considers the drum beat to be 'driving' the brain rhythms into the appropriate frequency for the altered state of consciousness.

The hart bouncing along in front, my way led me along the shore of a large lake on the other side of which I could see white marble buildings with people in white robes moving amongst them. It is difficult for me to describe why I 'made up' this scene rather than another but it seemed right somehow. My way led past a house which I recognized as 'my house,' described earlier in this Chapter. I entered this house and went straight up to the top floor — the 'roof space' — where I found the Indian ladies weaving their saris and embroidering their slippers (see Chapter 4.) This time they appeared to recognize me and looked pleased and welcoming. The first time I found them there they took little notice of me.

Arriving in the roof space with the busy Indian ladies and the view of mountains at each end I immediately looked for the door into the WOM's room, tapped on it and entered. He was there as before, also seemed pleased to see me, greeted me and then I went out again, following the hart. This time I went through one of the windows at the end of the room onto a balcony from which I jumped a considerable distance to the ground and followed the hart, who seemed to be rapidly disappearing into the distance. I followed the power animal further round and then realized from the rapidly speeding up drumming that it was time to return to the earth.

The shaman asked me to be rushed up the tunnel by the wind and return to my body — which I promptly did. Stretching and breathing deeply I returned to my ordinary reality.

Clearly I would probably get more out of this experience with prac- tice. I would be able to use tape recorded drumming and practise as much as I liked. Also, it would be well worth my while, if I pursued this, to learn to visualize well.

Learning to have hypnagogic imagery

We cannot leave this fascinating and important branch of conscious- ness without considering how readers, if they wish, might learn to have personal experience of it. This is really not difficult but it might take some persistence. It should be easier for those who have practised meditation and have some control over what they allow their minds to think.

This is the method I suggest. Go to bed a little earlier than usual. If the room is warm it might be a good idea to lie on top of the bedclothes rather than underneath — to indicate to George, your personal uncon- scious mind, that this is not the usual going-to-sleep procedure. Have a dim light in the room, say a small wattage lamp some distance away. Then go through a relaxation procedure involving tensing and relaxing all the muscles of your body in turn starting at the feet and working your way up through the lower legs (left and right in turn) knees, thighs, stomach, chest, hands (in turn), forearms, upper arms, neck, face, scalp. The exact order of relaxing the limbs is, of course, not important. While the relaxation is proceeding say (mentally) to George — treating him/her just as though it is a different part of you (as it is) — 'Relax ... relax.' Imagine as clearly as possible that all the tension is draining away from every muscle and sinew in the body. Imagining the tension as a sort of grey mist floating away through your feet is quite a good idea. The more you practise this the better you will become and after a week or two you may find that you can become very deeply relaxed after just a minute or two. It is perhaps a good idea in addition to tell George that you are now going to count slowly up to ten and as you count you will become even more deeply relaxed. Then count

slowly up to ten, pausing after each digit to say (mentally) 'Relax ...
relax' on your outward breaths. After a week or two — or more — you
will be able to see how you are getting on and judge for yourself: you
may be able to cut the procedure down to just the slow counting and
imagining the tension disappearing.

Having become very deeply relaxed try to hold your mind calmly
and placidly almost without thought and start the following procedure
to get you even more deeply relaxed — but without falling asleep. Lift
your right forearm (the left if you are left-handed) and hold it vertically
upwards, the weight being supported by the bed. If you find the point
of balance you will be able to do this with no strain. However, if you
fall asleep your forearm will drop to the bed and wake you up again.
(If you find that this can occur without your waking up then put some
crinkled-up brown paper on the bed so that when your arm falls on to
it rather more noise will be made. This should be enough to do the
trick.) The whole aim is to become as deeply relaxed as you possibly
can while remaining awake. Remember that practice makes perfect.
Many people tend to give up far too soon. When you have learned to
do this really well and can lie on the point of sleep but without actually falling asleep, then the hypnagogic imagery hopefully will start.
When it does, try to observe it without critical analytical thought. If
you start asking yourself questions then, if your experience is the same
as mine was, the imagery will immediately switch off. However, the
more I learn about consciousness the more I realize that every human
being is different, so I hesitate to be too dogmatic about any of this. A
psychiatrist might suggest, as I did earlier, that the imagery is being
produced by the right brain hemisphere — for normal right-handed
people — and that using the analytical critical faculty will switch the
brain activity from the right to the left hemisphere. That will switch off
the imagery. However, I understand that this picture of events may well
be an over-simplification too. Better just have the experience!

You may find that at some point of deep relaxation you are cataleptic — in other words you will be unable to move a muscle (except for
your eyes). Do not be in the least alarmed: this occurs when going into
dreaming and is perfectly normal but we usually do not notice it. If you
are in this cataleptic state you may be able at some time, if you wish,
to have an out-of-body experience. (This was referred to in Chapter 3.)
If you are alarmed just wait and the catalepsy will disappear as you
awaken. But giving up like this is not the way to have personal experience of altered states of consciousness!

A final word about this procedure. Be happy and optimistic about it. Remember, you are doing it because you are curious about something which shows every promise of being very enlightening — in other words, you are doing it for fun. Remember this! Do not make a serious business of it!

CHAPTER 6

The Hypnotic Trance State and
the Role of Belief

The hypnotic trance state is of enormous importance, primarily because of the implications it has for us in regard to the mind and consciousness. It provides powerful evidence for a quite different way of regarding the physical universe. Perhaps we can even say that it opens the gates to the inner universe. We shall see what I imply by this as we proceed.

But first, let us consider the normal way of looking at the state of hypnotic trance. Most people have, at some time or other, seen a stage hypnotist put subjects into a hypnotic trance. But this is not what I mean by 'normal' since they usually choose the deep-trance subjects because they are easy.

What is usually done (not on stage) is first to relax the body, often by tensing and then relaxing all the muscles in turn, starting at the feet and working up to the head. Then the mind is relaxed by directing the thoughts to peaceful scenes such as the countryside. If this is done then gradually the mind 'lets go' and its normal analytical and critical faculty goes into abeyance. This is the state of hypnotic trance. A hypnotist gives instructions to a subject as to what to do with their mind. The subject can, when taught, almost equally well do it themselves, in which case it is called auto-hypnosis.

Alternatively, the normal subject may be put into this state by, for example, having suggested to them that they gaze fixedly at a point on the ceiling, or at a bright object, just too far behind them to be comfortable so that the eyes are tired as a result of the strain. The hypnotist then suggests that their eyes are becoming tired (which they truly are) and will shortly close and that their whole body is becoming relaxed. In this way he persuades the subject that what he suggests is true and is then able to go on to more advanced things.

For 'easy' subjects (very suggestible, as a result of 'belief' in the hypnotist — and roughly 10 per cent of subjects fall into this category) it may be enough for the hypnotist just to say 'Sleep!' in a commanding tone If the hypnotist has correctly judged the subject, they will then go into the same state as above. Usually a stage hypnotist picks out by a 'suggestibility test' the very best (deep-trance) subjects. They will then immediately do practically anything he suggests. A typical suggestibility test is as follows. The hypnotist asks the audience to link their fingers and hold them on their heads. He then asks them several times to squeeze and then tells the audience that they will be unable to free their linked hands. By this simple procedure he easily finds the subjects who cannot release their hands and whom he then invites to the stage for the demonstration. Every fair-sized audience has, as mentioned, about one in ten of such deep-trance subjects suitable for a demonstration.

What is happening during the hypnotic trance?

This account does not purport to give the complete story of hypnosis. Many other excellent books do that. My purpose here is to illustrate and emphasise an important fact which is well shown by the state of hypnosis. If the conscious rational critical mind can be kept out of the picture then, for the subject, the physical world can be 'altered' in radical ways to make it in some respects entirely different. The subjects themselves can also be made entirely different.

The good subject, say a rather shy clerk interested in cricket who volunteered for a hypnosis demonstration, can be told that he is a mechanic who is madly keen on football and is watching an exciting football match. He will 'see' the match taking place in front of him and will behave accordingly, waving his arms about and shouting appropriate words. His personal unconscious mind has accepted the suggestion of the hypnotist and dramatizes a suitable outgoing persona and physical world in which a football match is taking place in front of him. Remember that the personal unconscious is well practised in doing this sort of thing as it does it every night in creating dreams. Someone who was in the 'normal' state would say, of course, that the subject was experiencing an hallucination.

We shall return to this point that the physical world and the way it behaves depends to a very large extent on what has been put into the unconscious by 'authority figures' in the particular culture in which the child is being brought up from the moment of birth. Anything put into the unconscious by authority figures and therefore 'known to be true,' that is, *believed*, can have a very powerful effect on consciousness.

Let us have another example. Some years ago a series of programmes on television dealt with various aspects of hypnosis. One of these programmes was as follows. Dr Stafford Clark, a psychiatrist and the programme's presenter, asked one of the volunteer subjects to walk along a line of paintings with him and say which he liked. As I recall, about half the paintings were representational, such as scenes of the countryside and seaside by Turner and others, while the other half were abstract, some by Picasso and other surrealist and abstract painters. The subject said that he much preferred the representational scenes and gave a number of reasons why, including the beauty of the trees and the natural soft colours of the countryside, giving him a sense of peace and tranquillity. He could see nothing at all to admire in the non-representational paintings, which he thought garish, tasteless and pointless.

The hypnotist, Dr Black, then put him into a hypnotic trance and told him only that he would now much prefer the abstract paintings to the representational ones. Brought out of the trance so that he was again completely 'normal' but with no memory of the suggestion, he walked along the line with Stafford Clark for a second time and was asked again which paintings he really liked. This time he showed considerable enthusiasm for the abstracts and thought the representational paintings to be no better than poor photographs. He liked particularly the rectangular patches of colour of several abstracts and, when asked why, gave a number of reasons including that the patches of bright colour were fresh and exciting.

At the end of the programme Dr Stafford Clark pointed out that all that had been done had been that the subject (at the unconscious level) had been *told* that he now disliked what he had liked before and liked what he had disliked before. He himself unconsciously devised the 'reasons.' Clark went on to point out that very few people ever think out carefully what opinions they should hold about almost anything. In the UK most people would say that they were Christian (at least they would have done some years ago) and this was because their parents (authority figures) had told them that this was the only true religion. They 'knew' this because their parents in turn had told them. Similarly, most people in Ceylon are Buddhists. The same applies to most people's political opinions. The majority hold the same or similar political views as their parents. Remember, all this is because certain 'truths' were put repeatedly into the unconscious mind by various 'authority figures.' 'Normal' scientists, it will be remembered, have been similarly 'conditioned' to believe in realism by the very authoritative university figures responsible for their 'education.'

Is mesmerism different from hypnotism?

It is well known that Mesmer considered that when he was doing his therapy, 'animal magnetism' was being transferred from himself to the patients. He had a large tub of water in his salon and this he 'charged' with animal magnetism; the patients grasped iron rods which he put into the water as conductors of this 'magnetism.' Frequently the patients fell back onto the floor in a deep trance state. Mesmer was very successful and had a large number of 'cures.'

Other 'mesmerists,' and Mesmer himself when he had only one patient, at that time usually used what were called 'passes' in which they moved their hands in sweeps down the patient's body and at a small distance from it, to transfer their 'animal magnetism' to their patients. The results seem to have been the induction of very deep trance states often including catalepsy.

It was found that some mesmerists were able to induce a trance in their subjects when they were not even in the same room with them and sometimes when the subjects were walking in the town and no prior arrangement had been made. This was clearly an example of telepathy. I well remember that Professor Richet demonstrated this to some colleagues by causing his best subject to fall into a trance and trace her steps to his house, where she walked, in trance, up to his room.

These days one never hears stories like this from hypnotists, and one begins to wonder whether the methods used earlier — before we came to believe what was occurring was just 'suggestion' — produced trances much deeper than they normally are today. 'Animal magnetism' has, of course, no place in normal Western science. Animal magnetism reminds one of the Indian 'vital force' called *prana,* which Western healers consider they are transferring to their patients when they do just what Mesmer did — by moving their hands in sweeping movements down the patient. *Prana* is variously called *ki* or *chi* in Japan and China (and, according to Max Freedom Long, *mana* in ancient Polynesia) and acupuncture is based on a theory that if this vital force is not flowing freely through the 'meridians' or channels for it (unknown to Western science) and is blocked in some way, then disease results. Acupuncture is thought to release the blockages and stimulate the flow.

Perhaps if one believes (knows) that this 'force' exists, is being manipulated in these ways — just as the normal scientists believe (know) that it does *not* exist — then certain results can be achieved which would be impossible without it. This point, that believing in something so strongly that it amounts to knowing and, as it were, 'creates' the phenomenon, will be returned to later. It is of course also relevant in connection with the well-known placebo effect in Western medicine.

It is my hope that some experiments will shortly be conducted by hypnotists who are willing to carry out exactly the procedures that Mesmer used and employ their imagination to picture the flow of animal magnetism just as healers imagine today that *prana* is being transferred. Certainly such healers sometimes get beneficial results, as we shall see in more detail in Chapter 13.

Hypnosis and belief

A friend and colleague in the Society for Psychical Research who is also a hypnotist gave me recently a good example of how effective a belief can sometimes be. He was working (as a doctor) in the Casualty Department of a London hospital and a young boy aged about eleven came in with a broken arm — a 'green stick fracture.' His arm looked as though he had two elbow joints. The boy was terribly nervous and would not let his arm be touched, even for the X-ray. A Junior House Surgeon and medical colleague of my friend did not believe in 'all this nonsense called hypnosis' then said to him: 'Now you can demonstrate to me whether hypnosis really exists by my setting his arm under only hypnosis. That would convince me.' My friend said to the boy: 'I have a special gas here that will not put you to sleep but will take all the pain away.' He turned on the oxygen tap and held the mask about ten centimetres away from his own face, He then held it the same distance away from the boy's face. (The surgeon made very sure that it was oxygen and not ether!) Within seconds the boy said: 'The pain is going up my arm.' The surgeon then touched the boy's arm and there was no reaction. The boy was lying flat talking to my friend who then nodded to the surgeon. The latter manipulated the arm, which made a cracking sound. The boy then looked at his arm and said to my friend: 'That was my arm. Did you hear it?' The surgeon did his work and there was no pain and no reaction whatever from the patient.

Had my friend talked to that eleven-year-old about hypnosis he would hardly have known what he meant. However, he merely said that the gas would take all the pain away. The boy believed him — he was an 'authority figure' — and that is exactly what happened, at once.

This illustrates beautifully the effect on 'the physical world' — and our own body is a part of the physical world — of a belief. The hypnotist did not need to use any normal hypnotic procedure: in the case of the naïve young boy the belief in the doctor was there without it. An older patient would be so set in his beliefs about what was possible and not possible that a hypnotic procedure would probably have been needed to convince him, at the level of his mind where it mattered, that the oxygen would take the pain away. And the rational critical part of his mind — the conscious mind — would have had to have been taken out of the picture first, by the hypnotic induction.

That same friend had another somewhat similar experience — of a rather older young man who came into the Casualty department with a badly burnt arm. My friend said to him: 'I expect you know that ether is an anaesthetic.' He replied: 'Yes.' My friend continued: 'I don't suppose you know that it is also a local anaesthetic.' He directed a stream of the gas onto his burn (he informs me that it is quite a good and useful disinfectant) and the burn went numb straight away, allowing the dressing to continue without discomfort.

The reader might think that these true stories are hardly examples of hypnosis as there was no procedure of putting the subject into trance. I tell them to illustrate that it is the *belief* that matters. When hypnosis is used it is to enable the belief to be established in the personal unconscious mind and to hold the normal conscious critical part of the mind out of the way — that mind that had been 'educated,' i.e. conditioned, to have a particular set of beliefs dependent to a great extent on our Western normal-science based culture.

The importance of belief

Belief has been mentioned several times so it would be appropriate to finish this chapter with some more examples of how it enters into many aspects of our daily lives as well as into the more dramatic hypnotic trance state, when it can be changed, temporarily or sometimes permanently. It was only in the last few years that I began to appreciate the enormous importance of a phenomenon which most scientists might consider irrelevant to science. Belief allows the possibility of explanations for so much which otherwise has long appeared to be utterly inexplicable.

The 'realistic' or materialistic framework in which most scientists are immured affects many psychical researchers, with the result that much of what they do is not understood by them. The results are clear enough but appear inexplicable. Explicable in this context means describable in normal scientific terms. Telepathy takes place but does not obey the inverse square law which it surely should do if it is a radiation of some kind. Psychokinesis undoubtedly takes place — but the mind (whatever that may be) is not supposed to be able to influence physical objects — except the brain, of course. Influencing physical objects by the mind alone is impossible in a normal scientific realism context. The evidence for precognitive telepathy is very good — and appears to make considerations of an inverse square law irrelevant anyhow. We psychical researchers seem to be in real difficulty: few normal scientists take any notice of our work because, no matter how good the evidence, it cannot be 'explained.' The basic reason is, I believe, that our fundamental paradigm — realism — is wrong, inadequate. Problems, difficulties, inconsistencies surely show us that this paradigm is unable to bear the load of both normal science and paranormal science. So we have to think again.

Mediums and their 'guides'

Let me illustrate the importance of this by examining the development of the so-called guides of mediums. I attended many years ago a class for the development of mediums at the Spiritualist Association. We first sat and relaxed for an hour on Saturday afternoons in a dim light. At the end the budding mediums were asked to 'give off' (as it was put) what they had experienced. Several said that they had felt the 'guides working on them.' They had felt what they called a 'developing cap' put on their heads and several said that they had observed clairvoyantly a figure standing behind a lady opposite. I remember descriptions of dimly seen figures of Chinese and Red Indians who were presumed to be the guides in the other world assisting in the development of the novitiate mediums. Each week the subjects *imagined* these figures working on them — *believed* they were working on them — and gradually they were observed with ever growing clarity. Now probably many of them are the regular guides of their mediums, hopefully doing useful work in ostensibly conveying information — sometimes correct information — from the communicators in the next world. The presence of these guides — in my view — is the result of a carefully and persistently held belief. Few such guides are ever found to have lived here, no matter how much effort goes into trying to trace them.

S.G. Soal made up a character he called John Ferguson and got excellent communications, ostensibly from him, through the trance medium Mrs Blanche Cooper (for a fuller account, see Chapter 8). Again, these agreed with the facts he had made up. In this case Soal was not interested in physical phenomena. His success was the result of his belief. He had built up what we might call a clear 'thought form' of Ferguson and the result was very successful. Charles Dickens used to say that when his characters were crystal clear in his mind they took over writing the book for him. He just described what they did — and was, in that respect, rather like a medium. I shall be using that phrase 'thought form' later.

Table tilting and levitation

A member of the Society for Psychical Research, Ken Batcheldor, did an experiment concerned with table tilting and levitation. He describes experiments in which the sitters drew cards at the start. One of those cards gave one sitter permission occasionally to remove their hands from the top of the table, where they normally all were placed, and to put them under the table and levitate it normally, by pushing upwards. But they were not to do that too often. Colin Brookes-Smith instrumented the table so that whenever a vertical force was applied in that way it was recorded. When the table was in this way levitated *normally*, sometimes the sitters *believed* that they were having success in levitating it *paranormally,* and their belief often led to genuine paranormal levitations — that is, with no hands underneath. What had been produced was, in Batcheldor's words, 'a temporary suspension of disbelief.' In other words, if you *believed* that the table could levitate paranormally it sometimes did. And believing that temporarily was quite good enough, as it were, to reverse the so-called law of gravity.

Spoon-bending

Now let us remind ourselves of relevant phenomena, of the spoon-bending type associated with Uri Geller. Arthur Koestler, Mrs Koestler and I travelled north some years ago to interview a family which, according to the wife's descriptions sent by letter to us, were regularly experiencing paranormal phenomena. I took several very heavy strong tea-spoons with me and, when we had all become acquainted, I gave the daughter of eleven one spoon and the thirteen year old son another. I watched the girl and Koestler watched the boy. Each held the spoon between only finger and thumb just below the bowl, keeping the other fingers well out of the way as their parents had instructed them, and gently rubbed it. Our eyes did not leave those spoons. After about one minute the little girl's spoon flopped over her finger like Plasticine. On that occasion the boy's was not affected. I immediately grabbed the bent spoon and felt it. It was cold, apparently normal and just bent, as though bent by normal large force. I asked the girl what she had been doing and she said that she had just been saying to herself 'Bend! Bend!' and she said that she knew it might bend because she had seen Uri Geller do it. In other words she had a strong *belief* amounting to saying that she *knew* it might bend — and so it did.[3]

I remember an informal but very illuminating experiment when Geller himself was in Professor Hasted's laboratory one Saturday afternoon some years ago. Geller stroked the upper surface of Arthur C. Clarke's Yale key for about a minute while Clarke's finger was on the round end the whole time, and he, Koestler and I watched it closely. It bent upwards. The key did not otherwise move from its position. There is not in my mind the slightest doubt about this, despite what most magicians inexperienced in the paranormal would say — not having been there. Geller *believed* it would bend with a belief amounting almost to *knowing*.

Paranormal healing

Several examples of the power of belief in paranormal healing are described in Chapter 13. One of many cases I have experienced relates to an old lady with an arthritic knee. The healer (in Streatham) held her hands on the knee and the old lady felt a growing heat. She said that she obtained considerable benefit from this. She probably imagined mysterious 'healing forces' unknown to science to be working on her knee — and came for healing once a week.

I put a thermocouple under the healer's hands and there was no appreciable change in temperature. I then asked the healer to stand to one side and I wrapped several turns of coloured wire around the knee and connected the ends to the terminals of a decade resistance box which, without any electric supply, would do absolutely nothing physical. Then I carefully set the knobs of the box to various numbers, looked wise, and asked the old lady if she felt anything. She felt a growing heat, exactly as with the healer's hands, and experienced the same benefit. I thanked them all and took my leave. What was helping her arthritis? Her *belief* in the healer. What were the healer's beliefs? She imagined what she called healing energy passing through her hands. The Hindus would perhaps call it *prana*. The result of all this belief was a useful therapy.

Exactly the same applies to much of normal medicine. However, most people including most doctors have a belief in the realism philosophy within which 'normal science' works. This structure works much better if the patient *believes* in the doctor. The well-known placebo effect is based purely on belief. If the patient *believes* that they are having a therapeutic drug then the effect is often almost as good as the real thing. Every doctor knows that patients who *believe* that they are going to get better stand a much better chance of recovery than do patients who have given up.

Many healers and patients all over the country believe in radionics. This therapeutic practice is based on the view that a blood spot or sputum sample is in some way 'in resonance' with the patient who gave it. After diagnosis locally by that apparatus using the sample, homoeopathic remedies can be prescribed. The apparatus can then be used to send out therapeutic radiations to that patient. The sort of concepts used by a radio engineer are used. All this makes no sense at all to 'normal' scientists and doctors, yet many patients swear by it. A colleague and I did a double-blind experiment many years ago under the Theosophical Research Centre auspices in which radionic practitioners were asked to sort a set of blood spots — widely used in radionics for diagnosis — into male and female patients. Every practitioner got about half of them right (different halves!). Another researcher in another experiment surreptitiously removed all the wiring from behind the front panel of the radionic box without telling the practitioner. He used it as usual and noticed nothing wrong. Surely all their successes are either the results of belief or else the patients get better anyway, as they usually would anyhow if one did nothing. But their belief may well speed up their recovery.

The Sheep-Goat and Experimenter effects

In scientific parapsychology there are two very well-established effects. These are the Sheep-Goat effect and the Experimenter effect. A group of subjects gets better results (more likely to show extrasensory perception — ESP) if they *believe* that it is possible than does a similar set of subjects doing exactly the same experiment with the same experimenter who *believe* that it is impossible. Similarly subjects doing an ESP experiment get better results (more likely to show ESP) when the *experimenter believes* it possible than with one who considers it impossible. The only differences between these pairs of conditions is the state of *belief*.

Let us now consider further belief among scientists and its likely effects on their experiments. It is well known that nearly all 'normal scientists' consider that belief does not affect their experiments and that they themselves are completely objective, as they would put it. (They also consider, of course, despite the ever-growing strength of the evidence in its favour, that psi is impossible.) I did an experiment with Matthew Manning some years ago in my laboratory in the University in which he caused, by some sort of mental effort, a volt-meter monitoring the output of an experiment, to drop its reading by a maximum of some 30 per cent. It returned to normal when he stopped exerting his effort. Matthew — a distinguished psychic — had many beliefs amounting almost to certainty that he could do many things 'impossible' according to normal science. I found three scientists in the Department at that time (the middle of August) and asked them to come and observe something of interest. I then asked Matthew to exert his effort, and the voltmeter reading dropped. I should explain that all three scientists thoroughly understood how the experimental equipment worked. They then suggested various nor-mal reasons why the voltmeter reduction should take place — includ-ing ridiculous things such as the effect of breathing on the apparatus, or mains voltage variations etc. All these we had already taken care of — for example, we supplied the equipment from a battery having a steady voltage and no fluctuations, and the voltmeter reading reduction would also take place with Matthew at the far end of the laboratory where his breathing could hardly have had any effect on the apparatus. When all normal explanations had been exhausted one of the three began to get angry, metaphorically stamped his feet, said: 'Well, there *must* be a normal explanation!' and retired angrily and hurriedly from the scene — hoping thereby to remove the uncom-fortable state of cognitive dissonance in which he found himself. The other two were what I call 'good scientists' and agreed that the phe-nomenon really had occurred and that they could see no normal explanation for it. They are probably exceptional! (That 'normal sci-entist' who angrily stamped out is now a professor in a south coast university.)

Rupert Sheldrake has recently been producing evidence showing the much higher scientific standards we have in parapsychological experi-ments than do most scientists practising orthodox science — because we know of the effects of belief and use blind conditions appropriately in our experiments.

The final experiment I shall describe shows that a strong belief can actually affect our otherwise normal experience of the physical world. I gave a lecture about many strange things in a University *conversazione* some years ago in early Geller days and then said that we would try to levitate something. I asked four members of the audience to come out and sit around a small table at one side of the lecture bench. (There was a similar small polished table at the other side.) I chose a bowl of flowers from several decorating the front of the lecture bench and put it in the middle of that table and asked the subjects to concentrate on the bowl of flowers and try to imagine its rising. I asked the audience to remain quiet and use their imaginations to help. In order to assist I informed them that millions of Hindus considered that God used a particular sound in the creation of the universe — the sound OM — and that I would play this creative sound from loudspeakers. This was done and, after a short interval, the bowl of flowers tottered unsteadily into the air, remained there briefly and then crashed down again. There was an almost primeval gasp from the audience. I then ended the lecture in a somewhat casual way and the audience rushed forward to examine the flowers and table. (Magicians don't usually allow that!) There was nothing that appeared in the least bit unusual. One lady, evidently a spiritualist, said that she had seen a 'greyish substance' under the flowers lifting them and a similar substance under the table legs lifting the table. Our professor of physics, a 'normal scientist,' was listening to this 'silly woman' from the edge of the group. Then he firmly pronounced his real truth: 'Well, I saw nothing!' — and departed rapidly from the scene.

I should explain that I was researching electromagnetic levitation of high-speed vehicles at that time and had installed a small electromagnetic levitator in the shallow table drawer, which was locked. The bottom of the flower bowl had attached to it a disc of aluminium, painted to match the bowl. The leads to the levitator passed down one of the hollow metal legs of the table and then along an underfloor duct to the laboratory next door, where my technician was awaiting the moment when he had to raise the voltage and produce the levitation. The levitator made a loud 100-Herz hum when operating, so I had to produce a similar sound to mask it. The bowl of flowers certainly levitated, but the table was screwed down and did not move.

We see, in large part, what we have been conditioned to see — what we *believe* we should see. That lady who 'saw' the greyish substance evidently had heard about 'ectoplasm' and she 'saw' that pushing up the bowl of flowers and the table. Our physics professor, if he ever knew, had forgotten that one of my research areas was magnetic levitation. However, he knew of my interest in the paranormal and considered it foolish and ridiculous. No doubt he still does.[4]

That physics professor had a dogmatic belief amounting to certainty that such mental levitation was impossible and therefore he did not see it. Thank goodness most sensible people, who have been strongly conditioned to normal realism by our educational system — which, as I have said, is really a conditioning system — are not so badly or excessively conditioned as are many 'normal scientists.' So far as I know, the rest of the audience saw that bowl of flowers levitate and they looked for the 'explanation' in terms of what they knew — strings and rods. Most sensible people know that the paranormal does occasionally take place, and for many of them their state of belief is not so strong that it completely prevents any experiences of it. As mentioned earlier, something like 10 per cent of the population have had one or more out-of-body experiences and an even higher proportion have had experiences of telepathy. Much the same applies to many other phenomena. The 'normal scientist' is so conditioned that not only does he have no such experiences himself (or he writes them off as something normal), he is unwilling to 'waste his time,' as he would put it, reading about those of other people, because he *knows* already that they could not have taken place.

A little quantum physics

Now let us introduce a little quantum physics to see why we have this state of affairs. As I am not a physicist I checked what I am about to say with Professor Amit Goswami recently and he confirmed that I had it near enough to *his* views.[5]

It is quite well known that the quantum physicists tell us that the world we experience depends for its meaning and reality on our perception of it. Before we observe something it is a cloud of possibilities. When we observe it we (in their language) 'collapse the wave function,' which is a measure of probability, and there is then something definite 'out there' to observe. Numerous experiments have shown that. In effect the physical objects that 'normal scientists' consider they are describing have had their wave functions collapsed billions of times. The more a wave function is collapsed by all of us observers in a particular way to produce a particular object, the higher the likelihood that the same effect will be produced next time. So the normal physical world has permanence and stability. However, many experiences are not so consistent. The same result does not occur every time. These phenomena we call paranormal. A strong belief, an expectation amounting almost to certainty, raises the probability that the wave function will collapse in that way and lead to the experience believed in. So we have our apparently normal physical world, fairly consistently the same day by day.

It is clear that since the advent of quantum mechanics the physical world has today lost its old permanence, consistency and solidity, certainly in the minds of most physicists. Some seem to me quite happy to use mathematical calculations — which always give the 'correct' answers. They do not go into the philosophical implications, which they seem happy to keep on a mental shelf. What we observe depends on what has been observed before. So far as I can see, normal realism is now hardly applicable. I would have thought that classical idealism — or perhaps I really should say, mentalism — would be rather nearer to a workable philosophical basis. That is the view that the world consists of ideas, thoughts — and nothing else. Of course I would not dream of being dogmatic about any of this. Some physicists consider that neither realism nor idealism would quite fit, but maybe something in between. I think something semi-permanent and, as it were, *given,* like thought forms metaphorically set in concrete, would fill the bill.

We considered earlier that there is no way of *proving* that there is anything 'out there' at all. No philosopher would disagree with that. And one of those rather illusory objects which superficially appears to be 'out there,' is our own physical body with its five senses, with which we think we are observing everything. It would be — in my view — difficult to imagine a more convoluted — no, muddled and confused — piece of reasoning. That it why I call it *'naïve* realism.'

All these data so briefly just reviewed — the data of my experiences — plus my reading of Eastern philosophy brought over here in the nineteenth century by H.P. Blavatsky and a very few others, have shown me that an enormous number of people, many in the East, believe that the physical universe is not at all like it seems to be and that the only reality is thought — consciousness. They call it a *maya* — which roughly translates as an illusion. However, the objects of this physical world have had their wave functions collapsed so many times that they have a sort of permanence. One way of expressing it is that we have a set of stable thought forms, which almost amounts to realism so far as most people are concerned. It is surely clear that all we each have for certain are our thoughts and that science is just the building of mental models patterning and ordering these mental experiences. It is surely perfectly clear that at least there is no way of *proving* that there is anything 'out there' at all. What is suggested is a perfectly valid way of considering the universe and it does seem to apply to, and make sense of, much in parapsychology which is otherwise completely inexplicable. But it will take what I think is the big forthcoming paradigm shift away from realism and to mentalism or idealism, perhaps by way of quantum mechanics, before it might become completely acceptable to the rest of the scientific community. Then we shall be able not only to show that the phenomena we are interested in really do occur very often (not all the time, when we are in the region of quantum uncertainty), but to 'explain' them too.

Belief and our physical world

I often wonder whether the physical world we think we know so well is the result of thousands of years of belief and conditioning of humanity (and perhaps other influences — it surely needed a start of some kind). In other words, by and large it has been created by us, and given consistency and solidity by our all believing in it most of the time. The clues that show some of us that it is not quite as we were told are all the facts of the so-called paranormal. A different *belief* — really a different *knowledge and expectation* — is needed to melt that thought form set in concrete and make it ideoplastic again.

Modern 'normal science' started in its current form, of course, with such people as Bacon, Galileo and Newton, some three or four hundred years ago. They did experiments (that is, gave themselves mental experiences) , devised mental models, tested those models, and in these ways, with their successors, arrived at all that is now called modern science — a magnificent set of models describing many of the thoughts we have, through our beliefs, set in metaphorical concrete. So the physical world has the (limited) consistency we know so well. It may perhaps be looked upon as having been extracted by the process I have tried to suggest, from 'the infinite plenum of all possibilities,' as Maharishi called it. 'Normal science ' is, as Kuhn suggested, 'puzzle

solving within an unquestioned paradigm,' that is, extending the
'thoughts set in concrete' which we call the physical world, in ways
which are perfectly consistent with what we already have and which
will therefore 'work,' that is, give us further experiences, congruent
with those we already are having. So we have the possibility of 'energy
from the vacuum,' and other matters which might be useful. All are
possible within the boundaries set by those 'thoughts set in concrete'
which limit what we can do now and are described by the models of
science, encompassed in our conventional understanding of the laws of
nature.

Those firmly held beliefs are not just superficial — they are held in
the personal and collective unconscious and operate almost all the
time. The times when they do not operate we call paranormal — or a
state of 'altered consciousness.' Every hypnotist knows that if the conscious rational critical mind can be temporarily removed from the picture by putting the subject into a trance, then the objects and laws of
the physical world can be drastically altered by just telling the personal
unconscious mind — which is incredibly trustful, helpful and believing — that things are different. In other words, the physical world can
be altered for them by changing the belief — or rather knowledge-
structure. Objects, including other human bodies, can be added to or
removed from the surroundings, or levitated in contradiction to the so-
called law of gravity, and so on. All these facts have been evidenced
earlier — but we are not perhaps drawing all the implications from
them that we might.

Altered states of consciousness are particularly important here
because most of what happens in states of altered consciousness has
not yet been set in concrete and remains almost infinitely ideoplastic,
so that anything from that infinite plenum of all possibilities would
appear to be possible. There may be limits I haven't considered. As I
attempted to show in Chapter 4, my experiences in the state of lucid
dreaming provide one or two examples which appear to support what
I am now suggesting. Remember that in lucid dreaming one is in full
consciousness with a full memory and is well aware that the physical
body is asleep in bed. Most importantly, one has the normal full critical faculty. In that state I had a good look at myself — or should I
rather say, I had a good look at the body or vehicle with which I
seemed to be perceiving the world all around. It was exactly like the
one I am using right now. My breathing was normal, my heart rate was
normal, everything else around seemed to be normal — except perhaps

that I felt particularly energetic, well and happy. The surroundings were just like the physical world — perhaps because I wouldn't know how — yet — to make them anything different. They might be considered a reflection of my memory store — of my experiences of the normal physical world. I did wonder whether the world of lucid dreaming is indeed the 'next world,' to which most ordinary people transfer at death. I think it probably is. But our consideration of that, and the experiments we might do to test it, we consider elsewhere.

Another experiment I did was to see whether gravity was operative. It was not: if I wished I could levitate — float in the air. I could therefore also jump off cliffs without coming to any harm. There are many other things I could learn to do which I have not yet been able to do, but I know that others have. I have carried out other experiments, but that will be enough to illustrate what I mean. In a lucid dream one has escaped from the thraldom of the normal physical world and almost anything — within limits, I feel sure — is possible. Perhaps the *physical* world was once — in the mists of antiquity — rather like this in some respects.

Some other of the world's cultures do not have the same beliefs about the world that most of us do in the West. They are not all naïve realists as most of us are most of the time. Some of them have, for thousands of years, had some quite different beliefs about what is and is not factual. The aborigines of Australia and their 'dream-time' come to mind as just one example. So far as I know, for these vast periods of time they have believed certain things about the world that, to a realist Westerner, would be considered nonsense. They are true for them — they 'know' that (very different from just 'believing' it) — and the result is that remarkable things are possible and part of their lives. They have knowledge, for example, of what is occurring hundreds of miles away in the absence of what we would call 'normal means of knowing.' *Their world is, in some respects, different.* One could multiply examples of this sort of thing from various other cultures.

In the East they have different views of the structure of a human being from ours — taught for thousands of years so that everyone 'knows' and does not just 'believe.' The result is that things appear to be possible that in our Western paradigm are impossible. They have quite different methods of healing that sometimes really do work — and they are quite different from Western medicine. One thinks of the system of subtle bodies that is taught in the East (and here in the West in Theosophical, spiritualistic and kindred circles). One thinks of the chakras, prana and kundalini and other powerful 'forces' we know nothing about in the scientific West. But trained psychics 'see' and otherwise perceive them, and various things are possible as a result. One thinks of acupuncture and the numerous and varied methods of hatha and raja yoga which traditionally lead to the psychic powers — or the so-called siddhis — leading to all sorts of interesting, valuable and intriguing possibilities. There are, for example, remarkable and effective methods of healing. Good research has been carried out on some of this. Shaffica Karragula, a medical doctor, and Dora Kunz, a gifted Theosophical psychic, have published interesting and remarkable scientific research on the chakras and health and disease, effectively linking Eastern and Western models. The world of a gifted psychic is quite different and enormously expanded from our normal world, and all sorts of things become possible. Often we cannot 'explain' them in terms of Western science — and why should we be able to do that? We seem to think that Western science is, after long centuries of darkness and ignorance, the real truth about us human beings and the world. One might seriously doubt such an arrogant idea!

CHAPTER 7

The Likelihood of Life after Death

The best evidence so far for the continuation of life after the death of the physical body seems to me to be the so-called 'cross-correspondences.' We shall have some suggestions to make later on in this book of how the persistent and open-minded reader might obtain their own first-hand evidence of survival — which would probably be more persuasive for them than reading about cross-correspondences, good though this evidence is for persuading the doubter.

The cross-correspondences is the name used for what appears to be the scheme adopted by a group of distinguished early (founder) members of the Society for Psychical Research after their deaths to provide good scientific evidence to us still living that they had survived. It was as follows.

First, it was well understood from the beginning of the scientific investigation of psychical research that the major difficulty with the 'communications' from mediums was telepathy from the sitter. In other words, any fact given by the medium as coming from the ostensible communicator which was immediately (or later) recognized by the sitter as true could more persuasively be explained as telepathy from the sitter to the medium. There existed excellent evidence for telepathy. It was felt on the basis of much evidence that in a 'satisfactory' demonstration of 'communication' from a deceased person there occurred a sort of fusion of the personal unconscious minds of the medium and the sitter and so everything in the sitter's memory store (both remembered and consciously forgotten) became, as it were, part of the medium's memory store and was available for 'dramatization' as a 'communication' from the deceased. The unconscious of a medium, it would be claimed, is well practised in doing this as it is part of a medium's 'training.' The dramatization would be very similar to that which occurs for everyone in the production of our dreams while asleep. The 'dramatization' would be as an ostensible communication from the medium's control or from the 'communicator' directly. This is what the medium has been trained to do and what she expects. She does not, of course, know consciously that this is occurring. She assumes the explanation of the 'hallucinations' she has, to be that given to her by spiritualists, that is, deceased people coming to her room rather literally in their astral bodies and talking to her. She 'sees' them by her clairvoyance and 'hears' them with her clairaudience.

In the cases where the sitter does not know the facts communicated and never did, but has to find out whether they are true from someone else, it would be claimed that we do not know the possible limits of telepathy and the telepathy might be from the person or persons who do know the facts. This is sometimes referred to as the 'super ESP hypothesis,' mentioned earlier.

The early Council members of the SPR, who appear to have produced the cross-correspondences, had devised a scheme to get round the telepathy difficulty. They said in their ostensible communications from another world that it was as follows. They were all well educated in the Greek classical literature and they devised puzzles based on this. There appeared in the SPR offices in London various scraps of quotations sent to the SPR by various mediums at the request of their communicators. The mediums did not know each other, lived in different parts of the world and (with one solitary exception) knew nothing of the Greek classics. (That one exception — Mrs Verrall in Cambridge — was not part of every cross-correspondence.) Those scraps of paper contained allusions to various incidents described in those classics. Each allusion was incomplete and not understood by the medium. The scraps of quotations were normally written by automatic writing, without the medium's conscious volition, and were often interruptions occurring to some other communication by automatic writing. The communicators (I shall cease using the word 'ostensible' for brevity) normally ended with a request to the medium to send it to the SPR in London. When the scraps were considered together it was found that some contained a part of a puzzle while others contained other parts and yet others gave clues that enabled those parts to be put together so that they could be understood.

The communicators said that they had devised this scheme in order to eliminate cross telepathy between the mediums (most of whom did not know each other) and so that the mediums would not understand what they were dealing with because they had no knowledge of Greek literature, and anyhow the scraps were incomplete. They had in this way provided evidence of their conscious thinking and planning presence, but not in this world.

I have necessarily rather over-simplified the communicators' scheme but it certainly does seem to have represented a big step forward in the evidence for survival. There appear to be only two (or three) possible explanations for these results. One is that the communicators really had survived their deaths and were communicating just as they explained. The second is what has been called 'super extrasensory perception' or super PSI mentioned briefly above, in which we have to imagine that the unconscious minds of the mediums (who, remember, did not all know each other) in some way got together to devise the whole scheme in order to deceive us about survival. The mediums certainly did not do it consciously and there is no evidence whatever for such wide-ranging powers of ESP. The third possibility (to which I attach no weight whatsoever) is that all those mediums in some way got together, with the distinguished SPR classics scholars, to devise a world-wide scheme to produce fraudulently evidence for survival.

My opinion, for what it is worth, is that the communicators devised and executed that plan just as they described it. They produced, as they intended, the best evidence so far for their survival of bodily death. The whole is usually referred to as the evidence for survival from the cross-correspondences. By the time the reader reaches the end of this book they should have enough evidence to hold a worthwhile opinion on the likelihood of life after bodily death. Needless to say, my opinion of the genuineness and success of the cross-correspondences is based not only on them but also on innumerable sittings with all kinds of medium and much experience of other altered states of consciousness.

Other views of life after death

Most of the world's religions teach that we survive bodily death but usually their ideas are not clear or coherent enough to discuss, and the evidence for their truth is generally weak and lacking in cogency. We shall therefore primarily consider here only scientific evidence — which is the firsthand experience of reliable witnesses. However, before we do that we should look at the views put forward by the Theosophists and by the Spiritualists — which are not very different — in respect to the life immediately after death. The Spiritualists assert that their views are based on the evidence of actual communication through 'mediums' who, they claim, talk directly to those who have survived their own deaths and who are in what they refer to as the spirit world. The mediums then, they say, are able to pass on the evidence for their identity given to them by the survivors. The 'normal scientists' would say that the visions seen and voices heard by the mediums are purely hallucinatory and of no value. They would go on to suggest that they could hardly be otherwise because human beings are only elec-trochemical machines and when they are dead that is the end of them. However, because of their blind religious faith in materialism, they do not usually take the trouble to examine the evidence carefully enough. Sometimes a medium gives information which is very persuasive that they are indeed in touch with someone who has departed this life. But unfortunately that is not always the case. As we shall see, what is going on in such a seance is very complicated and not at all clearly under-stood. It often appears that an invisible presence talks and gestures to the medium who, because she is psychic, can apprehend them through the use of 'clairvoyant' and 'clairaudient' powers. And, it should be said, it seems so to her too. (I shall use the feminine pronoun when referring to mediums because women greatly outnumber men medi-ums.) One very rarely meets a fraudulent medium — even though, it must be said, there are many people around claiming to be psychic who are not very good at it. (We are all of us psychic to some degree, but have been conditioned by our Western normal science-based culture to think that information can come to us only through the channels of sense.) Mediums often clairvoyantly perceive symbols such as stars or crosses or flowers in addition to a 'communicator.' They will say such things as 'My guide is showing me a cross shining in the air above the communicator. Was he a believing Christian?'

The Theosophists and the Spiritualists have systems in which the physical world is the 'lowest and densest' of a number of worlds or 'lev-els of consciousness.' The Theosophists were told of this ancient scheme (it is part of what Aldous Huxley called the perennial philosophy) by H.P. Blavatsky, their prime Founder, who got it from the East. She was also herself psychic. The Spiritualists got it from the 'communicators'; according to them it came from the nearest of those subtler worlds and sometimes from further afield, the information being communicated via mediums. In the perennial philosophy of ancient Greece and in some other ancient mystery schools the neophyte for initiation into the Mysteries was, it is said, taken into the 'next world' and shown what hap-pens at death. We have already considered this sort of experience in the more modern context when we examined lucid dreaming, shamanic journeying (Chapter 4) and out-of-body experiences (Chapter 3). We have yet to acquire the final bit of evidence that the 'worlds' of all these experiences/states of consciousness are in fact what we have referred to as the 'next world' and which most Theosophists call the 'astral plane.'

Mistakes in the traditional views

Certain aspects of this theory of 'subtler worlds' can be subjected to scientific experimentation and, as we shall see, are found to be rather fundamentally misunderstood by their proponents. We shall consider this now.

Psychics can often observe a coloured nimbus surrounding the body of a living person. This is also the origin of the halo often painted round the head of a saint in medieval paintings. They infer that this so-called 'aura' is the part of the 'subtle body' which is sticking out all round the denser physical body, the rest of it interpenetrating the latter. They state that this is the body being used for an OBE or a lucid dream and that it is also the body in which we find ourselves immediately after death. However, an experiment carried out many years ago shows that this is not correct in quite the way they think.

The experiment was as follows. I asked for and got help from the appropriately talented mediums/psychics of the Spiritualist Association of Great Britain (in Belgrave Square, London) in carrying this out. Using one at a time I stood in front of them and asked whether the psychic could see my astral body. They all said that they could and that it projected about 25 centimetres all round my physical body. I than stood behind a screen but near the edge so as to obscure my physical body and asked them whether they could still see my astral body. They all in their separate experiments said that they could. I then moved much further behind the screen and asked them again. They all said that they could not now see my astral body. I then explained that I proposed to move near the edge of the screen and further behind it at random times and I asked them to tell me when I was standing near the edge of the screen from their observation of my astral body. They all said that they would have no difficulty in doing this and so I moved near the edge and further behind at random times. They called out to me: 'Now you are near the edge.' ... 'Now you are further behind.' ... and so on. All were quite confident that they were right. Unfortunately there was no correlation whatever between my position relative to the edge of the screen and their observations of my astral body.

What did this show? It showed clearly that when a psychic is working at both the physical level of consciousness and the astral level of
consciousness so that she is observing both my physical and astral bodies at the same time then that automatic machinery of the personal
unconscious mind I have called George puts the two bodies on the
same centre line for them to perceive because they are both owned by
the same person. There is no good reason why 'he' should put them
anywhere else. The experiment shows that the astral body is clearly not
in the same space as the physical body and the two do not have any
spatial relationship.

This may not be clear to the reader: it is certainly not to nearly all
psychics. We naturally think that there is only one space — the physical world space — and everything goes on within it. This is, of course,
not true. The dreaming world, for example, is in quite a different space.
It still has three dimensions, at least to my experience, and time still
appears to move in the same way at the same rate (as estimated by us)
as it does in the normal physical world. However, suppose you tell me
(this is an example suggested by Professor H.H. Price) that last night
you dreamed that you were sitting under a palm tree. Suppose I then
asked you how tall that palm tree was: five centimetres? twenty five
metres? and whether it was at the foot of your bed or outside your bedroom door. You would surely reply to me that these are meaningless
questions: the palm tree was not in physical space at all but in your
dream space. These two spaces are very similar but they certainly do
not interpenetrate. There appear to be a number of different spaces in
this sort of way. They are spaces in which the human consciousness
can function in various 'altered states of consciousness' and we shall
return to this most important philosophical matter later.

The 'controls' or 'guides' of mediums

The perceptive reader will by now have been acquiring a fair idea of
the mental model into which psychics/mediums fit and 'explain' their
experiences. They believe that we are surrounded by a 'spirit world' to
which we go after death; that it is made of 'subtle material as yet
unknown to science' and that it interpenetrates this world; that we have
an astral body made of this same material which we inhabit exclusively
after death and, before death, which we use when our physical body
and our astral body are separate as in dreaming, during out-of-body
experiences or other ASCs. They believe that during a successful

seance the so-called dead come to them (but they have no way of demanding this) and talk to them and they hear them with their clairaudience and see them with their clairvoyance. Not all mediums have these two faculties equally developed: some 'hear' but do not often 'see' very much and vice versa. Most mediums have a 'guide' or 'control' who looks after their medium and acts as an organizer of the 'communicators' on 'the other side.' They often say, during a sitting, such things as 'My guide is showing me ...' I propose now to describe the year-long experience I had when attending a weekly Saturday afternoon developing circle of a Spiritualist group.

This weekly group was primarily a number (about ten) of people who wished to develop their mediumistic faculties so that, in many cases, they would be able to act as mediums. The circle was led by an experienced medium. We met early on Saturday afternoon, went to a room high up in the building, and sat in a circle in upright chairs, around it; the Leader was part of the circle.

We first relaxed, and the Leader said a prayer for help, guidance and protection and that we were all wishing to be psychically 'developed by spirit.' Then we sat quietly imagining that we were being in some way 'worked on' by entities in the 'spirit world.' After about an hour of this we were asked to describe our experiences. Some members of the circle said that they felt a 'developing cap' placed upon their heads. They imagined that in some way this would be helpful. Some others said that they could 'see' an entity placing hands on the head of 'the lady opposite' and that the entity was in the dress of a Red Indian chief. The Leader of the group explained that this was probably the guide of the lady opposite and that in due course the guide would make himself known. Other members of the group faintly 'saw' Chinese 'guides' similarly. Sadly I myself saw nothing but I was clearly not clairvoyant.

As the Saturday afternoon developing circle continued week after week the guides became ever clearer and the faculties of clairvoyance and clairaudience of some of the members slowly improved. The group was finished after a year.

It seemed to me fairly clear what was happening at that 'developing circle.' What we might call 'co-personalities' (see Chapters 12 and 18) were being developed as a result of somewhat tenuous suggestions, followed by implicit belief, followed by strong and continuing thought. I noticed particularly the excited discussions that followed the least scrap of tentative information about the 'guides' and how the images of the guides became steadily stronger and clearer after an hour's intensive dwelling in thought on them and belief in them each week. During that hour the budding mediums were imagining those Red Indian and Chinese guides standing behind them and 'working' on them in some way. Each feeling of 'pressure' on the forehead or indeed almost anything else that physiologically occurred during that hour was thought to be the action of the guide or the process of the development.

It is important to realize clearly that what has been described above is the result of a strong and continuing belief in something. It is my strongly held view that belief is one of the most important features of a human being. It is particularly important in connection with those subtler areas of the mind connected with altered states of consciousness. We discussed this in more detail in connection with hypnosis in Chapter 6. There we considered that hypnosis is a state where the conscious critical and analytical mind has been put temporarily into abeyance by a process of progressive relaxation and the personal unconscious mind ('George') is being directly talked to and given suggestions by the hypnotist. We saw there how radically the 'physical world' including the physical body can be changed — added to or sometimes subtracted from its normal state by a brief suggestion from the hypnotist. If only a brief suggestion is given to George then 'he' is perfectly capable of filling in all the necessary details to give it verisimilitude — after all, he shows every night when you dream how good he is at producing these, including all that is necessary for a perfectly good and acceptable scene in the physical world. It is important to realize too that an actual trance state is not necessary if the requisite strong belief is held anyhow. This was certainly the situation I discovered at the development circle I have described.

Before leaving this there are one or two important matters still to be considered. The first is that the reader might be considering that the 'co-personalities/mediumistic controls/guides,' the construction of which I have described, were an example of a complete delusion and a waste of time. This would be quite incorrect. What was constructed was a 'piece of mental machinery' which could then be used to acquire paranormal information appertaining to possible surviving personalities. Without that 'guide' it might not have been possible, or would have been more difficult, for that medium to acquire veridical information concerning deceased 'communicators.' (Whether the information came from the memory store of the sitter or from a 'real' deceased communicator is something which would have to be carefully considered in a particular case.) This explanation of the formation of a medium's guide is not, of course, any proof that they were all formed in that way. Perhaps occasionally a guide is a surviving personality: each must be judged individually.

There are, as we shall see in the next chapter, two major kinds of mental medium: the clairvoyant/ clairaudient type and the trance type. The former gives sittings in a more or less normal state except that they are perhaps a little more 'withdrawn' than usual. The trance medium is by no means in a normal state but goes into an auto-hypnotic trance at the beginning of the seance and is 'controlled' by the guide, who actually talks to the sitter through the medium's body. Some mediums function more effectively 'normally' and others more effectively in trance. Some of the trance mediums remember nothing whatever of a sitting; others remember nearly all. In my experience there is often not a lot to choose between normal and trance sittings. In interpreting and understanding the origin of the information that comes from them the problems are much the same.

CHAPTER 8

The Seance

The seance — mental phenomena

A typical seance

It is not my policy in this book to describe much that I have not personally experienced, but I propose now to give a brief account of a sitting with a medium experienced by a friend who lived opposite to us for several years and whom, with her husband, we knew very well. Her husband, a tall thin man and an accountant, died of lung cancer in hospital just before Christmas 1970. Having heard over the time we knew each other a number of conversations on the possibility of human survival of bodily death, she wondered whether it might be possible to try to communicate with him via a medium. She came over to us one evening, explained that she was not sure whether her husband survived or not, and asked me whether I could arrange an appointment for her with a good medium in order to try to find out.

This provided an excellent opportunity for a good controlled experiment. I knew that the proposed sitter had had no experience of mediums and I was glad to agree to her request. I telephoned my friend the well-known medium Ena Twigg, and asked her to arrange an appointment for 'someone I knew.' I gave her no other information. She gave me a date and time and I passed them on to the widow across the road. A little before the sitting I gave her careful advice on how to conduct herself during the sitting. She was to be warm, friendly and encouraging but very careful to give no information to the medium about her deceased husband. She had no tape recorder with which to record every word spoken by herself and the medium (the ideal) but she did have two daughters, the elder of whom was a secretary. So she appeared at the seance with her elder daughter plus pad and pencil. I had instructed the daughter to record every word spoken by all three of them.

The evening after the appointment the daughter brought round to me a carefully typed manuscript containing every relevant detail of the sitting. She was quite excited and said that her mother was the same. The medium had opened the door to them and at once said that they had brought in with them a tall thin man who was the husband of the elder sitter. He himself, she said, gave her this information. She could see him with her clairvoyance and hear him with her clairaudience. All this occurred in the medium's pleasant sunny room in July 1971.

The medium often spoke as though it were the deceased husband speaking. At other times she spoke as from herself. In giving this account I shall put the medium's remarks in inverted commas, the medium's speech as though she were the communicator in italics, and my own comments in brackets:

'This is someone who has never communicated before.'

I feel so ill. I feel so ill. I can hardly speak, I feel so weak. I can't breathe very well. I have not been over here very long. Less than a year ...

'I can see a big letter D and then two big capital D's.'

(These are actually the initials of his first name and of the pet name of his elder daughter. This makes it quite clear that the idea that a deceased communicator is speaking directly to the medium just as in a normal conversation can hardly be correct: he would hardly need to produce letters in this way.)

Didn't want to die in hospital. They let me come home but I had to come back. They couldn't cope and I had to be propped up because I couldn't breathe. They gave me oxygen and an injection.

(All this was perfectly accurate.)

'I see him riding a horse.'

(Not understood by the sitters but the other statements made were correct.)

'You have a Persian carpet somewhere in your house. Take care of it. He is particularly fond of it.'

(This last was obviously from the medium but it was quite correct. There were many statements about their life together, their visits to the country, their search for old things to buy for their house, his love of paintings, his fondness for his mother, and about the women in his family.)

'There must be another child.'

I want to send my love to A.

(There was another child whose initial was A.)

And my swallowing was so difficult. My mouth was so dry and they just moisten it. They used to put ice on my mouth.

'Married twenty three years.'

(This was correct but it was twenty two when he died.)

'He mentions a photograph of his father with a moustache.'

We resemble each other.

(This was correct too.)

There is a dinner suit and three evening shirts. See if someone can use them. Don't leave them there.

(This was all correct and very typical of him.)

See to the apple trees. They were good trees. We have got a lovely garden.

(All this was correct.)

Somebody has a walnut tree.

(The latter was not understood at the time of the sitting and the daughter had marked it 'not understood.' The family later showed the manuscript to friends of theirs who lived nearby. The wife there said to the widow that the bit about a nut tree had been marked 'not understood.' 'It's that tree down the garden' she said, indicating with her hand. Your husband and I discussed it during the summer before he died. 'But,' she added, 'you and the girls were not there at the time.')

It would be stupid if all that remained of a man of my age was a handful of dust and a memory. Given the opportunity, I could be more vital and forthcoming in this world than I could be even when I was on earth. So continue: think we should do some kind of experiment. If you will co-operate, I will. I do like to feel you are involved and directly concerned. So we will pursue it.

That is sufficient to give the general flavour of this sitting. Some of the statements made were very evidential but others were rather vague. When I received this manuscript I listed all the statements made in three columns: correct, incorrect and not understood. The medium made 172 separate statements in a sitting lasting one hour and of all the statements 85 per cent were correct. If we omit the statements which were not understood or vague and merely count the correct and incorrect, then 95 per cent were correct. It is important to realize that, with the exception of the reference to a walnut tree, all the correct statements were recognized as such by the sitters at the time.

Let us now discuss the various ways to look at this experience — the models which represent what was happening. First there is the medium's explanation of her experiences, which we might have some difficulty accepting exactly as she gives it. We shall later on have better ways of representing these facts of experience but for the moment it will be helpful to know how a medium would describe what was occurring in a seance such as the above.

If asked for an explanation the medium would say something like the following. You may think that you are just that physical body I can see, but actually there is much more to you that you may know nothing about. You have other bodies, in particular an astral body. I can see it with my clairvoyance; it is composed of subtle matter as yet unknown to science and is rather bigger than your physical body so that it interpenetrates your physical body and projects all round. The colour of the projecting part, the 'aura,' depends on your emotions. If you are a very spiritual person then the aura around your head tends to be purplish, which is the reason for that colour being shown around the heads of saints in medieval paintings. When you die your physical body disintegrates but your astral body remains and you go into the next world — the astral world, which is also made of astral matter and interpenetrates this one — and there you meet your deceased relatives and friends. Normal decent people go into the Summerland, which is very like this world only much more beautiful, and selfish unpleasant people go into a very gloomy place, which has led to the stories of hell. When we have a seance and if we are lucky, deceased relatives and friends of the sitter will come to my room. I see them with my clairvoyance and hear them with my clairaudience. I have no way of compelling them to come. (This Spiritualistic Summerland reminds one strongly of the place many near death experiencers find themselves in when at the end of a complete NDE.)

So what is wrong with that explanation? It is certainly what the medium appears to experience and it is what has been told to mediums by other mediums from time immemorial. We shall consider later on in more detail what is wrong — and we shall also discover that our normal explanation of our daily consciousness leaves a great deal to be desired also. Here let me say again that mediums are amongst the most honest and genuine people I know: one rarely meets a fraudulent medium. However, they are not scientists and are rarely aware of the shortcomings of their rather literal explanation of the experiences that they do genuinely have.

Before we consider in some detail what is perhaps a better and more accurate description of what probably really happened at the seance I have just described let us look at an experiment which was carried out by an old colleague of mine when I was an academic staff member of the University of London.

The John Ferguson experiment of S.G. Soal

S.G. Soal, a former President of the SPR, was having sittings some years ago with the London trance medium Mrs Blanche Cooper. She put herself into an auto-hypnotic trance at the beginning of the sittings. At Mrs Cooper's seances a voice, not her own, appeared to originate from mid-air. We shall be considering later possible mechanisms for this. Here our concern is with the factual material received in this way. A psychologist, if accepting these facts at all, would probably suggest that the source of the information was a secondary personality of the medium, just as if the voice were emanating from the lips of the medium in trance. Most such 'secondary personalities' say that they once lived on this earth and are now in the next world, their work being to pass on information from deceased communicators. Sometimes such communicators claim to be speaking directly, using the medium's vocal chords — in which cases the voice usually alters. However, not many 'control personalities' (as they are usually called) can be traced from the facts they provide in this way. In Dr Soal's case the control personality and Dr Soal's deceased brother Frank both appeared to be passing on what looked like very good evidence concerning Frank. Facts which Dr Soal had long forgotten or — in one example — had never known, were put forward.

During this series of seances another communicator appeared and said that his name was John Ferguson, originally from Brentwood in Essex, who sent love to his brother Jim and his wife. He gave his age, the date and manner of his death, and the general subject of his work. Soal later remembered a James Ferguson, another boy at school with him in Southend, and vaguely recollected facts he had given about his father. Soal had lost touch with James Ferguson years before.

Soal now visited Brentwood for the first time to acquire facts about the locality. He formed in his mind a series of 'fruitful conjectures' about John Ferguson. He received back from the voices at the next seance some of the facts he had noticed or speculated about. Soal again visited Brentwood and interviewed the postmaster. It was clear that no persons having the names given in the seances had ever lived in the roads also named. Soal invented more theories around the personality of the fictitious John Ferguson. Interesting and ingenious allusions to these appeared at the seances. Later on John Ferguson said that he had lived in Glasgow, where he had received further education and, eventually, been buried. Soal looked at a map of Glasgow and then asked for street names in Glasgow and the whereabouts of the cemetery where John Ferguson was buried. He received all this information from the seances as requested and then wrote to the keeper of the cemetery who confirmed Soal's suspicion that no people with the names stated were buried there around those dates.

Summarizing, it seems that the new communicator, John Ferguson, gave many facts to prove that he really had lived on earth, yet most of the so-called facts existed only in Dr Soal's imagination. (One is here perhaps reminded again of Charles Dickens the novelist, who said that sometimes the characters in his books became so 'real and positive' that they took over writing the book from him.) Eventually Soal's dead brother Frank, with other controls, realized what was happening and said that John Ferguson's mind was a blank. 'He caught at any thoughts flying around: he'd have believed he was Jonah if you had told him so.'

Let us consider another similar example. The Irish poet W.B. Yeats was once having a sitting with the automatic-writing medium Geraldine Cummins. Her personal unconscious mind ('George') used her autonomic and muscular system to produce writing. In this instance the writing was describing an old castle and the people who lived in it. She read it with interest and said to Yeats, 'Shall I let this go on? Are you interested?' Yeats replied, 'I certainly am: that is the plot of my new book.'

There is no doubt that information in the mind of a sitter somehow penetrates into the consciousness of a medium and is dramatized in various ways by the unconscious machinery I have, for convenience, called George.

There is another device that George sometimes uses to make material overt: the Ouija board. Here the recipient(s) puts the fingers gently on a pointed piece of wood called a traveller which then slides over the polished board pointing to the various letters of the alphabet which, with the words Yes And No, are inscribed upon it. Another version of the Ouija board is the well-known party game in which a polished table is used together with an upturned glass. The letters of the alphabet are again put around the edge, and the sitters place the tips of their fingers gently on the bottom of the upturned glass. If success is achieved the glass moves to the various letters, spelling out messages, while all the sitters stoutly maintain that they are not pushing it. They consider that it is moving of its own accord and all they are doing is maintaining their fingers in contact with the glass. Usually, of course, they are pushing it, but unconsciously.

Some mediums go into trance and produce what is called automatic painting or drawing. These are sometimes very like the artistic productions of famous deceased artists. The medium explains that this is a way the deceased artist is using to prove their survival. (The well-known British medium Matthew Manning used to do this sort of thing in his younger days.)

We shall now consider another example of this kind of psychic happening and then go on to consider and assess the material of the seance held with the widow of the accountant and her daughter.

The Philip experiment

The Philip experiment provides an example of an outstandingly successful experiment which serves to clarify and confirm the suggestions we have somewhat tentatively been putting forward as 'explanations' of various matters considered above.

It was carried out in Toronto by a group headed by Professor George Owen, who was once a Council member of the SPR. Other members of the group included Mrs Iris Owen and various other members of the Toronto psychical research society, including a psychiatrist. The purpose of their experiment was to discover whether they could establish communication with someone they had brought into existence by imagination only.

The group wrote a fictitious story set in seventeenth century England and it involved a stately home, the history of which is well known and is nothing like the story they devised. The story they invented involved a nobleman named Philip who lived in that stately home with his frigid wife, and a beautiful gypsy of whom Philip was enamoured. Philip installed his gypsy lover in a cottage on his estate. His wife discovered her and accused her of being a witch. She was consequently burned at the stake. Philip, who had done nothing to save her, was tortured by remorse and eventually killed himself.

The Owen group read history books concerned with the period in which they had set their story and made a sketch of their imaginary character Philip. They also obtained photographs of the site.

When all this was clear in their minds they sat round a table and tried to communicate with Philip who had, of course, in their story, died several hundred years ago. They had very little success until they tried the effect of changing the solemn 'scientific' atmosphere and kept their seances light and cheerful, making jokes and singing. (Here they were adopting methods Spiritualists had long found successful.) When they changed the atmosphere in this way they very quickly obtained contact with Philip, who produced raps on the tabletop on which they had all lightly placed their fingertips. Philip used a code on which they had all agreed: one rap for Yes and two for No. Philip, who was imagined as standing near the table in his 'astral body,' produced very positive raps. He answered all sorts of questions which confirmed the facts they had decided on in their story and occasionally extended it, the extensions not always being historically accurate. Philip's opinions tended to depend on who was present. For example, he had no objection to smoking when the only smoker in the group was present; at other times he disliked it.

Philip's raps were quite clearly paranormal, that is, no one was, consciously or unconsciously, rapping the table. This was perfectly clear: the table top was a thin round disc which was mounted on a narrow central post. The light was always good (the group having decided from the beginning not to have sittings in darkness). When a vibration transducer was attached to the surface of the table the displacement of the table varied with time in a way which was the reverse of what would have been obtained if someone had physically rapped the table. (If a table is rapped the surface is displaced at once to the maximum and then restores itself to its original equilibrium position over a short time. The paranormal raps produced a more gradual build-up to the maximum displacement.)

A most interesting feature of this experiment occurred during one seance when the raps were fairly weak. The group said, 'Come on Philip, you can do better than this. If you can't produce stronger raps we can always send you away: we only made you up, you know.' The raps then practically died away completely and the group had to strengthen Philip's identity by clear imagination in order to build the (physical) raps back up to a reasonable level again.

On one occasion, after a successful visit by Matthew Manning who did some spoon bending, amongst other things, the group asked Philip if he could bend a key left on the table in the locked seance room overnight. George Owen described to me how, when he entered in the morning, the key was indeed bent.

This production of physical energy — and clearly the physical raps (and the bending of a key) involved the deployment of physical energy which was certainly not being consciously expended by anyone present — is of fundamental importance to science. It has been suggested — and I certainly agree — that if a Nobel prize were awarded for a parapsychological experiment then this should win it. (We shall be referring to this deployment of 'physical energy' later, when we consider the philosophical implications of what has been learned in this subject.)

As I have pointed out, the phenomena I have described were always obtained in a good light and were strong enough to occur in the presence of more than one sceptical observer. They have been photographed and have appeared in radio and television programmes a number of times. The group was kind enough to allow me to sit in on a seance which they convened specially for me when I visited Toronto and I have not the slightest doubt that everything was genuine and took place just as I have described. I sat with my eyes opposite the edge of the thin table; the lighting was good, and certainly no one was producing the raps normally. All their hands were clearly visible, finger tips still and gently touching the table top. Later Philip produced raps under my hand on request, and I am in no doubt that I did not produce them!

I should mention that when I asked the Owens whether the experiment had been successfully repeated by other independent groups — always important in scientific work — Iris sent me a list of them. Some of these groups had used the Philip story and others had made up their own Originally the group hoped to be able actually to see Philip. They had no success with this but who knows what might have occurred had they continued with the experiment? (After some years they all became somewhat bored by it.) The possibility of seeing the imaginary Philip as well as 'hearing' him and so communicating with him does not seem at all unlikely. 'Hallucinatory experiences' are by no means uncommon.

An intriguing thought occurred to me when I read the original papers on the Philip experiment. There are, I believe, lots of groups practising 'black magic' in various of our communities and probably trying to 'raise the devil.' If these groups had the clarity of thought and the persistence of the Toronto group it would not surprise me in the least if they were not in the same way able to 'communicate with the devil.' However, the devil would, of course, have been created by themselves. Like Philip it would be a 'thought form' but nonetheless able to deploy physical energy. Maybe they would even see him, complete with horns and a forked tail! Who knows what dark and undesirable events might follow after raising from the unconscious an archetype of that peculiarly unpleasant kind?

Let us now consider what all this implies in our interpretation of the sitting with which we started this chapter. The first thing to remark is that it would be simplistic to maintain that the deceased husband came in his astral body, and was observed by, and talked to, the medium, who passed on her experiences. That clearly will not do in view of Dr Soal's semi-imaginary communicator, the completely imaginary Philip and Geraldine Cummins' passing on of Yeats' plot. The true picture is clearly more complex. In the model we have of the mind (and shall later, in the final chapter, be considering in some detail) we imagine George acquiring the information in some way and floating it up into the conscious mind of the medium as hallucinatory visions and voices. So what is the likeliest source of this material? Surely it is the memory stores of the sitters. They had just as clear, if not clearer, memories of their family member than Soal and the Owen group had of their 'communicators.' Is it not now perfectly clear that immediately recognized information from an ostensible communicator is not good evidence that they are in some sense 'there' and communicating. On the other hand, of course, it is not proof that they were not. One must always remember that most 'ostensible communicators' are not scientists and they do not know all this.

The material presented to the medium's 'George' for dramatization as from a communicator (for which George was trained) includes the medium's conscious and unconscious guesses concerning possible communicators from her observation of the sitters. It also includes the contents of the memory stores of the sitter(s). In 'good' cases it also includes material put into her memory store in some unknown way by possible communicator(s). We can imagine a sort of fusion of minds at the unconscious level — which certainly seems to take place.

The perceptive reader will no doubt be thinking at this point: 'But what about that nut tree? Only the husband knew about that. Surely that proves that he must have been present?' It is certainly true that we are now on much stronger ground. To 'explain' that without the husband requires much more wide-ranging ESP from the living than there is any very good evidence for. In addition the 'cross-correspondences' provide enormously strong evidence for human survival of bodily death. So, you might say, the husband/father is surely highly likely to be involved when his nearest and dearest are similarly involved in trying to get evidence from him? Again we must remind ourselves that he was not a scientist and not conducting a scientific experiment to try to prove survival. He was eminently in character. Anyhow, the two sitters were highly delighted with their success — and so was I.

We shall be referring later (Chapter 11) to attempts by putative deceased scientific entities to explain to us how they were trying to communicate with us. And, according to them, it is not at all easy!

Let us now turn to the other type of phenomena of the seance room — physical phenomena.

The seance – physical phenomena with ectoplasm

Physical mediumship

The physical phenomena of mediumship are paranormal occurrences which everyone present, whether psychic or not, can see and hear and sometimes touch. I gave examples from my own experience below. Here it is appropriate to say only that during the production of physical phenomena the medium is usually in deep trance. For the less extreme phenomena such as 'independent voice' (disembodied voices coming from the space near the medium) the medium has not always been in trance but sometimes in my experience engages in the conversation with the voice or voices just as the sitters do. Where the phenomena include materialized forms these appear to be made from a substance exuded from the bodily orifices of the medium in trance and which was called ectoplasm by the French investigator Charles Richet.[6] Ectoplasm, which has already been discussed, has been described as temporarily densified semi-physical 'etheric' material from a subtle body of the medium. 'Etheric' material is described in Theosophical books as the non-physical substance which forms a sort of mould for the physical body and which carries the prana or 'vitality.' I have carried out experiments (Chapter 7) involving etheric material as psychically observed by clairvoyants and it appears not to have position in physical space. I cannot therefore see how it can be a mould for the denser body. (It may, however, be a sort of 'information field.') At present much of this area of science awaits elucidation and all it is possible for me to do here is to describe as accurately as possible my experiences and leave it to later workers to do the scientific 'modelling.' This work is orders of magnitude more difficult than 'normal science.' I have made an attempt to model a human being in Chapter 18.

As mentioned earlier, when ectoplasm has been used to produce materialized forms during a seance the medium was, in my experience, at the end completely exhausted and had to be carried out to rest. So far as it goes this would appear to be confirmation of the Theosophical statement that the etheric material used to produce the ectoplasm was taken from the medium's body — and was so not available to carry the vitality needed for normal life.

Recently I have been having experience of physical phenomena not so far involving visible tangible human forms which appear not to involve ectoplasm. The two mediums, both in trance during the seances, are perfectly fresh afterwards. This is described below.

In the case of mental phenomena there is nothing to 'see.' The psychic/medium passes on her mental experiences (a psychologist would say 'hallucinatory experiences') to the sitter. Usually she interprets them too and sometimes does not mention that her impression that the communicator was deeply religious was obtained by her seeing a gold cross in the air over the head of the communicator. A major difficulty of a researcher is persuading such mediumistic subjects actually to describe what they are experiencing rather than their interpretation of it. (George selects all sorts of interesting ways of passing on to the conscious mind the material he is acquiring, from the sitter's memory store or elsewhere in the unconscious, in a way that is not at all understood.)

Regarding physical phenomena, there most certainly is something tangible to experience. Again, as we shall see, there are various ways of interpreting the experiences acquired in physical seances. But let us start, as before, with a description of actual experiences I had when studying physical mediumship.

Early investigations by scientists

A great deal of good and soundly based scientific work has been carried out to study the physical phenomena of seances. Some of the best ever was done in Paris near the beginning of the twentieth century. It was organized by the professor of psychology at the Sorbonne (University of Paris) and the researchers included the distinguished philosopher Henri Bergson, Pierre and Marie Curie and Charles Richet (mentioned above), all professors at the Sorbonne. They studied a famous Italian medium, Eusapia Palladino. The investigators had a most complicated system of instruments designed to monitor phenomena and record any physical occurrences. Also, the monitoring was in a separate laboratory, thereby removing the investigators from any influences present in the seance room. The medium's chair was on a weighing machine and other furniture was electrically wired so that their movements could be registered. Every noise and comment in the seance room was recorded and a reasonable light was maintained, variable as desired.

During these tests a large number of physical phenomena were observed, including tables levitating and raps produced some distance from the medium, whose weight increased by the weight of the table when it was levitated, showing that the force was coming from her. (Later this was clearly shown again in the Irish Goligher circle, briefly described in Chapter 8.) There were other phenomena such as curtains billowing out, a musical instrument being played, investigators touched and faint lights seen. Sometimes hands and arms were observed which did not belong to anyone present.

Sadly, Pierre Curie was killed in a traffic accident before these experiments were completed. The investigators gave the results of their work and the famous astronomer Flammarion suggested that levitation should be in no further doubt.

It really is difficult to see how better tests than these could have been arranged. Nonetheless the SPR refused to endorse them and sent their own team of three experts in the detection of fake physical phenomena and conjuring to Naples (where Eusapia lived). They took a room and equipped it with their own materials, buying objects such as musical instruments which were required. Eusapia brought her own 'cabinet' — in the form of a curtain across a corner of the room — behind which the objects could be placed on a small stand, and she brought her own table, which they thoroughly examined.

From their report it is obvious that those three investigators were hostile and doubting in the extreme. They certainly did not wish to believe; quite the contrary. Though they observed all the phenomena they felt that they must have been subject to hallucinations or had not observed clearly. They questioned their senses rather than their experiences. Doubt remained! But I wonder whether there was good reason for it. At this distance it looks to me (and no doubt my view is based on similar experiences of genuine paranormal phenomena I have had) more like prejudice. (I should mention that their report was nonetheless positive.) It has become clear to me over the years that before most investigators can fully accept that any phenomenon really occurred they need to have some sort of a theory or model in their minds as to how. In other words, the facts of experience are not enough. This point is illustrated by many experiences I have had and described elsewhere in this book. We still have sceptics who are putting forward the most far-fetched and ingenious suggestions to 'explain' the paranormal phenomena produced by Eusapia Palladino, who was just an uneducated Italian peasant and not within a million kilometres of membership of a Magic Circle! I do not suggest for a moment that this should not be done but to me it often indicates a lack of experience of such physical phenomena by investigators who really consider it all to be impossible.

There is one remark I should like to make about physical phenomena and a reasonable attitude towards it. Sometimes a medium is 'caught out' in fraudulently producing phenomena. In my view this is a criticism of the investigators and not of the medium. The medium is normally in trance during physical phenomena and consciously unaware of what is occurring. Her personal unconscious mind ('George') knows what is required and does his best to produce it. If paranormal movement of objects is desired then he does his best, selecting the easiest way to produce the desired result. If the medium's movements are not under proper control so that they can get an arm or leg free then George will move the object by using an arm or leg. If this is not possible then he will have to use a paranormal means, if this is possible. Eusapia Palladino used to say often that she would 'cheat' if she could. This was not fully appreciated by some of the early SPR and other investigators — and indeed by some of today's inexperienced investigators. (I had a similar experience of George's doing the best he could in experiences with Ingo Swann and Matthew Manning, described in other chapters.) It is important to remember that 'George' is naïve, very helpful, obliging and amoral — and limited in what 'he' can do. But he has an enormously important job to do in connection with the structuring of our normal consciousness and with other levels of consciousness too.

My early experiences

The way I found out about the existence of the first seances I shall describe was quite intriguing in itself. I liked to go on an occasional Saturday to London from Rugby, where I lived and worked, and look around some of the biggest bookshops. One day I was looking at the Occult section of the second-hand department of one and found a booklet describing some of the most amazing physical phenomena of Spiritualism I had come across. I wrote to the address of the author, not expecting to receive a reply, saying how interesting I had found his book and asking him whether he was still holding the seances described there. He replied quite quickly and invited me to attend. He suggested that I should come early in the afternoon so that we could talk before the seance in the evening. I was happy to accept so travelled to London in the morning of one Sunday in 1953 and appeared at his house in Battersea after lunch.

I found my host to be what I would now describe as a 'rabid Spiritualist.' He believed literally everything that 'spirit' told him and would have been horrified if I had expressed doubts or reservations about anything. Needless to say, I chose my words carefully or I should have been instantly dismissed. He wished to be, as he put it, 'scientific,' and asked me to inspect the room where the evening activity was to take place to check that there was nothing there that should not be there. He lived in a normal small semi-detached house in Battersea and I inspected his upstairs seance room carefully. It was a perfectly normal bedroom except that there was no bed and the sparse furniture was around the walls so that the middle of the room was clear. A circle of upright chairs had been set. There was one window with a substantial blackout and only one door. The ceiling was normal as were the walls. At his request I looked for places of concealment or hidden doors but there clearly were none. The central light, a bare bulb, had draped around it a red handkerchief. Across one of the corners of the room was a rod carrying a curtain to form a 'cabinet.' I do not remember ever seeing the curtain actually drawn across that corner. In that corner was a large armchair.

We went to his living room and had some tea. He had on his small table a lamp and, propped up at an angle near it and facing the lamp, were two 'plaques,' that is, two rectangular pieces of plywood each about 40 cm or so by about 25 cm and each carrying a strip of wood as a 'handle' on the back for picking up the plaque when it was face down on the carpet. The plaques had been earlier painted with luminous (phosphorescent) paint and were being exposed to the light to make them glow brightly in the dark. My host explained that it was with these that the spirits showed themselves.

After tea and more conversation we went upstairs for the seance. After a few minutes more Spiritualists began to arrive, came up the stairs and took their places on the chairs. By around 7.00 pm there were about eight of us. The red light had been switched on and the blind drawn. We talked quietly and expectantly. Some time later a noise was heard downstairs and the medium came up and sat in his big armchair. It was always a relief to everyone when he arrived. Sometimes, I later gathered from experience, he either did not appear at all or was too drunk to climb the stairs.

After very brief greetings activity commenced. The medium sat in his chair, closed his eyes and went (ostensibly) into trance. My experience during the next year showed me that he was quite genuinely in trance. There was nothing pseudo about his performance as a medium.

I shall now describe briefly what went on at a typical seance during the next year or so when I attended every Sunday. For brevity and as customary I shall omit such qualifying words as 'ostensibly' or 'it appeared that.'

The medium's Red Indian guide, Great White Feather, opened, and speaking through the medium in trance said:

> G.W. FEATHER: Greetings my children. It is I, Great White Feather. I come unto you with the blessing of the spirit world and the great white spirit whose loving power joined you all together in his heavenly name. We come unto you that we may help and aid thee in your spiritual progress. We come that each day and each night we may help you on this path to perfect enlightenment. The Great White Spirit gives unto all his divine healing power. He gives and shares his blessings, the treasures of heaven, unto each one of you. Your spirit guides are forever continuing to attract the children of the earth that remain in the shadows unto the warmth of his holy light. I pray you to cherish the blessings and gifts from the heavenly kingdom, the spirit world, and I, Great White Feather, pray that each one of you will go forth with the work of the Great White Spirit. I bless you. Fare thee well. Great White Feather. Peace be unto you.

Grey Horse, another Indian guide, then controlled the medium: 'Indian. Indian,' a deep voice called.

The medium rose from the chair. 'I bless you all,' he said, and then shook our host by the hand: 'Grey Horse, I bless you.' He greeted all the sitters similarly:

> GREY HORSE: I have come for a purpose — very good purpose. I am spirit guide. I guide those who go in mist. I help rescue. Guide to path of light that leads to spirit world. I give you blessing. Peace to you.

A third communicator gave the name of Joan Woodhouse:

> Excuse me coming like this. I did ask permission to come. I did
> not come on my own, I have come here with a guide. Now I
> know, you see. I told you the spirit world would put everything
> all right. Joan Woodhouse. I told you, you see; that man was not
> responsible for my passing. The spirit world is going to put it
> all right. He will be quite all right. He did not have anything to
> do with it. I told you weeks ago ... it is not the only reason for
> my coming through. It will help to prove survival. I told you
> several weeks ago that he had nothing to do with it and it will
> be proved. Grey Horse is calling me now. I must go. I will come
> again if I may.

The medium's expression altered:

> Gleetings, honolable daughters, gleetings honolable sons. Long
> Fu. Yes, I very happy to officiate during this service. I take
> control. No earthly light! Blessings.

Here our host switched off the light and we were in darkness. After a
fairly short interval the plaques rose from the carpet and we saw our
first materialized form: 'Hassan.' He came and looked closely into the
face of one of the sitters whose 'Chief Control' they believed him to be.

> HASSAN: Blessings upon thee my son and upon thee my daugh-
> ter. I come to tell thee I have found the land upon which thy
> house and temple will stand. Upon it I have placed my blessing
> and anointed it with holy water. Now I await the Great White
> Spirit to direct me further. Then with thee I will remain to build.
> Peace to thee.' Hassan then greeted all the other members of the
> circle in turn. 'Peace to thee. I bless thee my children.

He then disappeared down through the floor and the plaques clattered
down. I should explain that the plaques enabled us to see him quite
clearly and the plaques were held in the same relative position until the
hands holding them disappeared — it seemed quite clear — down
through the floor. They then bumped onto the carpet and all was dark
again.

So the materialized figures went on appearing. Another bearded

Eastern character was next with more blessings and promises of wonderful things waiting.

The next one came self-illuminated (light appeared to be coming from his cupped hands, which he held in front of him) — another Eastern character:

> Peace. Peace to thee. I come to thee once again. Thou wilt sup
> at the Master's table.

The next one was the spirit wife of our host. She also came self-illuminated and dressed in a nun's costume. She called out 'Bud' to her husband:

> See, I have come. I've come in the purple ray. I've come with a
> lot of spirit children because today is Sophy's birthday on earth
> so we have allowed the spirit children to gather flowers and to
> bind them up for each one of you. I bless you all.

The radiance dimmed and White Rose, as she was called, disappeared. (Whatever does 'come in the purple ray' mean? Nobody seemed to wonder.)

Sophy was next heard chatting in the cabinet. 'How many are you?' Eight. 'All right kids, I want eight bunches of flowers.' Now another nun appeared. She helped Sophy bring the flowers. We all had a bunch of apported flowers.

So it went on for some three hours. Another Indian, Brown Owl, was the next figure. Then the squaw of Great White Feather. etc., etc.

Lady Jane Seymour, the 'special helper' of one of the sitters, then appeared. She told the sitter concerned that the ring she had received at the last seance was highly magnetized. She said 'I have returned that I may now work with the magi for the apportion (sic) of objects.' (What does 'highly magnetized' mean? Nobody appeared puzzled or troubled by this. I presume that 'apportion of objects' meant the production of apports — objects brought paranormally into the seance room from elsewhere.)

On this occasion King George V, looking exactly like his photographs, was the last visitor. He said 'I have joined the band of great power. I have come to tell you that Mary and I will work with you for this special religion.' As he was going, King George V said: 'I have come in a dark suit.'

On another occasion Sir Oliver Lodge appeared looking exactly like his photographs (big bald head and bushy beard). He also went all round the circle showing himself with the plaques. I could hardly wait to hear what he would say to me — a fellow electrical researcher. Sadly it was much the same as he said to the others: 'God bless you my son. Keep up the good work.'

On yet another occasion an Indian wearing a huge diamond in his turban appeared and said that he was the architect of the Taj Mahal. He also just wandered around blessing everybody.

The most interesting thing that ever happened to me at all those sittings, each on a Sunday evening and the series lasting over a year, was the arrival of an apport which I was able to see well in every detail from beginning to end. On that occasion and while the red light was still on near the beginning of the seance, the medium tottered out from his corner, eyes tightly closed, and held out his cupped hands towards my host. Over the top of his hands there was a pink glow which extended five or six centimetres into the air at its highest point. It looked rather like the glow one gets as a Crookes' tube is evacuated, or like the coloured glow in a fluorescent tube. I gazed intently at this from a distance of perhaps 15 centimetres looking all over and under the medium's hands. I remind the reader again that this was in a good red light: I could see clearly that everyone was seated and there appeared no way in which such a phenomenon could occur. As I gazed I could see something taking shape in the middle of the glow, mistily at first and then more clearly. It was a rose. The rose fell down onto the medium's hands and the pink glow died away. He picked up the rose and handed it to my host, who was sitting next to me. My host put the rose into a vase containing water which had been set ready on a sideboard. It was a perfect rose and looked as though it had been recently picked; there was nothing unusual about it. This occurred quite often and was, I was told, the gift of my host's deceased wife. At one of the most astonishing experiences of my life no one turned a hair!

Some — most — of those Sunday evenings we had as many as thirty full materializations. In one we had an Indian, his squaw and a papoose. I was allowed to hold the papoose. (It felt exactly like cold suet pudding.) The seance usually lasted some three hours. The medium was absolutely exhausted at the end and had to be carried out to lie on a bed for half an hour.

If the medium had been fraudulently dressing up he would have needed a large portmanteau of clothes. He came in with nothing but his ordinary clothes. The same applies to all the sitters. Also, the door was locked at the beginning of the seance and, for what it was worth, I had searched the room. It was not a large room and there was nowhere to hide anything. Needless to say, I had looked inside the sideboard.

A final remark or two are necessary in connection with those experiences I had over forty years ago (and of which, of course, I still have my detailed notes). The first is regarding 'ectoplasm.' The materialized figures were constructed of ectoplasm which, the theory goes, was extracted by the Controls from the body of the medium. (I read all this in my father's Theosophical books while I was still a schoolboy.) Ectoplasm, I was there told, was densified 'etheric material' — a 'semi-physical material as yet unknown to science which interpenetrates the dense physical body and carries the vital energy of life (prana).' If much of the medium's vital energy body (as it is sometimes called) is missing for some three hours it is not surprising that he is subsequently depleted of energy and eventually 'driven to drink.' I tested this theory a great many years ago and found that though many psychics say that they can clairvoyantly perceive the etheric double they cannot tell where the physical body is if it is *only* the etheric double they are allowed to perceive. The same applies to the 'astral body'- which, the old books said, also interpenetrates the physical body and projects all around forming the so-called aura.

The second remark refers to the rather revolting smell of ectoplasm (at least in my own experience of it). The smell of the ectoplasm in the materialization seances I have described may, of course, have been due to the eating and drinking habits of that particular medium, of course! When the materializations described above took place there was a very distinctive smell of what in the old advertisements for a particular brand of toilet soap was called B.O. (body odour). It reminded me of the smell in a very crowded tube train in the rush hour on a hot summer's day when it was raining. I do not see how that could have been faked.

The final remark concerns the substance of the seances I have described in such detail above. I have said already that my host would have been horrified if I had doubted anything. However, would the reader seriously think that Sir Oliver Lodge, a great and distinguished scientist, would really have behaved in that way if he had been there? Does King George V really have nothing better to do than to attend seances in a little house in Battersea, bless us all, and make reference to his suit? Does the architect of the Taj Mahal ... Really!

Does this not remind one a little of the Philip experiment and those other similar matters described above? Do we really need anything at those seances except the unconscious hopes and expectations of those Spiritualists? Ectoplasm appears to be 'ideoplastic' — mould-able by thought. Has George (or perhaps all the Georges of all those sitters) been up to his dramatization tricks again? He gets lots of practice every night with our dreams.

Over the years, I have had many 'scientific' communications from 'the other side.' To the Spiritualists who received them they looked very scientific. In every case they were pseudo-scientific gobbledy-gook. I have had two requests by 'the other side' to investigate their seances. In neither case did I find anything worth investigating.

The Goligher Circle

Before we leave the consideration of what 'ectoplasm' is we should spend a few moments considering the experiments done by an Irish mechanical engineering academic and his resulting theories in the famous seances of the Goligher circle in Belfast many years ago. This was a private 'home circle' for physical mediumship and Dr W. John Crawford (a Queen's University mechanical engineering lecturer) per-suaded the family to allow him to attend. This group was producing table levitations and Crawford tried photographing them. He found that the photographic film showed something normally invisible to the eye — something he called 'psychic structures.' 'Ectoplasm' was exuded from the bodily orifices of the medium, Kate Goligher, densi-fied and formed into cantilevers to levitate the table. Strangely, Crawford could put his hands through the space where the ectoplasmic structures were, as shown by the photographs and by the levitated table, and could feel nothing. Crawford put the table and all the sitters on weighing machines and showed that most of the weight of the table during levitations was transferred to the medium. (A little of the weight was taken by some of the other sitters.)

Crawford's experiments were most valuable in showing just what was occurring. There seemed little doubt that the theory was true — that a substance of some kind was certainly taken from the body of the entranced medium and used for the manipulation of the table. It would then appear reasonable to suggest that the same substance was used in the production of the figures which walked round the circle in the Battersea seances. It was presumably also used in the levitation of the trumpet in the North London seance described below. Ectoplasm was often photographed in those remarkable seances held near the beginning of the twentieth century, some of which are briefly described below.

Other physical seances

All those years ago — before and after I first came to London — I attended many other physical seances. At one — where the medium was tied to his chair — I entered after all the Spiritualists were sitting down and when a red light was still switched on. We were all sitting in a large circle and the only thing in the middle on the carpet was a trumpet with phosphorescent rings painted around it. However, while the light was still on, the Control gave me a special demonstration. I was asked by the Control to hold my linked hands out in front of me. The trumpet levitated off the carpet and encircled my linked hands quite rapidly some five or six times before descending gently back to the carpet. Everyone present was clearly in view and sitting still.

Later the medium's jacket, which had been sewn up down the front by one of the sitters before I arrived, was removed from him during a few seconds while the light was turned out. The medium remained tied to his chair; his coat had been placed on the floor, still sewn up. He operated the lights by a switch near his hand on the chair arm.

I have no expert comments to make on phenomena which occurred in the dark or were otherwise mysterious, as I am not a skilled magician. However, perhaps I should say that a stage magician would maintain (assuming he did not believe that any of the phenomena I have been describing were genuine) that I had omitted vital parts of the description. He might, while giving the same description as mine, precede it by the words 'What appeared to happen was this.' I can only reply by saying that I have had long talks with many magicians and am well aware of what to look for in close-up magic. Magicians who have listened carefully to my descriptions have told me that if I am accurate then they do not see how that could have been done under those conditions. One of the leading magicians in the UK has given me his opinion that stage magicianship has little to do with whether psychic phenomena take place or not and certainly what I have experienced could not all be explained in that way — at least, one should perhaps add, by him. This does not stop some magicians, who appear to be even more prejudiced than some normal scientists, from suggesting that all psychic happenings are fraudulent because they are impossible. How can one answer such prejudice?

The Scole phenomena

I have for the last few years been attending what appears to be a quite new kind of seance in which physical phenomena take place but without ectoplasm. The people who are organizing this refer to the phenomena as 'energy' phenomena. There are here two mediums — a husband and wife combination, both in trance during the 'experimental sessions' as they call the seances — and they are used in the same way as described above in the Battersea activities but at the end of the sessions they are not in the least exhausted. If the ectoplasm/etheric body theory has value then here, it would appear, no etheric material is being extracted and used for the physical phenomena. However, in my view this throws some light on a possible philosophical approach to modelling these sorts of phenomena. We shall consider this in Chapter 18.

The sessions which I shall now briefly describe took place over several years at Scole in Norfolk and were arranged by Robin and Sandra Foy in the basement of their house. The two trance mediums we knew as Alan and Diana — a married couple. Three senior members of the Society for Psychical Research were invited to witness the phenomena and their development. For most of the period during which we witnessed the sessions and the development of the various phenomena, some of them new, the three SPR researchers consisted of two past presidents, Professor David Fontana, a psychologist, and myself, an electrical/mechanical engineer; and one other senior member of Council, Montague Keen, a farmer, journalist and editor. We had each of us a vast amount of experience of psychical research. We were approved by the ostensible communicators as being scientific with the requisite experience and with reasonably open minds. The communicators appeared to know well that researchers, in accordance with the well-known 'experimenter effect,' tend to fall into two classes: of 'catalysts' and 'inhibitors.'They were anxious to avoid the presence of anything which would make the desired phenomena more difficult to produce, while eager to have competent scientists. Their main aim was to produce good and new evidence strongly indicating human survival of bodily death and occasionally using modern scientific aids (with our help, as appropriate).

We are, as I write this, in the final stages of producing a long paper which will be a complete volume of SPR Proceedings. All important phenomena, with all the details necessary for a complete understanding, will be described in that paper (see Reading List.) Hopefully it will be followed by a book containing more detail together with possible speculation which would not be appropriate for a scientific paper suitable for the scholarly SPR. The following is therefore a brief sketch of some of the more important features of a long series of experimental sessions taking place over some five years. We were involved for about the last three of those years.

The sessions were held in the brick cellar of the Foys' house. The floor of the cellar was of concrete, the arched ceiling and walls of brick and it was approached by stone steps. At the beginning of every session, the door at the top of the steps was bolted and would have made a loud noise had it been opened at any time during the session. The only other opening was a small former coal chute securely blocked off from the inside by a stout wooden panel screwed firmly into the wall. Every session was tape recorded and the record was later typed so that very full records are available. Robin and Sandra together with the two mediums wore around their arms luminous bands so that we were able to see that they remained in their seats while phenomena were taking place. These bands were held on with Velcro tape so that their removal would have resulted in a distinctive noise. The circular table, which was about a metre in diameter and around which we sat, also carried luminous tabs near its edge, one at each of the four cardinal compass points. On the centre of the table was a glass dome as once used for housing a stuffed bird, and this was mounted on a plinth, itself supported by six small Perspex pillars. Music was played on a second tape recorder and occasionally changed in character in accordance with the communicators' wishes.

After a short time with the lights out to give the mediums time to get into trance, the first communicator always opened the proceedings. This was a somewhat loud and distinctive androgynous character called Manu who welcomed us and gave us preliminary instructions. He spoke through Diana.

There were major differences in the Scole phenomena from those of the other physical seance which I described in some detail earlier. The first difference was that the principal communicators were normal educated Western people, with the possible exception of one or two who sounded like Western-educated Asians. The principal communicator

(Mrs Emily Bradshaw), speaking through Diana, rapidly followed Manu and seemed to be a well-educated lady having an upper-class English accent of around the turn of the century. It was some time before we felt we knew her well enough to address her by her first name. I don't ever remember having this kind of problem before! A little later we had other voices: Patrick, said to be a former priest, spoke through Alan. He sounded very tired and said that communicating with us was 'like jumping into a bath of custard.' Emily Bradshaw jocularly wondered what researchers would make of that when written up. We were told that all the names we were given and by which we addressed the communicators were pseudonyms and that they were interested in demonstrating human survival and did not want us to waste time trying to trace their earth lives.

On one occasion Patrick said that he had been told to stand right back. Then a string of bells hanging from the ceiling started to ring and a hoarse and croaky independent voice was heard which sounded as though it was coming from a little above the table. We were told that he was Joseph, and Robin Foy stated that he was 'one of our scientists.' A 'spirit light' no larger than a pea appeared in various parts of the room. This light touched our hands, alighted on a tab, settled and illuminated from the inside a Pyrex bowl which was also on the table and then visited various points around the room including the top of my head. It felt just as though a pea had landed on my head from a height. It appeared to go right through a hand and then through the table, appearing underneath. When it hit the table or a glass object sharp raps or pings could be heard. An occasional inspection of the arm bands showed that the arms of everyone in the Scole group appeared to be in their usual positions. The light then appeared — completely silently — to describe high-speed figures-of-eight and then circles. Sometimes there were segments missing from the circles. On several occasions the small sphere of light remained stationary near me and I observed it closely. There was no sign of any filament in it or other clue as to its nature. It was just an isolated sphere of light. On more than one occasion the light entered a crystal and remained as a small point of light moving around within the crystal, or permeating light throughout its structure. In one case the small sphere of light settled on the open palm of a guest investigator who then enfolded the light within his hands to satisfy himself of the absence of any physical link. In another remarkable example the small light shone from within the clear light bulb near the ceiling, the filament of that bulb emitting no light. The small light on another occasion agitated the water within a glass held by Professor Fontana, his face being immediately above the glass, precluding entry of any physical device. On many occasions the light entered the chests of investigators who then reported internal sensations, the light then leaving from a different part of the body. Often the light illuminated the feet of sitters below the circular table despite the screens formed by the vertical wooden barriers dividing the table up into four quadrants. Another interesting phenomenon occurred when the light appeared to build up from a diffused glow into materialized objects on or floating above the table and taking the shape of small draped figurines or a vague 'face' with apparent movement of the lips. Some then rose to the ceiling before disappearing, sometimes gently brushing against our hands on the way. On other occasions the light performed gyrations in front of one sitter while being completely invisible to neighbours, as though screens had been placed beside it and directed towards each of us in turn. We experienced nothing even faintly like the ectoplasm of traditional physical seances.

Another somewhat croaky independent voice said that he was Lawrence and promised to speak to us shortly. He was followed by one who introduced himself as John. Lawrence then picked up a ping pong ball carrying a luminous tab which was in the Pyrex bowl. The ball was heard to bounce as it was dropped and the bowl was dragged across the table. The light then returned, appearing to describe acrobatics. Emily said that she would be back shortly and declared that 'SPR this side, SPR your side: the place is alive with them.' She declined to give names — yet.

The party atmosphere changed dramatically as Joseph returned, speaking through Alan. He apologized for remaining anonymous and offered to answer any questions. These dealt mainly with the afterlife, the relationship to lucid dreaming, the role of near death and out-of-body experiences in relation to the next world and various ontological issues. One question asked how the communicators knew that it was time for the sitting. The reply was that there is no time as we know it where they were but they felt a sort of pull when the sitting was about to commence. The communicators appeared touched by our offer to do what we could to help produce examinable phenomena under the right control conditions and the sitting ended with Joseph explaining that on their side they desired to make people aware that there is something more to life than living and that death is nothing to fear, just an extension to life. 'It's a good thing happiness is involved in this work. It isn't all darkness and gloom: it is love and it is light.'

Emily Bradshaw suggested a series of sittings, some of them devoted to particular aspects of the varied work they had planned.

That is a very brief description of our first sitting with the Scole group with a slight admixture of events from later sessions. I shall go on to describe some phenomena of particular interest that occurred during some of those various other later sessions.

On one occasion the Perspex bowl was illuminated by the communicators brightly enough for me to see the adjacent sitters. Within it appeared to be a large crystal which brightened and dimmed in turn. I was invited to feel the crystal and did so. It was about 10 cm long. Then I was asked to feel it again. I attempted to do that but, though I could see it apparently present as before, I could not feel it but only the smooth base of the bowl. I saw the silhouette of a large hand casting a big shadow and then an arm crossing the light. We observed vague figures and sometimes shapes building up with varying degrees of illumination. The crystal appeared and disappeared and this still occurred when my head was in the opening of the bowl so that it would have been impossible for a hand carrying the crystal to have put it in or taken it out of the bowl. Not infrequently we experienced table vibrations, sometimes accompanied by a jerky clockwise movement of the table.

When this display ended the room felt colder and darker. Joseph indicated a desire to speak to us. He said that he and his spirit friends existed in a land of pure thought and light, but light entirely different from that on earth. He said that it was difficult to explain such concepts in terms we could understand. (I often wished that they would just explain and leave us to decide whether we understood or not!) The rest of the session was devoted to the problems and techniques of communication and the extent to which negatively disposed sitters would inhibit the production of phenomena and whether the use of infra-red viewers and photography, for which we were constantly pressing, would constitute a further obstacle. We also asked whether we might suggest or introduce some experiments of our own. His answer distinguished this investigation from any predecessors. He said that the experiments they had embarked upon had been thought out by a team of spirit people from their side with the sole aim of providing evidence of an after-life. They had never thought of carrying out experiments based on our suggestions. They wanted to perfect their experiments to the point where they produced repeatable successful results. We made no progress in regard to our own experiments and have never understood why non-invasive instruments such as an infrared viewer should adversely affect phenomena. (The tape recorders alone would produce more physical effects than would an infra-red viewer.) I shall have more to say later concerning possible psychological factors involved. I was quite unable to persuade the communicators to agree to attempts to read the numbers I had put on my bookcase or in my pocket during the sittings.

Our sittings were conducted, as described earlier, in a specially prepared room in the house of the principal protagonist. In view of this it is worth mentioning that the group have held sittings with others present in several different locations such as Germany, the Netherlands, Switzerland, Ireland, Spain and the USA. Two sittings each in Ibiza and USA were attended by one of us investigators (Montague Keen). There was no facility for preparing the room beyond checking the blackout and placing luminous strips at the cardinal points of a central circular table. The usual effects were obtained with, interestingly, perhaps more and better phenomena when the audience consisted of believing spiritualists than of critical scientists. (This was probably the result of a combination of the sheep/goat effect and the experimenter effect.)

We did not know whether the 'spirit lights' were 'self-controlled' or operated from a different level of consciousness from ours, but they appeared to 'know' exactly where to go. On request, they were able to touch our hands or heads with unerring accuracy in the pitch darkness.

Any 'normal' explanation of these phenomena would presuppose a minimum of two requirements. The first assumes complicity by all members of the Scole group in deception of a highly-skilled kind. The second requires the existence of concealed apparatus to produce all these effects. Our regular searches failed to discover any such hidden apparatus. In addition the phenomena were replicated overseas in the presence of one of the investigators, of many independent and expert witnesses, and in situations making prior installation of such equipment impossible. We rarely searched the group members but cannot, in any case, imagine what sort of equipment would have been needed. And it has not been suggested by critics. In Ibiza everyone was dressed in very flimsy clothing and it would have been apparently impossible to have concealed any apparatus.

Now I turn to a different kind of phenomenon using photographic film. Well before our investigation sittings began, one of us (Montague

Keen) had discussed with Dr Richard Wiseman a suitable protocol likely to pass muster with sceptics. Dr Wiseman — a specialist in deception and a member of the best known UK society of stage magicians — had provided us with a security bag in which it was proposed to place an unopened tub of 35 mm film in the hope of obtaining spirit messages and/or photographs. This bag was left with the Scole group and, at our next session, Emily said that it was an excellent bag and expressed herself optimistic. (She said that she and her colleagues were not part of the photographic team.) At the next meeting I opened the packaging and took out a tub of 35 mm Polaroid film bought by Mr Keen. I removed the chemical cassette to await development after the sitting and placed the unopened tub in the security bag, which I then sealed. I took it down to the experimental room and placed it on the floor within one of the table quadrants inaccessibly between my feet and those of Mr Keen. After the sitting we opened the bag, took out the film tub, extracted the roll of film and put it through the electrical developer machine upstairs. The film was projected onto a large screen and it showed star-like scatters with some lines and a small cog-shaped light with a shadowy substance behind. Normally of course there should have been nothing at all on the film, which had — it seemed clear — been neither opened nor exposed.

We carried out various experiments of this kind in collaboration with the communicators using different security bags. They were obviously experimenting and learning just as we were. A slightly later film showed *inter alia* the word 'man' rather crudely written in lower case Greek lettering. We wondered whether it was an attempt to represent 'Manu.'

After various attempts of this kind we received something really interesting on a film we had sealed with white sticky tape and left on the table between experimental sessions. The communicators were obviously having great difficulty in penetrating the three layers of plastic of the security bag but they did get stars onto an unopened film. The other cassette still apparently sealed by our sticky tape (but obviously not fully secure as was the other film in the security bag) contained substantial evidence. We opened this, developed it and projected it and found a poem written in four lines along the whole of the length of the 12-frame film strip.

I do not propose to go any further into this as we are at present concerned primarily with the physical phenomena, and the full and interesting analysis of this and other material received and taking many months of careful detective work is to be found in the SPR Proceedings. Clues appeared to show clearly that several early and distinguished members of the SPR Council (and concerned with the cross-correspondences described in Chapter 7) were involved.

More and equally interesting but quite different physical phenomena were produced at later sessions. These concerned the production of spirit voices on tape, instructions concerning which were given to us through a clear roll of film carrying also a diagram, all closely linked to the tape-recorded discussions between members of the communicating Team and ourselves and between the Team and someone previously unknown to us and referred to as a spirit scientist. In connection with this, one of the communicators, Joseph, asked whether we could get a small piece of germanium, bring it and leave it in a small dish on the table. No one but I appeared to have heard of germanium (which is a semi-conductor used for making computer chips before silicon was used). I volunteered to try to get some and later Joseph asked whether a coherer had been mentioned. It had not, but I volunteered that a coherer had been invented by Sir Oliver Lodge and used in the early days of radio, long before germanium. A coherer was an early detector of electromagnetic waves and acted as a detector/rectifier when high frequency current passed through it.

I did as requested and the spirit scientist, speaking as an independent 'energy voice,' apparently from the air, said that he was relaying messages and informed me, in answer to a question from me, that silicon would not serve instead of the germanium. The germanium was intended to enhance communication of a quite different nature from what had been attempted before — from other areas or dimensions of life. The 'scientist' said that the germanium would hopefully be used as a focus but not simply a focus. We were not, he said, dealing with electromagnetic waves but pure spirit vibrations and waves. (This made absolutely no sense to me! However, it made more — normal — sense at a later stage, as we shall see.)

The spirit scientist (energy voice) asked us to mount the germanium and apply some pressure between two threaded screws to be used as terminations. In answer to my question 'he' said that one screw should be flat and the other pointed. I said: 'Like a crystal radio set?.' He replied: 'There's some polarity involved.' I said then that the radio waves would be rectified, when they could be made audible. The reply was that the need to rectify anything was not anticipated. There was clearly a misunderstanding on the meaning of 'rectify' and I explained that it meant take out half the waves — not put something right. He replied, 'Very well.'

It was agreed that we would arrange the mounting as instructed, and I was then asked to bring a device 'to amplify what is heard.' This should have a 'high impedance input' but considerable 'gain' would not be needed. 'The two terminations upon the germanium will be used as an input.' 'Hopefully the output will be heard.' I replied: 'There will be a small loudspeaker.' I was concerned that the metal point might crack the brittle germanium and considered making a point on a coiled piece of wire to add resilience. Then I realized that I was reinventing the crystal detector from the early days of radio and designing a rectifier, so I asked the communicator whether a more modern silicon diode would not be better. The reply was that the device was not to be used as a diode and should be made exactly as described. A piece of rubber was therefore placed under the germanium to add a measure of resilience.

Shortly after this I brought along a box containing an amplifier and a tape recorder, connected the input to the germanium device and we awaited results. I had been told that this device was not to have an AC supply so I arranged for it to be battery-supplied. I was very puzzled as to why a relatively small additional alternating current should cause problems as both the tape recorders for the recording of the sessions and for playing the music took much more alternating current than the new device would have required. However, we eliminated the mains unit as requested.

We had been told to expect white noise (rather like the sound of the sea). When the device was switched on there was no sound as expected. However, when the communicators started their work the speaker emitted crackles and bangs and then a sound was produced very like a steam train accelerating from a station. We finally had the rushing sound rather like white noise. These sounds were somewhat puzzling as they appeared to have no normal explanation. Some sitters considered that they could hear whispers. The communicator Edwin informed us that all this was still at the exploratory stage but eventually it should be possible to communicate without mediums — not directly but with the help of personalities like himself. Here the communicators considered that there was something wrong with the amplifier — but felt that there might be a sketch on one of the films that were to be put on the table at the following session — with all the usual safeguards — which I was unable to attend.[7] One of these films had a diagram and a short message for me on it asking me to connect two small coils in series between the germanium device and the input to the amplifier. Using normal theory, the coils could act like an aerial and pick up radio waves but the direction of the connection shown would mean that the pick-up from one would cancel out that from the other. Connected so that the signals picked up would be additive, the germanium device would then act to rectify the signal picked up; the amplifier would then produce a larger signal for the speaker. This would in effect produce a normal crystal radio set but with no means of tuning it. (It will be remembered that the communicator said that the germanium was not being used as a rectifier, as I have assumed in this description.)

However, there was dissatisfaction on the part of the communicators with the amplifier: it never became clear to us why but it was blamed for the excessive white noise and it was replaced with a simple cheap tape recorder from which the internal microphone had been removed. This recorded what sounded like voices and also orchestral music. All in all it was difficult for us to see how these facts could be interpreted as evidence of fraudulence because the events and interventions by us appeared to be spontaneous. And a radio transmission sent especially for us to pick up we would probably not have heard. More detailed analysis is to be found in the full paper.

The film carrying the diagram appeared to have on it a reference to Fox and there had earlier been some reference to a communicator called Talbot but it did not appear that the photographic pioneer Fox Talbot was involved and Emily suggested that the whole message should be re-examined. We gathered that perhaps Thomas Edison might have been involved and so a copy of a squiggle which appeared at the far end of the diagrammatic film was sent to the Edison National Historic Site Office in New Jersey. The archives technician responded with samples of Edison's handwriting including an initialled squiggle by Edison which was virtually identical with ours. Edison had an apparent interest in communication beyond the boundaries of the earth but it was felt that this might be followed up later.

Two other ostensibly physical phenomena appeared in other sessions. In one Emily Bradshaw had earlier said that she would bet 'half a crown' that the experiment would be a success — and it was not. During the next session a loud bang occurred on the table accompanied by a triumphant exclamation from Emily, 'Debt paid!' and an 1890 half-crown coin was found on the floor. On another occasion we were told to expect some specimens for an experiment. A strip of aluminium and a strip of ferrous material were ostensibly apported to the session, arriving in the central glass bowl, and I was asked to have these carefully measured and then to bring them back and leave them on the table. Later I was asked to have them measured again. I took them to my university and their weights and dimensions were accurately measured. When I took them back to be measured again there was no difference. That experiment — whatever it was meant to be — was evidently a failure.

An earlier apport the Scole group claimed to have received — the most extraordinary — was a pristine copy of the *Daily Mail* of April 1, 1944, featuring a front-page account of Mrs Duncan's prison sentence under the eighteenth century Witchcraft Act, and which was apparently intended as evidence that the spirit of Helen Duncan, a physical medium herself, was a benign observer of the Scole proceedings. The newspaper was printed on wartime newsprint and not on the postwar paper used for reproducing copies of old issues. Robin Foy has expertise in this field as he was once in the paper-making industry, though he recognized that the paper could not be regarded as fully evidential. Nonetheless a later report from a paper industry laboratory confirmed that the paper was genuine wartime newsprint.

An unusual apport we received came when we were asked to put an empty plastic film tub on each of three cardinal compass points and then leave them for an hour after a sitting. We later found one to contain green crystals, another a liquid (presumably water) and the third a quantity of grey ash; we were to await further instructions. At the next sitting the tubs were found to be empty. We still do not know the explanation for this.

On another occasion an apport appeared in the Pyrex bowl. A light entered, swirled around the bowl and caused it to glow. At the end of the session we found a screwed up piece of paper in the bowl. It was found to carry some indecipherable writing and three ammonite shells, one of them broken. The paper was torn all round and bore scorch marks around a burnt section.

An experiment carried out abroad which I did not attend but which Mr Keen did, involved a tape recorder from which the microphone had been removed. Mr Keen had concealed a new tape in his room so that he was sure that nothing was on it. The tape was unwrapped, put into the tape recorder and then forwarded to random points and 'played' so demonstrating that there was nothing on it. The tape was returned to the start. When the sitting commenced the recorder was started. Nothing was heard during the seance itself, but afterwards, when the half-hour tape was played, two sharp clicks, a whistle, crackling and a high pitched sound followed by a noisy but unintelligible voice were audible. The communicator Edwin had been heard during the sitting exhorting an unknown entity to try to be clearer. Edwin said that he could hear someone but we could not. The fact that non-random messages were recorded on a machine lacking a microphone was strongly evidential of a paranormal origin. It will be remembered, however, that it might have been theoretically possible for a radio signal to have been detected (but there were no means of tuning) and recorded — as described above — but, it seemed to me, highly unlikely. This experiment was repeated two evenings later, this time with rather clearer messages.

There were many phenomena we observed in these Scole seances that I have not described but which are fully treated in the paper (see Reading List.) Many puzzles were given to us by the indefatigable Emily Bradshaw in collaboration with such putative characters as F.W.H. Myers, the poet Wordsworth, Professor Henry Sidgwick, Edmund Gurney, Lord Rayleigh and others. These appeared on paranormally received writings and sketches on film from unopened tubs put on the table or locked in a padlocked box as requested and later opened, developed and projected. Solving these problems needed much library and other research.

The conundrums and puzzles, cross correspondences and other communications from Emily and a number of very distinguished scientific and literary members of the SPR and others (such as Wordsworth) certainly seemed to us to be evidence very strongly suggesting survival of those personalities and a continuing interest in the topics which occupied their attention during their lifetimes.

I should finish this piece with one or two remarks concerning what I have learned as a result of that long period of investigation. It will be appreciated, of course, that the 'scientific conditions' were not all that we might have desired. The sittings were held in the cellar of the chief proponent and not under conditions that we had ourselves provided. Even though we frequently searched the cellar, we did not do this every time. The same applied to the group consisting of the Foys and the two mediums. We did nothing to ensure that the mediums were genuinely in trance when they appeared to be. We did not attempt to imitate fraudulently the various phenomena we observed and we did not recruit a team of stage magicians to try to do the same. It must be remembered that we were invited guests asked to *observe* phenomena which were not of our choosing. Bearing this in mind, we did all we could to tighten up the conditions within the bounds of politeness and friendliness. We frequently asked for permission to bring in an infra-red viewer so that we could be absolutely certain (and not just reasonably confident) that no one had moved from their seat. We were told that perhaps later ... We occasionally asked for phenomena to be repeated as we could see how critics would react to some of the events. This was not usually complied with for reasons given by the communicators, who said that their work had now moved on. It is our view that complete trust and respect between all present give the optimum conditions for good and advanced phenomena. It should also be said that we formed a warm and friendly group while still taking reasonable scientific precautions against many of the expected criticisms of sceptics. But certainly everything was not always scientifically 'watertight.'

It is my view — which I believe my fellow-investigators share — that had we not been the sort of overtly sympathetic people we are, we should not have been invited. But it is perfectly possible to be warm, friendly and sympathetic without abandoning good scientific standards. Continuous suspicion would have completely spoiled the atmosphere that we were at pains to build up — for good scientific reasons. Also, we got to know all the members of the Scole group, mediums and hosts, extremely well over the years that we saw them regularly and one of us went to various other countries with them. They were there joined by experienced scientific investigators and seances were held in strange rooms where there appeared to be no opportunity of fixing anything scientifically improper. This made little difference to the phenomena. There was never a breath of suspicion that things were other than open and honest. Again, it must be said, this is not scientific evidence that it was so, but it has some value nonetheless.

A final point must be made. It has slowly become my view over many years of investigation — and I briefly implied this above — that if investigators have such tight precautions that they can be *absolutely certain* that every paranormal phenomenon is genuinely occurring, then this may, indeed will, inhibit the occurrence of those phenomena. Nature sometimes seems to need that final defence of her mysteries. I have referred before to a number of aspects related to this point. Often

paranormal phenomena will occur only if you *believe* that they will —
or at least are very likely to do so. Perhaps a completely open mind is
sufficient, and this may be needed only during the time that it is important. (I gave much evidence in support of this point in Chapter 6.) But
— I say again — a view that paranormal phenomena are quite likely to
occur does not mean that good scientific conditions cannot be maintained. However, it shows very well — if it is true — why sceptics, and
those who seem to consider that if mediums and proponents could possibly have produced phenomena fraudulently then they will have done
so, rarely if ever experience good strong evidence for the paranormal.
The moral for successful experiments in this field may well be
'exclude the sceptics' (in the bad sense of that term) and include only
good open-minded scientists who have had experience and *know* that
paranormal phenomena are possible and sometimes do take place. And
make sure, if it is humanly possible, to do what is possible appropriately to meet the objections of the sceptics, who are bound to raise
their heads later, if not at the time.

CHAPTER 9

The Psychic's Experience

It would be a good idea at this point in our study of consciousness to consider what it is like to be 'psychic,' but to do so free of the rather ridiculous and prejudiced views that the average psychiatrist has. This is presumably the result of his education and lack of experience of those altered states of consciousness that were not included in his university education in psychiatry: most psychiatrists appear to think that psychic experiences are signs of pathology and of no intrinsic value. (The standard 'treatment' for hallucinatory voices is, I understand, tranquillizers.)

In my experience all really strong psychics have been psychic from birth. They tell of experiences which they did not realize were unusual until they became old enough to talk about them. A majority of psychics are Spiritualists because, as many have told me, the first time their experiences were taken seriously and sensibly discussed was when they entered a Spiritualist church. Some of them attended a developing circle and spontaneously went into trance and were told afterwards that the voice of a 'control' (or Guide) of which they had no knowledge spoke through them. The experiences they had had were here associated with a 'next world' to which we all go, according to the Spiritualists, after death.

What sort of experiences do psychics have that the rest of us normally do not have — or have only very rarely? One psychic told me that as a small girl she was very puzzled by the behaviour of the grown-ups in that, when someone came to the front door and rang the bell they were politely invited in and asked to sit down. However, when someone floated in through a wall, she told me, they were completely ignored; in fact sometimes the grown-ups were so very rude as to sit in the same chair with them. She also told me that she was very puzzled also at the 'death' of her grandmother. When the coffin was being carried out of the house to the hearse everyone was crying or otherwise showing great sadness. She shouted down to them from her upstairs window, 'Why are you all so sad? Grannie is here with me.'

Many psychic children — and sometimes other children too — have 'imaginary playmates.' This sometimes worries their parents who consider that they are having hallucinations. Yet again, psychic children — and sometimes other children — have spontaneous out-of-body experiences on numerous occasions and have the experience of floating out of their bodies and down the stairs; then they wander around the house at night. They do not realize that everyone does not have such experiences. Many 'normal' children have some degree of psychic faculty when they are very young and one child psychologist researcher I knew got a Ph.D. degree for his telepathy experiments with children which showed that they can often demonstrate telepathy when they are old enough to communicate (say about three years of age) but that this has usually declined to zero by the time they are about seven. The 'conditioning' to the normal which they get from the moment of birth is evidently sufficient to suppress any incipient psychic functioning by this time. The poet spoke of the shades of the prison house closing around the growing child!

Experiences of famous psychics

Here I think the reader may be interested if we consider the sorts of experience had by famous psychics and mediums, or sensitives as they are sometimes called.

Mrs Gladys Osborne Leonard

Mrs Gladys Osborne Leonard did an enormous amount of valuable work for some well-known SPR Council members. She was the medium who produced the 'communications' from Sir Oliver Lodge's son Raymond after his death in World War I conflict, which resulted in the famous book *Raymond* which caused so much controversy.[8]

Lodge said in the Foreword to her autobiography that she was one of the best mediums he had known. Mrs Leonard while young enough to have 'nursery breakfast' saw visions of the most beautiful places:

The physical wall or door would disappear and in its place would gradually come valleys, gentle slopes, lovely trees and banks covered with flowers of every shape and hue... Walking about, in couples usually but sometimes in groups, were people who looked radiantly happy. They were dressed in graceful flowing draperies ...

Some instinct made her keep quiet about them but she thought that everyone must see these views even though the grown-ups showed no signs of it. She says that one morning she was allowed to have breakfast with her parents and saw the Happy Valley unfolded before her in place of the wall. Remarking on how beautiful it was she was at once surrounded by the whole family in a state of anxiety and annoyance. 'This was not in line with their conventional way of looking at things.' She was forbidden to see or look for the Happy Valley again. Her family believed in 'a heaven of harps and crowns, kept specially for those who refrained from 'probing into things they were never meant to understand.' Gladys clearly considered that the Happy Valley was the 'world' to which we go immediately after death.

Gladys' 'Guides,' she explains, made several attempts to draw her attention to Spiritualism when she was in her early teens. (Most Spiritualists consider that almost all of us have 'Guides' — a little like Guardian Angels.) Like so many young potential mediums she came upon a Spiritualist church and surreptitiously visited it. She experienced there a demonstration of trance mediumship when 'a fat anaemic-looking young man became a vivacious pert little girl of apparently seven or eight years old with a strong foreign accent.' He/she picked out various people in the audience and gave descriptions of other people which were answered in only one way with 'Yes' or 'That is correct.' She was somewhat disappointed with it all. However, she went again and this time a slim delicate looking middle-aged woman 'gave a blood-curdling howl and became a North American Indian.' She continued with the 'same boring procedure' as the time before. However, this time Gladys got a message herself from her cousin Charley correctly describing his death by drowning as a result of cramp. The medium went on to say that Gladys had 'guides' who were preparing her for a special work similar to the medium's own. This did not impress her but she came away remarkably comforted with the thought that 'those who died were never in the grave at all, only their outer coverings, and their real selves in new healthy bodies escaped to a better land. ... We should hold out our hands that they might take them with pity and understanding ready to help us in whatever way was the best and right one.' Unfortunately she told her mother, thinking that it would be a great comfort to her. This was received with 'deep anger heightened by fear.' Her mother told her that this was vile and wicked and terrible things would happen to her if she followed such evil practices. (In those days the prejudice against Spiritualism was very great.) So she had to give it up — until one day in the future when she would be a free agent.

To a normal psychiatrist or psychologist there is, of course, nothing especially mysterious about such transformations of personality as those she observed in the church, which can be easily produced via hypnosis. However, the production of information as a result which is recognized as true by a sitter and is characteristic of a deceased relative or friend is not so easily explained by the orthodox view, which is usually that it is coincidence, combined with good guessing or 'cold reading' and feedback to the medium by 'body language,' etc. I feel fairly sure that this is indeed sometimes part of the explanation of a medium's performance but it is certainly not the whole story and in the case of the very best mediums is far from the truth.

Gladys grew up and trained as a singer but caught diphtheria and went into hospital. Afterwards one of the nurses, a Spiritualist, invited her home and she experienced her first table seance. She told her mother again and got the usual warnings of a dreadful fate if she 'dabbled in such things.'

One day (in 1906) she went to stay in a town thirty miles from home and awoke in the middle of the night with a feeling that something unusual was happening. She looked up and some five feet above her saw a 'large circular patch of light about four feet in diameter.' In this light she saw her mother quite distinctly looking several years younger than she had looked a few hours earlier. 'A pink flush of health was on her cheeks, her eyes were clear and shining, and a smile of utter happiness was on her lips.' She explained that the vision seemed to convey an intense feeling of relief and a sense of safety and well-being. It was a few minutes past 2.00 am. In the morning she received a telegram from her brother saying: 'Mother passed away at two o'clock this morning.' She was deeply impressed and felt that all she had heard from the Spiritualists was confirmed. (I have lost count of the number of people who have described to me seeing a recently deceased loved one appear to them in the middle of the night in just such conditions as that.)

After some laryngitis trouble Gladys' voice did not improve so she abandoned her intention to train as a singer and took part in plays which required only speaking. She soon met her future husband, who was sympathetic towards Spiritualism. In a play she met two young lady members of the cast who were interested in Spiritualism and, during a period in the play when they were not needed, had table sittings with her. Nothing happened for a month or more though they sat every evening until eventually the table did move and spelled out messages by tilts. After several messages 'from all their mothers' a 'communicator' appeared who said she had married Gladys' great-great-grandfather: her name was Feda. Gladys had heard about her from her mother but had taken little notice. Feda had died while giving birth at age thirteen to a son in the year 1800. Feda explained by tilts of the table that she had been around since Gladys was born and wanted her to develop her psychic powers so that she could put her into a trance and give messages that way. This was repugnant: she wanted to be a clairvoyant/clairaudient medium. They continued sitting and got helpful messages 'from their mothers' and especially from Feda. Feda asked for a heavier table so that she could 'show her strength' and they got a heavy oak table with piano legs; it took three men to carry it in. When their hands were on it she says that it moved like a feather-weight.

Many interested groups of people (not psychics) have produced unusual table movements by carrying out this procedure. Messages are probably, in my experience, more easily produced by a Ouija board or an upturned glass on a slippery table top surrounded by the letters of the alphabet. The results are usually not so distinctive and characteristic of survival as when one of the group is a medium. (Remember that 'George' in the unconscious is very obliging and amoral and tries to help when he can. If there is no one from 'the next world' around and the 'sitter' wants a 'message' he will make up a suitable one and move the glass accordingly. George will gladly tell you how many letters will arrive by next morning's post — but is usually wrong. He will never (in my experience) admit that he doesn't know and has no way of finding out!)

Gladys says that in these sittings they often saw the forms of Feda and other spirits silhouetted like clear-cut shadows on a white wall. I find this difficult to understand but I have no reason to doubt her word. She was eager to have a *tangible* experience of 'the other side' and this occurred during one of the sittings with her two friends. They noticed an 'atmosphere' which seemed 'different' from the usual and then saw a reddish glow in one corner of the room a little like a fire. The letter D formed within it. They were using a chair instead of a table on this occasion and when they inquired what that meant the chair tilts spelled out 'Death in this room,' explaining that the D stood for a man's name. The following week a man whose name began with D did die in that room. They again asked to feel something and were asked to remain still. She then became aware, she said, of something unpleasant between herself and one of the others. It pressed against her. She then saw on her friend's shoulder a small black patch which grew and extended until it became a long, thin, dark hairy arm moving towards her friend's neck and giving her a feeling of intense fear. Her friend screamed and rushed for the door, which was locked. They all considered this a well-deserved lesson for their dangerous curiosity — for which they had been warned.

This kind of experience — which is not at all uncommon (I have heard of a number of such cases) — is the reason why Spiritualists almost always pray before a sitting and ask for protection. Usually then there is no difficulty. (When one is dealing with the mind in this way what is *believed* is of great importance.) A few days later when they sat again Feda came and told them that they had profited by their lesson and that Gladys should start developing properly as a trance medium with Feda as her control. She now agreed. The little group of three had to go separate ways so she found a developing circle and joined it. Here she developed very rapidly and felt what is often felt by developing mediums — tingling in the body and pressure in the temples as if a band was around the head. She felt impelled to stand. She says that it was like a dream. A sound came from her lips. The leader of the circle touched her hand and said to the spirit he assumed was trying to control her that all would be well and that he would soon be able to speak. That touch brought her back to normal consciousness.

It was not long after this experience that fortunate circumstances brought one of her two friends back to her and she also met another lady with some experience of Spiritualism. They were all taking part in the same play. With some effort they found a quiet spot in the theatre below the stage and began sittings there. The theatre was new and the Managing Director one night also came down into that 'engine room' and paced up and down while the three girls kept very quiet. Gladys felt sleepy and 'slept.' After what seemed a long time she awoke to find her friends in tears having received messages through her from their deceased relatives via Feda. Feda explained that the man who had been pacing had contributed great 'power' and enabled Feda to entrance her. Gladys later, during World War I, met him again when he came to her for a sitting and Feda told him how she had influenced him to come down the stairs. (I am not at all clear what is meant by 'power' but it is frequently referred to by psychics and is clearly of great importance to them.)

Most mediums have had a 'healing' side to their mediumship and Mrs Leonard was no exception. One of her first contacts with 'healing' was when she had severe problems and great pain with the stumps of broken teeth left in her gums. A certain Miss Macgregor 'made passes over her' for some half an hour (her procedure is described in Chapter 12 of Mrs Leonard's autobiography.) She says that the pain, swelling and discoloration almost completely disappeared. A little later she describes having nineteen stumps extracted under ether and chloroform and she describes hearing the voice of a discarnate doctor issuing from her lips as she was being given the anaesthetic. This other doctor was giving somewhat forthright advice to the doctors on 'this side' concerning the anaesthetic. (One can only imagine what they thought!) The severe post-operative pain was again removed (she said) by Miss Macgregor.

Gladys' 'healing guide' was a North American Indian named North Star. Such guides, she said, are able to 'direct the healing forces through a suitable medium' to a subject who needs them. She adds that it is easier to heal others than oneself.

That is probably sufficient to provide a reasonable view of the initiatory experiences that showed one of our best UK mediums what was to come.

Statements of other mediums

Information as from a hallucinatory figure observed and described by the psychic medium is often mixed with symbolism. As I mentioned earlier, she will say such things I mentioned earlier as: 'I see a cross (or a star) shining over the head of this person. Were they very religious?' If the sitter asks a specific question such as: 'What is the name of the communicator?' then often it appears difficult to get an answer. Surnames are almost impossible to obtain though there appear to be notable exceptions. Mediums say things like: 'I have a feeling of a mother figure. Is this your mother (or grandmother)? Have they passed over to the other side recently?'

Often in a sitting there are long periods of somewhat desultory conversation with the medium which gives the sitter the feeling that time is being wasted. This is perhaps usually because very little paranormal information is being picked up by the medium and they go on in the hope that the flow will improve. In a word, mediums vary in their skill over a very wide range from strong through every gradation to very weak. And what they can get depends very much on the establishment of a good rapport with the sitter. It is enormously important for a sitter to be warm, friendly and encouraging, never meeting any statement with a direct negative but saying perhaps that they will think about it carefully and perhaps the meaning will come. If a really good 'hit' appears then it is usually a good idea to tell the medium, as this will encourage them to continue along that line.

It is perhaps strange that the mediums who were practising many years ago seem to me to have had a great deal more psychic ability than appears to be the case today. I remember well that I had, many years ago, a regular yearly sitting with a trance medium called Lilian Bailey. She was in great demand. I would appear at her front door at the appointed time and she would open the door to me hardly, if at all, remembering ever having seen me before. We would then sit down in her seance room and she would immediately go into trance, remaining so for exactly one hour. Her guide (or control), a man called William Henry Wootton, who claimed to have been killed in the 1914–18 war, would then take over. He would greet me and continue (in his male voice) just where he had left off one year ago. 'He' remembered everything he had said to me before and produced occasionally some very good evidence — for survival and also ESP. After an hour he would say that the 'power' was now almost exhausted and regretted that he had to go. He would say 'Goodbye' and Mrs Bailey would slowly come back to normal, sounding a little weak at first. 'Was that all right?' she would say. She then showed me out. I usually put her (small) fee on her mantel as I left.

Some years earlier I had several sittings with a very famous medium called Estelle Roberts. She had, I remember, signed portraits of the King of Greece and of Mr McKenzie King (a former Canadian Prime Minister), both of whom had had regular sittings with her. With me Mrs Roberts rarely went into trance but worked in full consciousness. She sometimes produced evidence of survival of quite outstanding quality.

Yet another well-known medium I regularly sat with (and sometimes appeared with at meetings, where she gave the Spiritualist point of view and I explained the scientific one) was Ena Twigg. I gave earlier (in Chapter 8) a brief account of a sitting with Ena Twigg experienced by a friend who lived opposite to us for several years and whom, with her husband, we knew very well.

It would be appropriate to finish this piece about mediums in general with a little about another world-class medium who spent just about all her time with SPR (scientific) investigators. She was an American, Mrs Leonora Piper.

Mrs Piper, a member of Boston society, was discovered by Professor William James of Harvard who 'retained' her for the SPR and put Richard Hodgson in charge of her investigation. Hodgson had recently come to the United States to form an amalgamation of the American SPR with the Society for Psychical Research when the former (started by the SPR earlier) got into financial difficulties. He managed it until 1905 when he died and it regained its independence.

Mrs Piper's mediumship was outstanding. She proved so good that she was brought to England (where she had never been) by the SPR, was met at the ship on arrival and stayed with Sir Oliver Lodge's family. The precautions taken to see that she obtained no information in the 'normal ' ways about the sitters who were brought to her was unprecedented. Lodge actually had her staying in his own home and followed by detectives when she went out to make sure of this. Nonetheless she produced outstanding results. She was never in the whole of her career discovered to have cheated. She produced large quantities of true information about the lives of sitters and their 'communicating' friends and relatives and not infrequently this was unknown to the sitters, who had to discover its truth by enquiry from others.

Her achievement which most impresses me concerned a friend of Hodgson called George Pellew. He was killed in an accident and after his death acted as a 'control' for Mrs Piper. Hodgson brought as sitters some thirty friends of the former George Pellew who were all introduced using pseudonyms. The Pellew control (known as GP) addressed them all in the appropriate manner and tone and recollected incidents appropriate to their past relationships. It was just as though the living George Pellew was seeing, greeting and talking to them all using Mrs Piper's physical body. I know of no better example of 'normal trance mediumship' than this.

Mrs Piper had a number of the usual kinds of control also — her initial one claimed to be a French physician named Phinuit. Later she had a number of high-sounding ones called Rector and others forming the so-called Imperator group.

It will not be necessary to give more detail about Mrs Piper's mediumship as the phenomena have been already sufficiently dealt with earlier. She is the subject of considerable writing in the SPR Proceedings and elsewhere.

Physical mediumship

Daniel Dunglas Home

D.D. Home was born in Currie near Edinburgh in 1833 and he died in 1886 in Paris. He was probably the most famous Spiritualist medium of all time. In a book of this kind it is important to refer briefly to various facts of his life because of their importance in connection with the major philosophical point being made, namely, that idealism is a more appropriate basis to our efforts to understand our daily experiences, and also the more unusual experiences of the paranormal, than is the generally accepted philosophy of today, realism.

D.D. Home during his seances often floated into the air in normal daylight and also in good artificial light in front of many reliable witnesses. On one famous occasion he actually floated horizontally out of one upstairs window in London and in through another. There is also another well-known occasion in one of his seances when a table carrying a number of items levitated and tilted over (with none of the items on it falling off) but the flame of a burning candle continued to burn in a direction along the centre line of the candle and not vertically into the air above, as it would have done normally. Big and heavy tables levitating while carrying several heavy men were relatively commonplace in his seances.

Another not uncommon feature of Home's seances included his plucking with bare hands glowing coals from the fire. He would sometimes blow on such a coal held in his cupped hands until it glowed brightly. In this connection he once famously put his face into the glowing coals of a fire He was never burned. On another occasion he placed a red hot coal on the head of a sitter, who said that it felt warm. He then drew the sitter's white hair over the coal and the hair was not burned. Sitters who had 'faith' were sometimes allowed to hold a glowing coal and it never felt more than 'warm.' Home would sometimes elongate during his seances up to as much as 7 ft 6 in (almost 2.3 metres), his normal height being 5 ft 10 in. He would also sometimes shrink to considerably less than his normal height. During these episodes there were often many reliable witnesses. These more remarkable phenomena occurred only when he was in trance and under the 'control' of his 'spirits.'

D.D. Home was a regular guest of the aristocracy at social occasions in Britain and also with crowned heads and other aristocracy all over Europe and Russia. He was married twice, firstly to Alexandrina (Sacha) who died of consumption caught from him; and then to Julie.

Both were members of the Russian aristocracy. With Sacha he had a daughter, Marie, who died in infancy, then he had a son, Grégoire (Gricha), with Julie.

Home was a personal friend of the Czar of all the Russias, of the French emperor and of the king of Italy. Amongst his friends he numbered numerous members of the aristocracies of all these countries together with Alexandre Dumas, Leo Tolstoy, Mark Twain and many other famous authors and scientists, including Sir William Crookes, for whom he carried out several experiments.

Home also conducted experiments together with another friend, the young Lord Adare (later the Earl of Dunraven) and Professor von Boutlerow. Home lived for some time with the young Lord Adare who attended many seances with him and had many experiences of his mediumship. Adare recorded these experiences in the form of reports to his father the Earl of Dunraven, who published them some years later in the form of a long paper produced by the SPR in a *Proceedings* (Vol. XXXV, 1926). As these accounts often included personal family matters Adare used initials to refer to individuals whose identity he wished to keep confidential. Lord Adare's reports to his father make fascinating reading and include aspects of Home's mediumship which are not often referred to in other reports. The seances took place after his first wife Sacha had died and she was a frequent attender there where she showed him much affection. Interestingly, there was never any sign of what was later called ectoplasm in Home's seances.

Adare's reports include several accounts of little 'phosphorescent' lights, two or three at a time, flying about in the air in the room where he and Home were sleeping. Also, one night, Home was put into trance and then led Adare down the stairs in complete darkness, saying that he needed no light.

Spirit voices and healing

Spirit voices apparently sometimes communicate directly with individuals, rather than through a medium. A psychiatrist friend of mine reports the following case.

Diagnosis of brain tumour

A formerly healthy lady, a housewife and mother, was sitting reading when she heard a clear voice inside her head. The voice said: 'Please don't be afraid. I know it must be shocking for you to hear me speaking to you like this, but this is the easiest way I could think of. My friend and I used to work at the Children's Hospital, Great Ormond Street, and we would like to help you.'

She had heard of the hospital but did not know where it was and her children were well. She was quite frightened. As a guarantee of sincerity the voice gave her three pieces of information. She found them to be true but nonetheless felt that she had gone mad and went, panic stricken, to her GP. Her doctor referred her urgently to the psychiatrist friend of mine (Dr Ike Azuonye, who has kindly given me permission to describe this case) who saw her at his clinic and diagnosed a functional hallucinatory psychosis. He prescribed medication and counselling. Two weeks later, the voice having disappeared, she went abroad on holiday. There she was still taking the medication; the voice returned and told her to return home immediately as there was something wrong with her and she needed immediate treatment. She was obviously worried so her husband took her home. By then the voices had given her an address to visit. Dr Azuonye saw her again but remained of the same opinion.

Nonetheless her husband took her to the address given and they found that it was the computerized tomography department of a famous London hospital. Arriving there the voices told her to go in and ask for a brain scan as she had a tumour in her brain and her brain stem was inflamed. As she now believed them, she was greatly distressed when Dr Azuonye saw her the next day. To reassure her he requested a brain scan, explained about the hallucinatory voices, said that he had observed no physical signs of such a tumour and the scan was to set her mind at rest. Initially this was declined on the grounds of expense with no clinical justification. However, eventually the scan was carried out, followed by a repeat scan with enhancement, and a tumour was found. The consultant neurosurgeon to whom she had been referred agreed, after discussion, to an immediate operation. The voices said that they agreed fully with that decision.

The tumour was removed and there were no later complications. The patient was told by the voices immediately after the operation: 'We are pleased to have helped you. Goodbye.' Her medication was gradually stopped and there was no return of the voices.

Some twelve years later the patient telephoned the psychiatrist to wish him a merry Christmas and to say that since the operation she had been completely well.

My friend presented this case at a medical conference later in the year of the operation, with the patient present. She was closely questioned. About half the audience thought this a clear example of telepathic communication from two people who had psychically diagnosed the tumour. Another group thought that even though there were no physical signs she must have felt something and her fear led to the hallucinatory voices. This group felt that she must have had knowledge, consciously forgotten, about hospitals, and that this was reproduced in her voices. The voices bidding her goodbye expressed her relief.

I suggest to readers that they probably now have a great deal more scientific information about other possibilities than did the 'normal scientific' audience at that medical conference and they accordingly might like to consider what they think is the likeliest explanation of those veridical hallucinatory voices.

CHAPTER 10

The Mediumship of Mrs Eileen Garrett

Another quite outstanding medium/sensitive of world class, and worthy of a chapter for herself, was Mrs Eileen Garrett. She was born in Ireland and had most interesting and unusual experiences when she was young. When she was older she moved to the United States (often returning to the UK) and there worked with a number of outstanding (and open-minded) scientists in order to try to understand her mediumship.

Early awareness

Mrs Garrett's parents both committed suicide as a result of religious intolerance (her father was a Catholic and her mother a Protestant) and she never knew them, being brought up in Ireland by a very strict aunt who rarely if ever gave her affection and never understood her. Her parents' photographs were on her chest of drawers and were referred to by her elders as 'poor Anthony and Anna.' She was told who they were when she was ten and was given their few belongings.

When she was alone in her room she learned to 'extend the nebulous cobwebby part of me' and could use this process to shut out the voice of her aunt, seeing then her lips moving but hearing no sound. This was perhaps the beginnings of her trance. She found when quite young that if she lay quite still, her head in the crook of her arm, she could 'reach out and touch the flowers and the sky' and was able in this way to banish the hurt she so often felt and, in the pulse of the living world within, 'know oneness with all light and life.'

Eileen Garrett used to play with three 'spirit children' (two little girls and a boy) only she could see and who first appeared one day when she was about four years old. (They disappeared finally when she was about thirteen.) She called them the Children and when she spoke of them to her aunt she was accused of 'making up things' and of lying and wickedness. When told of this the Children just laughed. The Children taught her about nature: sunshine, flowers, wind and rain. They loved everything that grew and flowered and opened up her sense of beauty. Eileen Garrett saw from her earliest years ordinary people surrounded by a 'nimbus of light' (the aura) but the form of the Children consisted entirely of this light. Everything grew up but the Children never changed. She never saw them approach, they just appeared — and went in the same way. When puppies and lambs were born they knew first and took her to visit them. She conversed with them without words on everything else alive. No grown-up ever believed anything she said and she discovered only years later that her methods of sensing were called 'supernatural' or 'supernormal.' The first person she ever met who understood her supernormal nature was Edward Carpenter, whom she met when she was 23.

When she was five she became aware that the whole of space was filled with coloured egg-shaped 'globules of light,' swirling and bursting. She discovered that these globules were 'filled with energy' gladly absorbed by all living creatures as vitality. (I first read about these 'globules of *prana*' in Theosophical books.) The air was filled with 'singing sounds' — no space was empty to her. She 'knew' plants, trees and rocks and other people 'by projecting part of herself into them, yet remaining herself.' She could do this, she says, even with people in a distant country who were unknown to her. As the only Protestant in a Catholic school she was early on 'exposed' both to her aunt's fearsome and forbidding God with His Avenging Wrath and at school to the consoling presence of the Virgin and Child. These two attitudes had no relationship to each other.

One day she was sitting lazily alone when she saw her aunt's sister Leon approaching her carrying a baby. She looked tired and worn and Eileen rushed to help her. Leon said that she must go and take the baby with her. Eileen rushed indoors to get her aunt to come and help but when they got outside could not find anyone. She was questioned carefully as to what she had seen and again severely punished for making up such a wicked story. It was only the following evening that they received the news of her aunt Leon having died while giving birth, together with the newborn infant.

Eileen wondered how she could punish her aunt for her cruelty and saw several baby ducks swimming happily on the lake. She knew her aunt loved her ducks and would be deeply hurt if anything happened to them. So she accepted this means for her revenge and grabbed each duck as it swam by and held it under the water until it drowned, putting each body on the grass beside her. To her surprise she noticed a smoky substance rise from each, assume the shape of a duck and run off. So she learned (she says) that all she had done was to alter the form of the ducks and not 'kill' them. She confirmed this lesson later with baby rabbits and birds until killing revolted her and she vowed never to kill again. She no longer went out hunting with her uncle.

Later, a few weeks after her uncle became ill and died, her door opened quietly and he came in, seemed pleased to see her, talked to her and asked her to try to obey her aunt's wishes. He said that in two years' time she would go to London. Then he quietly disappeared and she never saw him again.

Some time later — after her marriage — she explained that 'incredible as it may seem she found herself *seeing* more easily and clearly with her finger tips or through the nape of her neck than through her eyes and *hearing* came to her 'through my feet and my knees.' (Some years ago I remember we had at an SPR conference a visit from several Chinese professors who described tests they had been making on children who could distinguish colours by 'touch.') These were, she said, what is now called clairvoyance and clairaudience.

She was very active in business during World War I, starting a very successful hostel for wounded officers. (Very few psychics are good at business.) She found that at this time her seeing and sensing were opening out into other types of perception. She saw fragments of incidents and episodes connected with people she knew and flashing before her like blurred pictures on a dark screen. These were sometimes precognitive and disturbed her a great deal. She might see a picture of a fire or explosion and next day read a description of it in a newspaper. Waves of nausea often accompanied such visions, she says, and she observed also an intense drawing upon the sex centres. She felt more alone and bewildered than ever, knowing that it would be worse than useless to consult medical men. However, it was at this point in her life that she discovered a useful way of coping with her overwhelming psychic experiences. She appealed to 'the Breath of the Universe' to help her build up some strength to assist her in shutting out the impact of those unwanted experiences. She then 'addressed the chambers of my mind as I had come to know them, asking each in turn to keep out the invasion of external impressions from my two selves.' She had in this way stumbled upon the technique of what was later called *auto-suggestion.* The invasion of things external diminished. If she relaxed her use of this process, impressions from without would immediately rush in. So she had to continue doing this each night 'as regularly as brushing [her] teeth.' She found now that the process of dealing with her impressions 'through the mastery of her two minds' became easier.

Soon afterwards two friends wrote to say that they had become aware of her presence in their homes and were troubled by this. She realized that she had probably been thinking of them while in a passive state and 'one aspect of [her] mind had therefore moved out and reached them.'

It is interesting in view of certain 'occult' doctrines about the so-called *chakras* and *kundalini* (outside the scope of this book) that at the time of this 'visioning of events' she describes becoming conscious of an increasing pressure at the top of the nose and between the eyes to the cerebellum. She located a spot in the forehead where the images began to register.[9] In her case the events seemed to move out through and beyond her, focusing at a point far distant, and needing some visual strain in order to see the detail. She felt that Mind was a greater phenomenon than anyone realized. 'While one tiny ribbon of it guided the mechanics of conscious thought, there must be vast realms of unfathomed and untapped sources which touched and linked all aspects of life with each other.' Man was but an incident in a larger scheme. It seemed probable to her 'that individuals had no comprehensive minds of their own, but had brains which were delicate mechanisms, which simply permitted them to participate, according to the degree of their capacity, in this evolution.'

Eileen Garrett moved to London and became involved in running a restaurant with a friend and later, after World War I, an officers' hostel. She found the hard work of managing her business interests there helpful in using up her tremendous energy and restoring her health, which was never good. She had long discovered that it was useless to consult doctors and psychiatrists about her condition: her family thought she was likely to go mad. Happily while in London she found someone who understood her experiences — Edward Carpenter, mentioned earlier — who said that she was born with *cosmic consciousness* and he was sad that she had been brought up by someone who tried to suppress her perceptions. He advised her to read all sorts of publications but not allow herself to get pulled into organizations. She went to many Theosophical meetings but found Theosophy to have no life for her. Carpenter advised her to read Emerson, Walt Whitman, Spinoza and Eastern literature: the *Upanishads* and the *Mahabharata.* He helped her to feel she was reborn and set free. Her experiences were not the hallucinations of a disordered mind but the true seeing and sensing of cosmic consciousness.

Mrs Garrett had a number of experiences in connection with her daughter's many illnesses, one of which must be mentioned. At a crisis point when her doctor expressed little hope she sent away the nurse and took her little daughter out of bed, where she was fighting for breath. She decided that the child must get better. Then she heard a voice telling her to be careful, to open the windows and get more air. She did so and then put the child back into bed and observed a figure smiling at her in a sympathetic and kindly way. She did not see him go but the child recovered. She now remembered her other visions — of her aunt Leon with her baby and of her uncle and his prophecy that she would go to London. She could no longer tell herself that all these visions were not true, and she resolved to find an explanation.

One man who stayed at her hostel told her one day that he was clairvoyant and recognized her 'mediumistic powers' covering healing, psychometry, clairvoyance and clairaudience. This excited her and she asked him to explain the meanings of some of those terms. He was a Spiritualist and gave her an explanation of that religion, telling her that he could speak to his dead daughter. He demonstrated this as though she were present, and Eileen sensed nothing. He then handed her his watch and asked her what she sensed about it. She held it and described what seemed to come to her as incidents in his son's life. These facts were true, she says, and showed him that she could 'psychometrize.'

He explained the Spiritualist view of what happened at death and afterwards. Eileen was shocked. From her experiences of what occurred at death (described earlier) she believed that there was a definite transformation leading to a new and vital state of being. Life after death could not, she believed, possibly be the same as that occurring in life on earth, as he stated. She wished to investigate more deeply and agreed to go with him to the headquarters of one of the London Spiritualist societies. The first meeting was as she had experienced before — the passing on of messages to members of the audience. She felt in no position to judge this performance. The following day she joined and went to many meetings, then enrolled in a psychic development circle. After the Lord's Prayer the circle did table tilting, which she later tried at home. There she got excellent results, including the address where her husband's cousin was born. Only later was she able to verify the truth of this.

The third time she visited the developing circle she went spontaneously into trance and gave evidence of sitters' dead relatives, who spoke to them all. This the group was not competent to handle and she was referred to a knowledgeable Swiss. He listened and she then went

had been present during her operation. Some months later she was lying in her hospital room when her vitality seemed to be ebbing away. Then the wardrobe tottered and crackled and explosive sounds came from it. Terrified, she rang for the nurse and the noises ceased as she entered. This made her more determined than ever to do what she could to try to understand psychic phenomena. Almost at once she received an invitation to visit the USA in 1931 and work with the American Society for Psychical Research in New York City. She expected them to be much more scientific than were the Spiritualist societies for whom she had worked. Sadly she found that most of them were Spiritualists too and did not even keep records of her sittings. Continuing her work she visited groups in Los Angeles and San Francisco and found their 'research' even less objective. All they were interested in, she said, was communicating with the dead.

A most valuable part of Eileen Garrett's autobiography comes when she explains in detail what she did in order to accomplish different kinds of psychic perception in connection with the experiments she undertook with several American psychiatrists and scientists at this time. The experiments were considered to be on telepathy and she was never asked to explain how she did the work.[10]

Eileen Garrett explains that in one experiment an investigator prepared a series of objects on a table and would also select some objects to hold in his mind. To determine the objects on the table she would use 'projection' and then clairvoyance. To pick up thoughts she would use projection and then telepathy. But on this occasion she could get the objects from the investigator's thoughts using only telepathy. To her surprise, she says, she found no one aware of these distinctions.

In another experiment she was expected to determine objects and the thoughts of an experimenter in Newfoundland while she was in New York City. She explained that she projected in this way: 'Everyone has a double of finer substance than the physical body ... and called the astral or etheric body by some ... This is not to be confused with the 'surround' which remains in position enveloping the body while the double can be projected.' (This 'projection of the double' is what is today called the out-of-body experience, described in Chapter 3.) When she projected the double she explained that it was done from the centre of the top of her chest. She was aware of a pull, with a fluttering which caused heart palpitation and accelerated breathing with a slight choking and a heady sensation. As she projected she remained aware of these sensations in her physical body.

While projecting, the double seemed to be in possession of all five senses It could readily pass through walls. She said that she could see the objects arranged on the table and pick up the thoughts of the experimenter at the site. All her perceptions were, she said, confirmed as true by mail later.

Eileen Garrett explained that all her steps in psychic functioning were induced by conscious changes in her breathing. In addition, in using precognition she had to 'conceive of standing outside of time' and perceive yesterday, today and tomorrow as a single curve. They presented themselves to her not in sequence but as existing simultaneously. Time lost all reality, so she seemed able to live in past, present and future at one and the same instant.[11]

The well-known psychical researcher, Hereward Carrington, did some word association and electrical skin resistance tests (which indicate stress) with Eileen Garrett to discover whether the reactions of Ouvani and Abdul Latif to certain key words were different from her own and from those of each other. If they were, then presumably they would not be using the same subconscious memory and were psychologically separate from her. She explained that there were striking differences but no final conclusions could be drawn. Similar tests were made in England soon after these but she was very critical of their quality.

At this time, and unable to get serious scientists to study her mental mediumship, she attempted to return to her work as a medium, but found that she could not produce results. Sitters thought that the scientific work had interfered with the activities of the control. This was not the view of the latter! Ouvani said that he would no longer give advice and personal evidence and wished to deal with more serious aspects of living and of research. This made her wonder again whether he had any reality apart from herself and whether his intelligence was superior to her own. She wondered whether trance mediumship really could give valid evidence of survival, whether the Spiritualists had conditioned her, and whether other sitters seeking other revelations might reach different levels of communication. Abdul Latif began to introduce healing, philosophy and religion. She realized that had she been born into a quite different culture with quite different traditions she might have produced widely different trance communications. Could her subconscious mind be a vehicle capable of expanding indefinitely and able to contact all possible realms of understanding which it might choose to reach? So she re-examined the mechanisms of communication.

Eileen Garrett described what normally occurred at a typical successful sitting where the control correctly described the communicator and gave their name together with advice. The sitter asked for evidence of identity and received correctly facts only they knew from earlier in their lives. They then typically asked for details of the place where the communicator lived and of their current activities. The communicators say that they are working hard but are rather vague about their present habitation.

Reflecting upon these details, she asked herself what was the value of this sort of information and how was it obtained? Ouvani had produced a great deal of it.

She first considered the trance state (usually the result of auto-suggestion). The control takes over and tells the sitter, with a description, what spirits are present. The sitter accepts this and agrees that the proffered evidence is true. But, Eileen noted, she herself is able to give similar evidence clairvoyantly. She could see dead relatives surrounding the sitter and receive the impressions of the messages they wished to transmit as a series of images and symbols. The difficult part was to interpret these: their meaning 'depended entirely on her limited human interpretation of them.' Ouvani was often questioned as to the process he used, and he described this in exactly the same way — as the interpretation of symbols, with word interpretations tried on the sitter until they were accepted. So there was little difference between the trance and clairvoyant states when it comes to obtaining information.

How does the subconscious mind arrive at these images and symbols? Examining herself, Mrs Garrett had become aware that she drew from the subconscious minds of the sitters the knowledge which helped her build these images. Was it not possible, she reasoned, that the control did exactly the same and was perhaps not aware of their source? And these images and symbols could be misunderstood. All this made her eager to work with trained scientists interested in serious studies of supernormal communication and mental phenomena.

But how could she continue to give such 'evidence of survival' when she was not sure it came from the alleged dead? She did not want to be a party to fraud. And she was gradually coming to reject the thought of the control as a personality. However, she certainly was aware of her supernormal functioning and wondered where it came from and what its purpose could be. Her faculties produced correct results, but how did they work and how was it she had them?

In 1933 Mrs Garrett returned from the UK to the USA and worked for two years with Dr J.B. Rhine at Duke University. He tested her for clairvoyance with his well-known Zener cards and she got unusually low results. She explained to Dr Rhine that she was sure that clairvoyance and telepathy depended upon 'an active radiation registering between two people or between an individual and an object.' As the Zener cards lacked this they did not stimulate her clairvoyant vision. Rhine did not at all agree. However, he admitted that he did not know what ESP really was (and neither did other investigators). Symbols 'passed through the mind of another' were made to live again and registered for her paranormally. If this were not so, she might instead merely get information about the person who designed the cards or about the substance of the cards or the place where they were made.

Eileen Garrett's interpretation was that a card symbol, when thought of, is projected through space like light. I have found one or two other psychics who described their impression of a symbol flying through space to them and we shall be looking later at ways of considering this in the light of more modern information. However, for the moment it is interesting and important to note that she had little success with pure clairvoyance, where someone else's mind does not come in at the time; and as with all psychics, what she *believed* is important too. She looked upon the 'surround' (the aura) as a 'magnetic field.' (No scientist or engineer would call it this! Psychics and healers often incorrectly use such scientific terms.) She emphasised that no successful work can take place without an ardent desire on the part of the experimenters to produce good results. 'Affirmation, faith and desire' are the energy stimuli needed. She felt that many investigators confused a negative attitude towards an experiment with objectivity and so deprived the sensitive of an essential 'energy.'

Dr Rhine also did some experiments with her on what he called psychometry, giving her fragments of handwriting carefully wrapped and sealed in envelopes. He wanted from her details of the sex, age, eyes and hair colour etc. of the writers. She explains that the excessive covering forced her to use clairvoyance rather than psychometry. She did not at all like this 'forcing of her supernormal sensing into arbitrary channels to answer specific questions.' She would often get impressions of the person who had prepared the envelopes. It was all very bewildering! She tried to answer Dr Rhine's questions but often felt that she was merely guessing. Dr Rhine had spent little time on the nature of control personalities in trance and she got little from him by way of answers to her deepest questions — the 'mechanisms of her supernormal powers and the meaning of trance mediumship.'

Mrs Garrett worked for a short time with an English psychiatrist who wanted to study multiple personality. He used hypnosis but, she says, never reached the controls. However, when she put herself into trance he was able to talk to Ouvani. The result of this work appeared to have given her a new ability to penetrate those levels of consciousness from which the controls obtained their paranormal knowledge. She also tried to develop automatic writing under auto-suggestion in order to reveal facts to herself, when she had later penetrated other levels of consciousness. She explains that she had never accepted the individuality of any trance personality communicating through her though she did accept that the information obtained was genuine. Her automatic writing she felt came from her unconscious mind but much also came from her 'superconscious.' The latter provided vivid pictures of unknown places, strange music and unknown languages, little to do with the subconscious dreams of the conflicts and problems of daily living. She wondered whether those stirring experiences were related to other lives she might have lived or to race memories. She felt that she was receiving knowledge from some ultimate source beyond the personal.

An important point emphasised by Eileen Garrett relates to the fact that medicine and psychology put such mediumship as hers into the same category as neurosis, hysteria and schizophrenia. She says that she showed no signs whatsoever of these symptoms and considered herself more sane, objective and practical than many other 'normal' people she met. (Her undoubted business acumen certainly provided ample evidence of this.) Her faculties she considered refinements of the physical senses everyone possesses.

Summarizing all the numerous kinds of scientific investigation conducted on her after seven years, she felt that little light had been thrown on the source of her supernormal powers. But she had made certain discoveries. Among the most important was the fact that her different psychic states were induced by the tempo of her breathing. (This reminds one of 'prana yoga' — the ancient Indian idea that the body's vitality, *prana*, is manipulated by the breathing.) Clairvoyance, clairaudience, precognition: all required, she said, a different rate of breathing. This was combined with auto-suggestion. She had learned how to do all this by her experiments as a child. Whenever she wished to try supernormal sensing she 'attached herself to the light and colour of the surround — the gently breathing envelope surrounding every object.' She did not know how clairvoyant vision began but its power and action she could intensify by accelerating her breathing. Her entire body seemed to become visual so that the whole surface of her skin became 'an all-seeing eye and an all-hearing ear.' And she had been aware from earliest childhood of fundamental symbols she seemed compelled to draw. They were linked with the shape of the printed alphabet and to her they became associated with types of people and their characters. The symbols which later presented themselves to her were always associated with certain types and temperaments. She was aware after many years of experience of seven levels of consciousness when she worked clairvoyantly, each associated with distinct physiological feelings. In the seventh she was identified with all life and all her powers of perception became one.

Research with Ira Progoff

After writing her book *My Life as a Search for the Meaning of Mediumship,* Eileen Garrett met a distinguished depth psychologist, Ira Progoff, who did the research on her controls that she had wanted for so long. The following notes are based on his book: *The Image of an Oracle.*

Ira Progoff explains that he proposed in his research on the 'control personalities' to use the new procedures of holistic depth psychology to draw forth from the recesses of the personality of Eileen Garrett and from the personalities of the voices who spoke through her some clues as to the nature and meaning of the phenomena of mediumship exemplified in Mrs Garrett's experience. Though she had earlier worked with many distinguished researchers including William McDougall, William Brown, J.B. Rhine, Gardner Murphy and Robert Laidlaw, none had used his proposed methods. Two control figures had dominated over many years: Ouvani, who described himself as a young Arab soldier of the thirteenth century who had died in battle, and Abdul Latif, a Persian physician of the seventeenth century. There were also other figures. Progoff wondered whether they were truly multiple or were actually one. He resolved to treat them all as persons, speaking to them individually; and talked to four control figures: Ouvani, Abdul Latif, Tahoteh and Ramah.

I propose to give here abbreviated extracts of the conversations to give the flavour of them, with my comments in brackets. Then I will give Dr Progoff's explanation of their nature and 'meaning.' It will be seen to be quite different from that of a Spiritualist — who would probably never have contact with control figures 'deeper' than Ouvani and Abdul Latif.

There were deep breathing, yawns and moans as Mrs Garrett entered the trance. Ouvani usually appeared first.

> OUVANI: I am summoned, so to speak, by my instrument, when she passes into the state of, may we call it quietism. It is our pleasure that one of us could come. Always of course I have come, unless there is a demand for Abdul Latif, may his name be blessed, in which case he will take his place.

Ouvani described himself as 'a simple Arab and keeper of the door.' He nearly always appeared first and 'left the door open' if another one of the controls was desired. 'Abdul Latif is the physician who serves a healing role by means of psychic mediumship.'

In one conversation Abdul Latif said: 'It may be that this is a soul gaining its experience because the soul is beginning in the stone and the stone is in the tree and the energy is in everything.' (This is 'standard' Theosophy, albeit expressed in a somewhat convoluted way!)

In another conversation Progoff asked Abdul Latif this question:

> PROGOFF: You describe how you and your group are in this instrument (i.e. Mrs Garrett) and how it could be better for you and better for the instrument if you could come through more freely ... That is, your instrument has this particular capacity with respect to this hypnosis and the trance by which you are enabled to speak not to her but to other people who do not perhaps have this capacity of the trance, of hypnotism. But are there persons like yourself and like your group who are in other individuals?'
>
> ABDUL LATIF: Behind the individuals? Yes, indeed.

At another time Abdul Latif said:

> A. LATIF: We are the world now. We are the world to come. And all our work and all that we are and all that we do is grinding out this experience, turning the unconscious into the conscious

in order to give experience. We are the dynamos, are we not? ...
We are here, we will be here, we will be there, but we are it, the
world.

(This reminded me of Jung's view of 'the purpose of life' which, he suggested in his autobiography, was 'to make the unconscious conscious.')

PROGOFF: In the day when Abdul Latif lived ... there were other
people, other physicians, other philosophers, other people of all
walks of life, now did these other people ..?
ABDUL LATIF: Are they here now, you ask me? Well of course. The
infinite has no conscience about this, they are poured in together
into this, to take their experience, to give their experience, that is
what we must do ... do you see?... The soul that has come into
what you would call the body — of a sick body — that soul has
taken that way because that's where he feels he will achieve his
best results ... the soul is using this to the best of its understanding
to get experience, experience, experience.
PROGOFF: And the next time it will be something different?
A. LATIF: And, as you know, the soul is hermaphroditic.
PROGOFF: The soul is neither masculine nor feminine but both?
A. LATIF: Both.
PROGOFF: And may come as either masculine or feminine?
A. LATIF: Exactly.

(I wondered here whether these items of 'perennial philosophy' came
from Eileen Garrett's studies of Theosophy or whether they can be
taken here as 'original and true' information.)

Progoff says of Mrs Garrett:
... there has been only one conclusion on which she has been
definite, and that is that the spiritualistic hypothesis of survival
and communication in terms of personal entities is totally
inadequate. The statements of Abdul Latif and (later) Tahoteh
and Rahman are indicative of her attempts to find more
satisfying answers to these questions.

On another occasion, after an initial word or two with Ouvani the
doorkeeper there were additional groans and deep breathing and
another figure with a different voice and accent entered.

TAHOTEH: I am known as he who is called Tahoteh.

PROGOFF: Can you tell me something about your nature?

TAHOTEH: My nature is universal. It is the breath of life. It is the breath of the elements. It is the breath of the tempest and the breath of the stars. It is the breath of the times, the breath of the sea, the breath of the running streams ... But I have been regarded as a symbol of good by some men and as a symbol of freedom by other men, as a symbol of what is within the makeup of man by others, as a symbol of that creative side of man. May I not then call myself truly in relation to you, the creative principle of life; and if I am then the creative principle of life and have been known as such in life, it is obvious that if I have been, I am ... In the orthodoxy of your age I have no place?

PROGOFF: No. No. We know not of you.

TAHOTEH: ... I am always in the heart of man in suffering. I am that symbol of man himself, many countered, many edged, many sided. I have been ... called by many names; according to the process of his understanding I have been named. I have been known as the winged messenger ... as he who travels by sea, by wind, by air. Phoenicians have made their statues to put upon their ships and men have made statues to put within the contours of their gods. I have been given many of the faces of man. But in your time I do not think that I have a face, eh? ... In life, if I have not a face; and yet I am a part of the history of man. Am I not there in every breath that he draws, in his every wish, in his every wilfulness, within his desire, within his concept to make, to create. May I not be the creator of his dreams ... and the disturber of his dreams? ... I am there, as we shall call it, as a rock, as the structure of the whole of man's admixture.

It is clear at this point, Progoff remarks, that Tahoteh wishes to present himself as a god — but in no sense comparable to the Western understanding of what God is. He does not present himself as an omnipotent being but rather as a principle of life and as one among many — as a member of a pantheon of gods as would be the case in Greece or in India. He is thus a personification of a basic principle of life and so a godlike figure but not an ultimate God. Progoff suggests that if we follow Jung's hypothesis we would consider these four 'control figures' to be masculine animus figures who personify various aspects of the unconscious of Mrs Garrett.

Later Tahoteh says, in explaining his use of the word 'entity':

> TAHOTEH: An entity is also an idea ... and can be clothed in any kind of form and shaped in whatever mental image you like. ... The spirit is at all times in a state of innocence. It is contained within this cup of the soul, and the soul is contained within another lining that is part chemical; and then there is the inlay of what man calls the etheric which partakes of both stages, and then there is the dynamism of the body ... nothing can be comprehended, nothing can be understood if it is not in form. (This 'etheric' again may have come from Mrs Garrett's contacts with Theosophy.)

And again:

> TAHOTEH: When the soul goes from the body the soul substance perceives within itself the experiences to be handed to the spirit. This you cannot destroy. ... Death means a time to rest before the next race that must be run ... you take with you the sum total of experience ... the soul chooses the limitation to produce the necessary experience. Man is becoming perfect and therefore godlike. ... The need of the Great One, that man shall perfect himself. (This is more perennial philosophy.)

Tahoteh then must be understood, in Progoff's opinion, as a symbolic personification of an inward or perhaps eternal principle of human existence. He comes through the psyche of Mrs Garrett. Events and perceptions that come through the prism of the psyche are expressed symbolically rather then literally. They tend to be personified and they present themselves to the world in a dramatic style. Tahoteh does this. People can be moved in dramatic symbolic terms even though they do not understand on an intellectual level. That suffices.

Progoff explains that the meaning behind the appearance of the control figures is a continuous development towards wholeness in the personality of Mrs Garrett. The first figures to appear, Ouvani and Abdul Latif, have been mainly concerned with personal material. With Tahoteh and Ramah (who follow) the subjects under discussion were

of larger scope and indicated a broadening of interest and experience
of the personality as a whole. Tahoteh — or Hermes, as he was also
known — was the Giver of the Word — the breath of experience. The
next figure was Ramah (Ra, Re or Rahm) — the Giver of Life. Tahoteh
is desireless in one aspect. Rahm said that the true desire in the aspect
of Tahoteh's life is not to be life but to help the experience.

PROGOFF: Tahoteh manifests through people's desires ...
RAMAH: Yes, that is it. But Re is desire ... the desire of life itself
at its essence — the essence of life.

The conversation with Ramah started like this. Deep breathing, groans,
moans, sighs, as Mrs Garrett entered the trance condition.

OUVANI: Eet ees I, Ou-van-ee. I give you greetings friend.
PROGOFF: Greetings, Ouvani.
OUVANI: Peace be with you and in your life and on your
work, and in this your household. And may I be of service to
you?
PROGOFF: Ouvani, last time you were gracious enough to ask
Tahoteh to come and speak with me; and I would ask now if
you would ask him whom you have called the giver of life to
come and speak with me.
OUVANI: But are they not both the giver of life, Sahib?
PROGOFF: Well, there were two of whom you spoke to me;
one was Tahoteh who is the giver of the word.
OUVANI: Oh, Tahoteh, or Hermes, as you remember he was
also known; and you must look for him under these
definitions ... and the other one, yes?
PROGOFF: You spoke of Ramah.
OUVANI: Of Ra.
PROGOFF: Rahm, — uhh, Ramah, who is Ra ...
OUVANI: I well comprehend why if you speak with the one
who fills man with the word you would want to meet he who
is and represents the word... He will speak only with some,
uhh, hesitation, so you wait a moment until he is in control.
You will be patient.

Deep and sustained breathing, grunts, sighs, moans, and groans from
Mrs Garrett as her trance deepened. Gradually these subsided and a

deeper and slower voice speaking with some difficulty and heaviness
was heard.

> RAMAH: I am known by many names. Many cultures have
> thrown their cloaks to obliterate, or perhaps even not to permit
> the light to penetrate but dimly. May I present myself as Re or
> Ra or Rahm.
> PROGOFF: I spoke with Tahoteh who described for me the
> meaning of the word as it comes to human beings, and the
> reality of the word and the importance of the breath and of
> experience. And he spoke to me of the reality of man's symbols.
> Now, you are the giver of life and I wonder if you can speak to
> me.
> RAMAH: I am the giver of life. I am the representative in man's
> mind of the giver of life ... Tahoteh may not have mentioned to
> you why the gods awake ... You realize I am sure that our
> people, what you will call the people that have sprung from our
> loins ... for we were as men, and this you know too.
> PROGOFF: Tahoteh manifests through people's desires.
> RAMAH: Yes, basically that is it. But Re is desire ... the desire of
> life itself at its essence ... the essence of life. That is why men
> have looked at the lawgiver, at the lifegiver. They speak of the
> Father ... they speak of the Son ... and they speak of the Light,
> or the Geist ... whatever you like, which is the somethingness.
> Whatever way they speak of it, it is all the same. But you
> realize that without this desire the plant dies. There are many
> aspects of Ra or Re.

Here Progoff interprets for us:

> What does it mean for a person to go into trance and emerge
> with a voice who says: 'I am the giver of life'? Bear in mind
> that such statements are not to be taken literally. They are
> spontaneous symbols which have on the one hand a
> psychological significance in terms of the personal needs of the
> individual; and on the other hand they express a perception of
> reality that derives from dimensions not bounded by individual
> personality. Here the ultimates of life are expressed in various
> symbolic forms so that they can be stated and perceived in the
> terms of intellectual consciousness. They mediate between the

dark depth level of personality where obscure insights into life are given, and the surface level of rational consciousness where statements can be made and people communicate with one another. The voices serve to connect the two realms of the psyche — and the psyche is a miniature replica of the cosmos. It is a microcosm which reflects the pattern of the larger cosmos ... when a symbolic factor like an image, personifying itself and speaking with a voice, mediates between the depth and the surface of the psyche, it is thus a reflection of a parallel process in the macrocosm by which the depth of life is brought to formal expression in the individuality.

Mrs Garrett had a strong organizational flair and Ouvani may be understood as the symbolic embodiment of this as it expresses itself inwardly, working upon the contents of the psyche of Mrs Garrett herself. The separateness of the four figures indicates the organizational effect of this executive quality. Ouvani is stationed at the aperture of the psyche where conscious and unconscious contents intermingle. Here he regulates the flow and the coming and going of those symbolic figures who personify the various organizational levels of the psyche.

Abdul Latif embodies a level of the psyche that is below the surface level of consciousness but is still concerned with personal affairs, both of Mrs Garrett herself and of others who come to her for clairvoyant and mediumistic assistance. Abdul Latif is thus the figure who has played the primary role in the mediumistic activities of Mrs Garrett. This is because he personifies a level of the psyche that is far enough below the sensory capacity of perception; thus his clairvoyant and mediumistic abilities. But he represents a level that is close enough to the surface to be concerned with personal affairs.

The level of the psyche below the one that Abdul Latif represents is personified by Tahoteh. Here the concerns reach beyond subjective factors. He is involved in the level of the psyche that Jung would call archetypal, the depth where the universals of existence are experienced and portrayed. Tahoteh describes himself as 'the giver of the Word' to indicate that he represents the symbolic level of experience. The Word is the Logos and this is the dimension for meaning in human existence. Tahoteh speaks as the personification of the transpersonal perception of meaning as this is presented to and in the psyche of Mrs Garrett.

Deeper still than this is a level of the psyche that is primal. It is more fundamental even than meaning. It is life itself. Where Tahoteh expresses the aspect of man's experience that approaches life with desire because the desire is perceived as meaningful, Ramah represents that desire itself prior to any meaning that it may discover and attach to itself. This desire is the elemental life force. It is the principle that moves at the ground of being in the larger universe, the macrocosm; and it is the primal principle that moves in the microcosm of the individual human psyche.

This research of Ira Progoff from the point of view of depth psychology seems to me — and I am not a psychologist — to cast much light on Eileen Garrett's control figures. However, she was an outstanding person of high normal and psychic abilities: it may be that what applies to her does not necessarily apply in the same degree to the general run of other mediums/psychics.

A psychic who has been trained gives the sitter what comes to them and it is clear that they have very little if any control over it. And, from the research with, and the views of, Mrs Garrett, much the same appears to apply to any control figures who appear to be passing on information from a deceased person 'on the other side.'

CHAPTER 11

Difficulties in Paranormal Communication

In the literature of psychical research there are reported 'communications' through mediums which appear to bear the stamp of the founders of the Society for Psychical Research in just the same way that the cross correspondences did, and strongly appear to be genuine attempts to enlighten us as to the difficulties and hindrances they were meeting in their attempts to communicate with their surviving colleagues of around the turn of the nineteenth/twentieth century and a little after. The Scole Report (see Chapter 8) concerning predominantly the physical phenomena aspects, appears to describe the latest attempt. Readers will be able to make up their own minds as to whether they consider that the 'communications' can be taken at face value. Studying these is additionally valuable in that it gives a good idea of the possible 'structure' of a human being at the 'subtler' levels of consciousness — again assuming that things are as they seem.

We have at present only somewhat tenuous ideas as to the conditions in which those early SPR members found themselves immediately after death (assuming the reader will accept the multifarious evidence that they did in fact survive) and the evidence they appear to have sent to us seems to be somewhat unlike the normal spiritualist communications from the 'Summerland' of the 'astral plane.' (The Summerland seems very like the region where I had my lucid dreams, described in Chapter 4.) Often in the latter the huge literature of spiritualism seems to indicate only slight difficulty in communicating and detailed descriptions are given of the lives and surroundings of 'communicators,' who appear to be experiencing conditions either (and usually) like the pleasanter parts of the physical world (or, more rarely, like the gloomier and less pleasant parts of this world). However, the Theosophical literature and the many traditions of the Eastern philosophical and religious systems of India and elsewhere, tell us that there are many 'planes' or levels of consciousness awaiting us after death — depending on our 'spiritual status.' Here we read of the 'second death,' in which the deceased person drops their 'astral body' and moves to a sphere or level from which it is much more difficult to communicate with us. In seances I have often been told by ostensible communicators that they would no longer be communicating with us as they had to 'go on.' The communicators in the Scole seances often told us that they were actually 'all one' and not separate individuals. (Mystics have described much the same thing.) This is clearly not the so-called astral plane of the lucid dreamer, out-of-body experient or shamanic journeyer, where one — in my experience — seems to be separate from other people, just as in the physical world. Actually I think that those who tell us that we are all one must be actually in a paradoxical condition of being both conscious of the unity of all life and yet aware of themselves as well. Clearly it is not possible for us ordinary people in physical life to imagine what this must be like unless we have had flashes of this sort of consciousness while meditating, or at other times while perhaps in the countryside on a beautiful day when all life seems to merge into one Reality in one form of the mystical experience.

In material I shall shortly be summarizing, the communicator, ostensibly Frederick Myers, referred to the 'Summerland' as the third plane. He then goes on to describe the fourth, fifth, sixth and seventh states. (If this is true and if it really was the surviving Myers, then there seems to be some agreement with that Theosophical literature mentioned earlier — with which Myers was of course familiar.) Sir Oliver Lodge's son Raymond, communicating through Mrs Osborne Leonard (see Chapter 9), said that he lived in an extension of 'the illusory world in which you live.' He said that the 'spirit universe is the world of reality' and they were in touch with it. (The Theosophical literature states that the astral world where one awakens after death is a 'world of illusion.') Spirit and mind belong to that world. He went on to say that they had something physical in their world and Lodge asked if it could be called 'etheric.' He confirmed this (without any clear definition of the word 'etheric'!) and said that mind was operative in that world and could create the illusion of anything that was necessary for the development of the soul. He said that the 'soul' is us, the 'essential you,' that makes mistakes, loves and hates, does good and can do evil. The spirit cannot be touched by anything evil. In trying to correlate the views of different 'occult' writers one must take some care with their terminology. H.P. Blavatsky, for example, appears to have used the word 'etheric' in the sense that Annie Besant and C.W. Leadbetter (and later Theosophical writers) used 'astral.' Lodge's use of the word 'etheric' appears to agree with the Besant/Leadbetter usage: they too describe it as 'semi-physical.' They state that we all have an 'etheric double' which carries the *prana or* vitality throughout the body, and further aver that some of it is temporarily used in physical seances to form the ectoplasm which gives tangibility to the materialized forms. As mentioned earlier in Chapter 8, this could account for the extreme exhaustion felt by some physical mediums after a long physical seance. In regard to terminology it must also be remembered that many 'occult' and spiritualistic writers obtained much of what they wrote about from Blavatsky.

We have earlier considered the difficulties of accepting what ostensible communicators tell us of their lives, remembering the 'communications' received from fictitious characters imagined by the sitter and remembering that it is not easy to tell the source of the information. In the case of a fictitious character it clearly comes from nowhere else but the sitter's memory store (without medium, control — when there is one — or sitter, having any idea of the 'mechanism'). Whether the medium is functioning in practically normal consciousness or is in a trance state with a 'control personality' delivering the information is quite irrelevant. Control personalities cannot tell, any more than the conscious medium can, from where the material is originating.

The communications of Frederick Myers

Let us then now consider some extracts from communications received from what certainly looks very much like Myers and see what we think. Rather than give direct quotations from the original sources — mostly from the SPR Proceedings — I shall briefly summarize in my own words, giving only an occasional quotation. A reader who wishes to have the exact words will find an accurate set of quotations in Chapter 8 of Paul Beard's excellent book *Survival of Death.*

First, Myers gives the impression that the speed of thought is greatly increased after death and advises the medium, Mrs Willett, to let thoughts slip past her and just to grasp what she can. And while a control is operating upon a medium's mind the control's thinking is similarly slowed to the normal human rate. The control Feda says that she often realizes that the communicator's thoughts have slipped past her and even if repeated still often cannot be caught. Communicators seem not to be able to tell how much of what they have sent has been picked up by the medium and so they are unable to rectify any mistakes or omissions.

The minds of mediums also differ greatly in their characteristics. Besides all being slow and dull in the experience of communicators, they have areas of incapacity or insensitivity and emotional blockages. So part of a communicator's meaning may be rejected. Myers, particularly, often castigated Mrs Holland for not getting what he so carefully and frequently sent. Everything about the process is imperfect. The medium's own mind imposes its own meanings upon messages sent, even though the owner tries to be passive; some trance conditions introduce even graver difficulties. And mediums' minds become tired so soon. Myers once said that a stupid sensitive might sometimes even be better than an intelligent one, and that worries concerning unconscious cheating and self-deception sometimes make things worse.

A very frequently quoted and very informative piece from Myers is as follows — as before with my comments in brackets:

> MYERS: We communicate an impression through the inner mind of the medium. (I presume that this means what I have called the personal unconscious mind.) It receives the impression in a curious way. It has to contribute to the body of the message; we furnish the spirit of it. In other words, we send the thoughts and the words usually in which they must be framed, but the actual letters or spelling of the words are drawn from the medium's memory. Sometimes we only send the thoughts and the medium's unconscious mind clothes them in words.

Through association-habits in the medium's mind, thought received can send off that mind in quite a wrong direction so that further matter is added by the medium, embellishing or distorting the true thought. Mrs Leonard's control Feda complained that she could not always make the medium's voice speak as intended. The mind went off on its own account and Feda could not stop the speech even though she knew it to be wrong. A sitting sets up a metaphorical and somewhat imperfect bridge in a region between the next world conditions and our conditions, from the resources of both sides.

When a communicator directly controlled the medium, Feda explained, there is in the medium's brain a bit of both minds and a communicator cannot think clearly nor remember well. And when 'the power failed' (a frequently used expression in seances) the medium's mind begins as it were to awaken and start behaving independently, introducing grave distortion.

One well-known researcher and SPR writer asked Feda how she distinguished the thoughts of the communicator from those in the sitter's mind. Feda explained that it was a quite different feeling and she tried to lean towards the communicator and to shut off the sitter. It is clearly a difficult and confusing business.

While we are considering the ostensible difficulties of communicators it will perhaps be worth while to consider how Myers thought of himself. It will be remembered that he was a Greek classical scholar. This is what he wrote through Mrs Holland:

> MYERS: I want to make it thoroughly clear to you all that the eidolon is not the *spirit* — only the similachrum *(sic)* ... if any one of you became conscious of my semblance standing near my chair that would not be *me*. My spirit would be there invisible but perceptive, but the appearance would be merely to call your attention to identify me ... It fades and grows less easily recognizable as the years pass and my remembrance of my earthly appearance grown weaker ... If you saw me as I am now you would not recognize me in the least ... I appear now as I would fain have been — as I desired to be in the very vain dreams of youth — and the time-lined pain-lined suffering face that some of you remember with tenderness is now a mere mask that I strive to conjure up for you to know me by ... Remember once again that the phantasm, the so-called ghost, is a counterfeit presentment *projected by the spirit* ...

The Theosophist might here be reminded of Mme. Blavatsky's statement that the spiritualists are communicating with what she called 'astral shells' and not with the 'real person.' However, it looks from what Myers said that this simulacrum can be used by the real communicator to convey genuine information.

Mrs Verrall, who was also a Greek scholar, has a comment concerning *eidolon* and *simulacrum*. She quotes Homer's description of how Odysseus met in Hades 'great Heracles, his phantom (*eidolon*); himself (*antos*) rejoices amid the immortals ...' Mrs Holland's script correctly uses the words *eidolon* and *simulacrum,* which mean much the same. Another classicist, Merry, states that *eidolon* is best represented by our word 'phantom' used almost identically with the Greek word for spirit as the immaterial ghost that remains when the body is dead. Myers in *Human Personality* translates a fragment of Plotinus as:

'The shade of Heracles, indeed, may talk of his own valour to the shades; but the true Heracles in the true world will deem all that of little worth...' Again we have some sort of confirmation that many 'communications' may be of 'shades' or 'astral shells' and not true individuals — not exactly the persons we knew. But — if all this is substantially true — then it is not so every time.

We shall have more to say about life being in one sense an illusion, a *maya,* in a later chapter. It was certainly suggested several times in the communications from Myers.

Problems of communicators

Communicators appear to have little means of knowing how far what they have said has got through to the medium. The communicator, the Rev John Drayton Thomas (the father of the better known Rev Charles Drayton Thomas): 'I am not always aware what Feda says when in control. I am mentally following up what I am giving and so am not always noticing what she says. Thus I am not clear as to whether she has given my thoughts rightly or wrongly.'

Every medium's mind, apart from the inevitable slowness and dullness of reception complained of by communicators, has as well its own particular personal incapacities, insensitivities, incomprehension and emotional blockages, all of which may make it reject part of the communicator's meaning or be impervious to it.

Myers, the impatient, constantly scolds the medium, Mrs Holland.

> MYERS: I feel as if I had presented my credentials — reiterated
> the proofs of my identity in a wearisomely frequent manner —
> but yet I cannot feel as if I had made any true impression upon
> them (i.e. the persons he was trying to reach through the
> medium). Surely you sent — what I strove so to transmit ... Oh
> it is a dark road.

And again:

> MYERS: Imperfect instruments: imperfect means of
> communication. The living mind however sensitive — intrudes
> its own conceptions upon the signalled message — Even now
> my greatest difficulty is to combat the suggestions of the mind
> whose hand writes this though the owner tries to be passive —

into trance. He told her later that while she was in trance he had spoken to her controlling entity who was an Oriental, had given the name Ouvani and was of unusual intelligence. Ouvani wished to prove the truth of survival.

Eileen rushed home greatly alarmed at the idea that any other entity could work through her body, but gradually she realized that her early withdrawals into herself to escape pain had led the way to this state. The secretary of the Spiritualist society, whom she then went to see, told her that she had had a sitting with Mrs Osborne Leonard during which the control Feda had informed her that she would meet Eileen and help her to continue her trance work. Another lady had also been informed by the same control that she would meet and help her. Through the latter she met most of the leading Spiritualists of the day, especially Mrs Hewat McKenzie and her husband, who had founded the British College of Psychic Science (now the College of Psychic Studies). He knew much more of mediumship than anyone else she had ever met.

For five years she worked under the direction of the McKenzies. They were the only people she met who considered that the control personality, as much as the medium, needed training. She never accepted that Ouvani existed separately from herself nor that the 'communications' were necessarily from the dead. They could, she felt, have been from her own unconscious. Eileen worked at the College as a trance medium until Hewat McKenzie died (in 1929). She felt she owed an enormous debt to his untiring patience and faith.

After yet another period of serious illness Eileen started to work again as a trance medium, more and more worried that her sitters did not develop self-reliance but were increasingly dependent on the messages they received. Then occasionally a new personality began to speak to some of her sitters. They told her that he had given his name as Abdul Latif and claimed to be a Persian physician who had lived at the Court of Saladin in the time of the Crusades. He was especially interested in healing work and serious philosophical problems and communicated with several London physicians. She discovered also that he apparently worked through a number of other mediums in various parts of the world.

Another period of doubt and illness led to some new experiences for Eileen Garrett. She had to have a throat operation and a voice recognized as speaking in Hindustani was heard in the operating room. Abdul Latif later informed G.R.S. Mead, a well-known scholar, that he

Short of trance conditions which are open to even greater
objections the other mind is our greatest difficulty. And they tire
and flag so soon.

And again:

MYERS: ... We communicate an impression through the inner
mind of the medium. (Surely here he is referring to what I have
called the 'personal unconscious mind' and he sometimes refers
to it as the subliminal mind.) It receives the impression in a
curious way. It has to contribute to the body of the message, we
furnish the spirit of it. In other words, we send the thoughts and
the words usually in which they must be framed, but the actual
letters or spelling of the words are drawn from the medium's
memory. Sometimes we only send the thoughts and the
medium's unconscious mind clothes them in words.

The medium's mind may rush in to add meaning not intended at all. A
thought received can, through association-habits in the medium's
mind, send off that mind in quite the wrong direction, so that further
matter is added by the medium, embellishing or distorting the true
thought. Mrs Leonard's control Feda said:

FEDA: ... Your father says that he refrains from saying many
things which he wishes to give lest they should come through in
a distorted form. Feda feels that also; for she does not always
make the medium's voice speak as intended. Feda touches
something which wakes the medium's mind and then it goes off
on its own account ... cannot stop her speaking if what she says
is wrong.

One direct communicator said: 'no one yet understands the unique
character of a sitting ... It is a no-man's land between the two conditions, yours and ours ... Here lies all the difficulty. Medium and sitter
are in part working in a condition which is not entirely theirs, and we
work in one which is not entirely ours. It is a pooling of resources
which creates the bridge. One gets out of one's depth sometimes on
both sides.'

Feda, speaking of such times when the medium is controlled
directly by the communicator, puts it more forcibly: ' In her brain there

is some of her own mind and also some of his ... In controlling it is, what may be termed, a co-operative mind. You see therefore why he cannot, while controlling, think so clearly, or remember so much, as you can.' The paper's writer here suggests: 'May not such a co-operative mind account at least partly for some of the memory lapses and inconsistencies which so rightly trouble psychical researchers?'

The medium's mind can become tired, especially towards the end of a sitting, creating a familiar situation mentioned earlier and described in spiritualistic jargon as 'the failing of the power.' The Rev John Drayton Thomas, again communicating with his clergyman son, says:

> It is as if the brain were tired out and it is no use struggling with it ... My thoughts wander and I have no grasp ... I feel my thoughts wandering. We notice this when the power goes while we control. When we were speaking through Feda, and it happened, we thought that she was getting stupid. Now we know what it is. There seems to begin a real waking of the medium's mind, an independent movement, and so we get mixed up with things in her mind. The two being mingled it distorts my messages.

The Rev Charles Drayton Thomas directly questioned his main communicators — his clergyman father, John, and his sister, Etta.

> THOMAS: Feda, how do you distinguish between thoughts coming from the communicator, and those in the sitter's mind?
> FEDA: It is a different feeling altogether, very different. I have trained myself to lean towards the communicator and to shut off the sitter ... Your father says, 'Even that would not prevent Feda getting a thought and not knowing it was from the sitter, if the latter happened to be willing'..

Sir Oliver Lodge quotes Edmund Gurney speaking through Miss Rawson:

> GURNEY: I have come to warn you for my friend to implore you not to let them call him. He gets no rest day or night. At every sitting 'Call Myers! Bring Myers'; there's not a place in England where they don't ask for him; it disturbs him, it takes away his rest. For God's sake don't call him. It is all right for

him to come of his own accord ... What we want for him now is to rise, and to forget the earthly things He can't help any more. His life was given to it, and that must be the help. He was allowed just to say that he continued. That was his great desire, but it will help nobody that he should be called back, and made to hover near the earth. In fact it will only make him earth-bound.

On another occasion Mrs Holland in India automatically wrote (the Myers control):

Oh if I could only get to them — could only leave you the *proof positive* that I remember — recall — know — continue ...I have thought of a simile which may help you to realize the 'bound to earth condition' which persists with me. It is a matter very largely of voluntary choice — I am, as it were, actuated by the missionary spirit; and the great longing to speak to the souls in prison — still in the prison of the flesh — leads me to 'absent me from felicity awhile.'

Myers and Gurney were using automatic writing with Mrs Holland and Mrs Verrall. Gurney wrote:

You have gone back dreadfully like a stupid child that forgets in holidays all it has learnt in term time — Why did you stop? Your hand needs to be pushed and dragged now — All the scrawling and thumping again I hoped you had done with for good — (*Change in writing.*) 'Yes — I know your arm is aching — Want of practice only I had many tries before it's not clear — *Don't scrawl.* Hold the pencil *tightly rigidly* if need be ... Try not to scribble so much — it is a waste of strength — The writing should be small and neat — When memory fails it is a proof of withdrawal — of having gone on to a higher plane — a nobler sphere — *Pen — thick pen.*

MYERS: Pencil is only fit for children — Page 27 Para. b — the third sentence needs reconstructing — it conveys a meaning that is misleading — The second packet of proofs have still several errors that have escaped revision — Kindly go over them again with great care — The real reason why I have never managed to write with your hand before is that your preconceived notions make it so difficult for us — You are always hoping and expecting one person or one particular class of message — instead of keeping a passive hand and an open mind.

Let us include in these extracts the best known one, also ostensibly written by Myers through Mrs Holland:

> MYERS: The nearest simile I can find to express the difficulties of sending a message — is that I appear to be standing behind a sheet of frosted glass — which blurs sight and deadens sound — dictating feebly — to a reluctant and somewhat obtuse secretary. A feeling of terrible impotence burdens me — I am so powerless to tell what means so much — I cannot get into communication with those who would understand and believe me. It will soon be three years now — and yet I seem no further from earth though perhaps no nearer than I was that January day. (He died on 17 January 1901.) The bonds of association have actual strength and anniversaries should be kept. No no not rapping or Planchette that is maddeningly cumbrous and inadequate — but friends — comrades fellow workers — sitting quietly in our own familiar room — a pen in the hand of a sensitive. That is the way. One does so little alone.

In the following extract the Gurney control, writing in pencil, tells the automatist that her hand will be left alone, and she is to write down a message transmitted to her brain. He then tells her to take a pen. She does so and the message that follows is in her ordinary handwriting. Then she breaks off, noting 'I am very restless, etc.' The script begins again in the writing of the Myers control, complaining that she is not giving the method of experiment a fair trial. Thus urged, she makes a fresh attempt in her ordinary handwriting and gives — not quite correctly — the first two lines of Myers' poem, *St Paul*. (Mrs Holland said later that she had never read this poem and was quite unaware until informed that she had quoted from it in her script. Nevertheless she supposes that she had probably seen these lines quoted somewhere, and that she reproduced them from her subliminal memory.)

Mrs Holland's normal handwriting goes on:

> To believe that the mere act of death enables a spirit to
> understand the whole mystery of death is as absurd as to
> imagine that the act of birth enables an infant to understand
> the whole mystery of life — I am still groping — surmising
> — conjecturing — The experience is different for each one of
> us — What I have felt — experienced — undergone is
> doubtless utterly unlike what each one of you will experience
> in good time — One was here lately who could not believe
> that he was dead — He accepted the new conditions as a
> certain stage of the treatment of his illness ...

Here Mrs Holland said that she was very restless and had taken an
absolutely purposeless walk through two rooms and the verandah —
she could not help it.

Myers again:

> Try and fix your attention — you are not giving this a fair
> trial — I feel that if I am released from my attempts to make
> your hand write I may be able to send something really
> convincing — But oh the difficulty of it. Put your left hand at
> the back of your head and sit still.
>
> If it were possible for the soul to die back into earth life
> again I should die from sheer yearning to reach you (— then
> in the writing of the Myers control —) to tell you that all that
> we imagined is not half wonderful enough for the truth —
> that immortality instead of being a beautiful dream is the one
> the only reality — the strong golden thread on which all the
> illusions of all the lives are strung — If I could only reach
> you — if I could only tell you — I long for power and all that
> comes to me is an infinite yearning — an infinite pain —
> Does any of this reach you reach anyone or am I only wailing
> as the wind wails — wordless and unheeded —
>
> GURNEY: Why did you let your hand yield to the writing —
> You have stopped and exhausted him now — and he might
> have gone on dictating — (Mrs Holland here said that this
> writing took just half an hour but tired her more than any she
> had ever done.)

Several days later the Myers control wrote:

> I begin to understand how unwise it is to try to urge you to
> efforts beyond your present powers. While you are alone it is
> useless I fear to try to convey my newly won dearly bought
> knowledge through your mind. I must content me with what I
> can painfully and laboriously scrawl by means of your hand
> — If I can only reach them — when I can only reach them
> we will do great things — but as yet we are only beginning
> — if indeed we have yet made a beginning —
>
> GURNEY: He is disappointed but it's hardly your fault — But
> go on trying — do your best — you can't help its not being
> better —

And again several days later:

> MYERS: Yet another attempt to run the blockade — to strive to
> get a message through — How am I to make your hand docile
> enough how can I convince them? — I am unable to make
> your hand form Greek characters and so I cannot give the text
> as I wish — only the reference — 1 Cor. 16-13 ('Watch ye,
> stand fast in the faith, quit you like men, be strong.') ... Oh I
> am feeble with eagerness — How can I best be identified —
> It means so much apart from the mere personal love and
> longing — Edmund's (Edmund Gurney's) help is not here
> with me just now — I am trying alone amid unspeakable
> difficulties —

The 'Stand fast in the faith' text is inscribed in Greek over the gateway of Selwyn College, Cambridge, which would be passed in
going from Myers' house to Mrs Verrall's, or to the rooms in
Newnham College where Professor and Mrs Sidgwick lived. The
road in which Mrs Verrall lived is named Selwyn Gardens, after
Selwyn College. The Greek inscription over the Selwyn gateway has
an error in it — the omission of a mute letter — on which Myers had
more than once remarked to Mrs Verrall. The fact that this text turns
up in the script again, more than a year later, and also in connection
with Mrs Verrall, but before Mrs Holland knew that there was any
significance in its first appearance, suggests strongly that it is not

a mere chance allusion. Mrs Holland had never been in Cambridge and had few friends or acquaintances having any connection with it.[12]

Here conclude the extracts from those old papers of SPR Proceedings. Readers having a special interest should have no problem in referring to the originals.

CHAPTER 12

Multiple Personality Disorder (MPD) and the Paranormal

The reader will certainly be clear by now that I am not a psychiatrist and not qualified to comment professionally on such matters as MPD (multiple personality disorder). However, I have had two experiences of the syndrome which I am able to describe. I should first mention that not all psychiatrists agree that there is such a thing as MPD. One very senior and experienced psychiatrist I know (Head of a university department) has had only two experiences of the syndrome and expressed himself as having very little understanding of the case I am about to describe. There appears to be a majority in the UK who consider that it does not exist at all but is iatrogenic, in other words, produced by the psychiatrists who believe that it is real. There are many such (both MPD cases and psychiatrists and psychologists who believe that it is real) in the United States with a majority, I gather, in California.

The case of John

The first experience I had of MPD involved a mature student (I shall refer to him as John) who attended one of the annual week-long summer courses on the application of science to the paranormal, which I gave at a Midlands university for some years. John approached me privately after we had been discussing mediumistic control personalities and told me that his first wife had been a 'multiple' (as they are often called). She seemed to have two quite different personalities which appeared spontaneously at different times. Her 'normal personality' seemed to be in control most of the time but occasionally the other one appeared.

The distinguished professor of psychiatry I mentioned above and with whom John had a long correspondence (of which I have a copy) said he did not think there was anything 'paranormal' in the occurrence and spoke — as so many 'normal' scientists do — of being a 'man of science,' not appearing to appreciate that the paranormal can be studied by the methods of science too and considered as involving phenomena not yet understood (modelled) by normal scientists.[13] The thought in his mind was probably that the MPD might be akin to 'spirit possession' i.e. like what occurs when a 'control personality' appears to come into, and take over, the body of a medium in trance.[14] Most of the psychiatrists appear to consider that the *alter* personalities of a multiple 'split off' from the primary personality as a result of childhood trauma such as sexual or other abuse. This applies in some 97 or 98 per cent of cases, according to the American psychiatric and psychological literature.

Besides telling me the story himself, John's testimony is summarized in a tape recording which he made in 1969.[15] He told me that these experiences started for him on their wedding night, and continued for many years. That first night, in a rented bungalow in Wales, he heard his wife talking in her sleep in the voice of a small child, three or four years of age. 'Zonni, Zonni (Johnnie, Johnnie), I's hungry, want to eat.' He replied, somewhat mystified, 'Can't you wait until morning?' 'I's hungry now, Johnnie. Want something to eat now. I want bread, butter, egg.' This sort of occurrence then went on every night for some 23 years. The voice referred to his wife (let us call her Mary) as a separate person: 'Dat udder me.' My friend referred to the voice as 'Night time me' (NTM).

Birthday gifts for Mary and the children were dictated, he told me, by NTM. His young son asked him what he should get for his mother's birthday. John asked NTM, who said, 'A pretty amber thimble with a pretty stone on top.' John managed to find such a gift and tried it on an appropriate finger of NTM to be sure of the right size. His son then gave it to his mother. She was astonished and wondered how her son could possibly know that that was just what she wanted. Her son was also very puzzled that she did not seem to know, as his father must have asked her, he thought.

NTM had some rather special abilities. Mary fell asleep after reading a book, which closed. However, NTM was chuckling at a picture in the book. John said, 'But the book is closed: you can't see it.' NTM said that she could. He remembered particularly and told me, of a picture of an old gardener NTM described and then told him the page number on which it appeared. John had no idea how she did this. She then described several pictures on pages which John requested and was correct every time. For years Mary could not stand in front of a bookcase without what he described to me as 'anxiety pains' in the stomach. She just *had* to walk away. Then the pains suddenly ceased. The explanation came from NTM in the middle of the night; he had asked her to look in the closed book again. She said that she was not allowed to do that any more. The 'Over There People' (OTP) had forbidden her to do this and she was never going to do it again. From that time Mary had no further trouble and she was then able to stand in front of a bookcase as long as she wished. NTM and the OTP came up a lot, John told me. He himself thought that they were deceased people (but he knew very little about such matters until he attended my course on psychical research).

John mentioned another characteristic of the book-reading business. Mary would always read before going to sleep in bed. Often she would fall asleep reading and NTM would come. John had difficulty in getting the book away from her. There was much pouting and arguing from NTM. John suggested that she may, despite her promise, have continued reading the closed book.

Once, John said, Mary's mother was dangerously ill in Australia. NTM said that she had asked Dr Campbell, a friend, to go over there and look after her. John told me Dr Campbell had died some two months previously. There were few occasions when NTM referred to Mary's father and this was another reason he had, John told me, for considering his wife and NTM to be separate entities, because NTM had no particular interest in visiting her 'father' over there.

On one occasion NTM asked him to get fish in Leicester for supper. He did so and brought it home. Mary said, 'How curious. I went to buy some of that fish myself at Lewis's. I got to the counter but something told me not to, so I walked away again.'

There were a number of ways of operating electrical devices which NTM claimed to have. For several years, John said, when they were in their previous house and when Mary went into a dark room with her hands full, the electric light would switch on. They used to joke that it was 'Henry' and that the house was haunted by him. On one occasion, Mary had said, she was driving home in the dark and was about to light a cigarette. Another car was approaching and she wished to dip her headlights but could not, because both hands were occupied, one with the steering and the other with the cigarette lighter. But quite suddenly the headlights dipped themselves. That night, when NTM came while Mary was asleep, she referred to this and claimed to have operated the switch herself.

There were other incidents like this. Mary was studying in Coventry and in the winter John started her car for her so that she could have the benefit of the heater when she drove off. On one occasion, John told me, he had done this and Mary was getting her books together in the hall. Suddenly the car, without warning, 'revved up' a few times and then ran quite normally. That night NTM chuckled and said that she had operated the pedal and the choke in the car so that the engine would not stop but the car would be kept warm for her.

On a number of occasions NTM claimed to be in places other than where Mary actually was. Once Mary came in from shopping and said that she saw someone looking out through the bedroom window. John said that he was alone but went up and looked anyhow. No one was there but the bedroom window, which was normally kept closed, was open. That night NTM claimed that she had run ahead of Mary and had shown herself to her through the window.

On another such occasion when Mary was driving him in her car they were running short of petrol. John said 'There is a petrol station just a little way ahead; we can stop there.' Without any sort of reasoning Mary said 'There are several cars there and we won't be able to wait.' She didn't seem to notice that she had said this. When they rounded the corner there were three cars queuing at the petrol pump so they drove on to the next one.

NTM also claimed at times that she went for a ride on a train. The railway was quite near. Several times she announced that she was going for a 'Wide on twain.' On one such occasion she announced on her return that the train driver had seen her. John remarked to me: 'If only there were a way to check that!'

John told me that he could always tell when NTM went away and when she came back because Mary gave a sort of bodily jerk. Even in the daytime Mary could always say, if asked, whether NTM was present or not, even though she was unable to say how she knew this.

John always made tea at the bedside, and NTM came before Mary had woken up and held her hand out for a cup of tea. John told her to hold out her finger and she would have it tucked into the tea cup handle by John so that she could drink. This ritual with the finger and tea cup did not appear to be essential: John told me that if he left the room and the tea had been poured, NTM would raise Mary in bed and readily take the tea cup in her fingers to drink it.

Once John asked NTM, while in bed, to write down her name for him. She wrote down Mary's first name and maiden name. He also asked NTM who she was and all he could get was: 'I am dat other me's happiness.' He told me that it was certainly a fact that whenever his wife was unhappy, through a family quarrel or anything similar, NTM would be away. If on such occasions he tried to talk to NTM when his wife was asleep she would just wake up, with no response from NTM. Once after such a family row NTM went away for three weeks. Then Mary jerked violently in bed after sleeping and NTM came and said: ' Johnnie, I had such a job to get back. The gate was fastened and I had to make a hole in the wall to get in.'

Often NTM recounted many incidents in Mary's early life in India. John would occasionally tell her about them and sometimes she was able to recall them with great surprise and wonder where he had acquired the information — until she later realized. On other occasions she was unable to remember the incidents described.

It seemed that NTM had what John described to me as the gift of precognition. On one occasion she foretold by one week the death of a young man friend in a car crash. On another Mary herself stated emphatically the winner of a horse race a few days ahead — which came true. He also told me that she made statements about conditions in one or other of his businesses which also proved true. He could give no explanation of that.

When John asked NTM where she was when she 'went over there' she said, 'I just be; I go over there and I just be.' That's as far as John could get her to go.

John had strict instructions from NTM never to divulge the secret of her existence to anyone. She threatened that if John ever did so she would go away and take DTM (Mary) with her, never to return.

Over the years John always had to look on his wife not as one woman at all. In all their dealings, he said, he had to consider NTM, who would veto anything proposed which she did not agree with. Talking to her in the daytime it was useless to suggest anything that would not be acceptable to NTM. John told me that he now saw that some of their marital difficulties, which arose after a few years, must have come from this source. One cannot look on a person as a child and a wife at the same time. Arising out of these marital difficulties a Harley Street psychiatrist was consulted. John was strictly warned that he must say nothing about NTM to the psychiatrist. If he did so NTM said again that she would take his wife away and they would never return. As John put it to me 'This didn't give the chap a chance.' The psychiatrist's diagnosis of their sexual difficulties was that they were anxious about having more children than they could afford; his recommendation was that his wife should have a small operation to prevent this happening and remove the anxiety.

Several years later when sexual difficulties continued — deprivation, so far as his wife was concerned because John could not take an interest in her sexually although he continued to be interested in others — he went to see another doctor in London. Before going, he said to his wife. 'What is the use of this: we got no answers from the other doctor?' She replied, 'Well, you went, but you didn't tell him anything did you?' John took this to mean that she was telling him that he had not told the first doctor about NTM. When he went to see the second doctor he told her the whole story of NTM just as he told it to me and I am now recounting it. The doctor replied, 'I don't know why you have come to see me for treatment: your wife needs treatment more than you do.' So John persuaded Mary to go in turn to London to see the second doctor, ostensibly about his own condition. This doctor revealed to her that she knew the whole story of NTM, recounted by John. Within six weeks his wife had left home, found accommodation in Leicester and, at the time that this account was first written by John, had not yet returned.

In the period of rather less than a year before going to the second doctor the relations between John and his wife had become very strained. NTM had ceased altogether to come to speak to him. This was why John had had to take his wife's comment about telling the second doctor everything as NTM's own instruction, which apparently it was not. One or two things happened during that period although NTM never came. Mary was talking in her sleep in Hindustani and clearly having a violent argument. John thought, when he told me about it, that it must have been about the question of her going away. As she argued she repeated many phrases and John noted some of them down on paper phonetically. When Mary was awake she was able to translate some of them. It was clear that she was having a great argument with a man called Bidgley, who had been their gardener when she had been a child in India, about this question of her going away from home.

Two other incidents which were rather curious also occurred in this six weeks or so period before she left home. On one occasion John awoke in the middle of the night to hear his wife gurgling and breathing very hard and deeply in her sleep. Then she started to talk, but it was clearly not her own nor NTM's voice. A male voice said, 'My name is Cess Kotawalla. I am using her mouth.' This was said with great difficulty and after various attempts. Then Mary awoke and said,'What is happening? I have such a funny feeling in my jaw.' John described what had happened and asked her who Cess Kotawalla was. She said that it was a little Indian boy she had known in childhood.

A second experience of this sort took place a few weeks later. John awoke to hear her gurgling and breathing deeply again. Her arm was hanging outside the bed. He lifted it and put it back into bed. It seemed completely weightless — a most curious experience, he told me. The voice started to speak again and said, 'It is too difficult: there are too many others, trying to come as well.' The voice then ceased and that was the last experience John had of that type of phenomenon.

At that point John said that his problem was to find someone who could recognize all these characteristics and suggest some kind of way of ameliorating or 'curing' the phenomena.

At that time the consequences of Mary's leaving home (she had by then gone) had been very distressing for the whole family. The two older children were grieving. The youngest daughter had had a complete nervous breakdown and was in hospital in London. Mary had started co-habiting with a colleague. She was at that time a fully qualified psychiatric social worker working at the local child guidance clinic and school psychological service and had formed the new liaison with the psychologist there. They were living together and John did not know what had happened regarding NTM.

A curious thing occurred at Christmas. One of the daughters visited her mother and the man she was living with, and said later, 'Dad, a most extraordinary thing ... he gave Mummy two presents for Christmas: a Wedgwood vase and one of those kid's recordings of that song 'Thank you very very very very much.' The latter seemed out of character for a woman whose tastes were for Wedgwood vases.

John is quite satisfied now, looking back, that in some way NTM was still functioning and had let the new man know in some way in the daytime through Mary that she liked the record. She may even have given some other excuse than her own pleasure for having it.

Mary was inclined to disown the whole story of NTM. This is rather difficult to maintain, John told me, because he has numerous birthday cards sent to him inscribed 'With love from both of us.' (He gave me several photocopies of them.) He also has a very upset letter she sent from Ireland, when she thought he was seeing another woman while she was away, and which concluded with the words: 'Now she's gone away.'

There were a number of times when their children also perceived the activities of NTM. On one occasion when they were down visiting the girls at their boarding school Mary picked up a stick and was throwing it in a curious stiff-armed fashion into the weir at Marlow. The elder daughter said: 'Mummy, stop doing that, you look like a little child.' Occasionally the children realized something unusual was happening when their mother fell asleep in the daytime.

There were many occasions when incidents like this occurred and not only in the last year, when John described to the children the whole story of NTM. They then recalled things like the thimble, and the weir at Marlow, and many other things that occurred when they were all living together as a family. He said: 'I should still like my wife to come home. I still care immensely about her and I would be most grateful if anyone, hearing this tape, can suggest any way in which this problem can be dealt with.'

The tape recording referred to was made early in 1969. In October 1969 John's wife died suddenly, without any warning, of a subarachnoid (brain) haemorrhage. This took place just before she and John were to meet to discuss her return home. John has wondered ever since whether this was NTM fulfilling her threat that she would never allow her to return home once she had taken her away. (Needless to say, the distinguished psychiatrist said this was nothing to do with NTM.)

Amongst the papers John gave me for safe keeping were a number of letters from the professors of psychiatry and of psychology whom John had consulted. One of them stated:

> Wife showed evidence of a secondary infantile personality manifested almost entirely during sleep and which did not constitute an alternative personality in the waking state. There was *some* influence during the latter e.g. dipping of car headlights. Intrusive actions either not noticed or immediately forgotten by the wife at the time.

He mentions Miss Beauchamp in *The Dissociation of a Personality* and *The Three Faces of Eve* (well-known books on MPD):

> An infantile, usually mischievous, personality is often found in such cases though usually developed a lot further than your wife's 'Night Time Me.' This is of real psychological interest.

Another of these professors called this a case of multiple personality/mediumistic possession. It is interesting that some physical mediums also have an infantile control which the reader will have noticed in Chapter 8. Their speech, in cases I have experienced, has been very much like that of NTM. The syndrome is so rare that few psychiatrists have had any experience of it. John himself thought that this was another 'unit of personality' to operate the body in the absence of its owner. John said to me that if his attitude or behaviour towards the voice were not 'to its liking' it would 'go away,' sometimes for a day, sometimes for a week or more. He asked me whether I thought this a 'form of exorcism.'

The first professor John consulted said some aspects of the case were not unfamiliar e.g. glossolalia ('gift of tongues' — from the Greek 'to babble'). He could offer an explanation of the voice up to a point, but not of the psychokinesis. John wrote to him later to say that he thought his late wife was around and able to influence the family in some way. The psychiatrist very understandably desired some evidence for this but John could provide none.

There is a most fascinating sequel to this entirely true story, told to me initially in confidence by John, an intelligent and successful businessman (not, I should emphasise, a scientist). Some time after the death of his first wife John married again. To his great astonishment he soon discovered that his second wife was also a 'multiple.' He wrote again to the psychiatrist, who was clearly somewhat at a loss. He (the psychiatrist) described the hypnagogic state as sleep approaches, and described the odd hallucinatory things that occur, involving auditory and visual hallucinations and 'other dissociative phenomena' occurring while one part of the nervous system was asleep and the other part was not, for instance, 'sleep walking.' He mentioned that all this can be produced by hypnosis. This did not help John at all. The psychiatrist went on to say that because the phenomena occurred twice John must in some way be responsible for their production or prolongation. He had 'strongly identified with the phenomena and become absorbedly interested in them. This interested identification had led to the recurrence of the phenomena, just as a skilled hypnotist working to produce such things artificially in the laboratory could do so.' He suggested that John will no doubt argue that that does not account for the clairvoyant aspects of the phenomena. He further suggested that psychical researchers many times find that most clairvoyants do not stand up to critical examination. (This seems a little beside the point to me: sometimes they do.)

When I met John's second wife she was living in a cottage not far from John and they were somewhat estranged. However, she did prepare his meals. We exchanged a few words and it was rather like talking to a housekeeper. John told me that he got into touch with the Professor of Experimental Psychology in another famous university. He also was unable to help. On the occasion when I met her John showed me one aspect of her syndrome. He had a store of chocolate bars in a drawer in the kitchen table for the second (child) personality, who liked chocolate. I got to know very little about the second wife's *alter* but she used to appear in the day-time occasionally when the primary personality fell asleep. She would 'take over the body' and eat a chocolate bar — but if the telephone rang this would 'wake her up' and it would be awkward suddenly to find she had a mouthful of chocolate when she didn't eat chocolate! What the child *alter* did on one occasion was to take the tele-phone off the hook — and forget to put it back. (John could not then communicate with his wife by telephone for several hours.) This sec-ondary personality was just like the other — a childlike personality talk-ing 'baby talk.' However, in the case of the second wife she knew nothing about it. In the case of the first wife, John had told her all about what was occurring when she fell asleep, from the beginning.

Sadly, a few years after he attended my course and told me at length about his experiences, then gave me his papers about it all, John suddenly died peacefully in bed. As both his first wife and he have died I felt that it was now in order to publish the interesting — and perhaps unique — material he had given me and which he did not wish to be lost to science.

An interesting point or two to be considered are the following. First, most of the more common cases of MPD appear to be the result of child-hood abuse. I do not think that this arose at all in either of the above cases. Certainly John never mentioned it. Secondly, as I shall go on to describe in connection with other cases, there seemed to be no Inner Helper or Wise Person associated with the above. It remains a more or less complete mystery — especially the question of what it was, if any-thing, in John that acted as a catalyst to cause these cases, if the sugges-tion of the first professor of psychiatry he consulted is correct.

The doctor's wife

Before I review briefly some published work on the more common and 'normal' cases of MPD, I want to describe one case I met personally at a conference in London on MPD. One of the speakers (an American professor of psychiatry who was very interested in MPD) gave a lecture describing this case and I discovered while chatting with him afterwards that it concerned his own wife. It was an instance of a doctor marrying his patient — so he certainly knew a great deal about the case!

While I was talking to him and his wife after his lecture — they were both delightful people — his wife had a sudden 'switch' and I found myself talking to the *alter* personality. That evening there were to be two social functions associated with the conference, a dinner preceded by a cocktail party. He told me quietly that both his wives (!) wanted to attend both functions. He had had to talk to them both and they had arrived at an agreement: one would attend the cocktail party while the other would attend the dinner.

This professor's lecture (which was part of a conference arranged and supported by a body interested in 'the paranormal' rather than psychiatry) had been partly about his work in attempting to integrate the two personalities into an unbroken whole. In such work hypnosis is a most important tool. It seemed to me that the case was so interesting and so rare that it would be of great value to organize a lecture by him to an audience of psychiatrists in London where his wife could actually 'demonstrate' and answer questions. They seemed willing so we all got out our diaries. The earliest date they could manage was some months away. 'Oh dear! he said, 'She will probably be reintegrated by then.' At this point there was an immediate change in his wife and a third 'personality' took possession. She whispered to the professor that she would not be reintegrated. He explained to me that this was her Inner Helper who was working with him to try to reintegrate her. He told me that this Inner Helper had various psychic gifts: precognition appeared to be one of them and, he said, she had never in his experience proved wrong. Sadly, he provided me with no evidence, and as so often happens, suitable dates were impossible to find and I never did see the hoped for lecture in London.

Common and important features of MPD

Many of the cases in the literature on MPD show potentially important and interesting features which were not shown by the long-term case I described first. Their potential importance seems to result from the implications they have for other human characteristics. May I explain?

I was once lecturing in Europe and found myself on the platform next to a distinguished American professor, the late Dr Willis Harman. He told me of the large number of cases of MPD in California and said that many had come to his attention because he was one of the Board of Regents of the University of California where studies of the syndrome were being carried out. He mentioned the sudden quite radical physiological changes which sometimes occurred when one personality was succeeded by an *alter.* In particular he mentioned a case where the first personality needed strong concave lenses in order to see clearly, while in their *alter,* vision was 20/20 (in other words, perfect). He said there were a number of such cases. Studies also showed that blood composition can change quite suddenly and radically with a change in personality. Sometimes allergies are quite different too. This puzzled me greatly as the body would appear to be the same and the only change its 'occupant.' Was there something drastically wrong with my understanding of what was going on?

The following week I talked to one of the senior optometrists in our university and explained this. She, a good scientist, said at once, 'Was a refraction taken?' — in other words, 'May I see the results of the standard eye tests?' After such an eminently reasonable question I at once wrote to my friend in the US and asked him for the evidence. A busy and much travelled man, he failed to respond but another friend helped me by sending several papers including the usual eye tests of MPD patients. There was no doubt about it: there was sometimes a radical change in the dimensions and certain other physical features of the eyes on a change in personality. I read also of a controlled test of ten MPD patients and ten people feigning this so that the examiner did not know which he had. There were 'significant differences in visual acuity, in the shape and curvature of the eye and in refraction, from personality to personality in the real patients, but hardly any among the others tested.' One woman had three personalities aged 5, 17 and 35. When the 5-year-old was examined she had a condition common in childhood known as 'lazy eye' in which the eye turns in towards the nose. This condition was not present in the 17- or the 35-year-old. In another patient the left eye had been injured so that it turned out. This appeared in only one of his personalities and disappeared in the others, with no evidence of muscle imbalance. (It amused me to read that some multiples have a drawer full of spectacles at home and are never sure which ones to take with them when they go out.)

I went back to my optometrist colleague and handed over these papers, suggesting that perhaps some experiments using hypnosis might be a good idea, as the use of hypnosis is the preferred method of treatment in most MPD cases. I could foresee drastic changes in the habits of the spectacle-wearing population if the dimensions of the eyes could be altered!

The reader might like to guess what was the result of this piece of research of mine into MPD and optometry. It was zero. The lesson I learned yet again was this. No scientist — and that includes most 'good' scientists — will alter their paradigm unless they have a real need to do so. My friend was getting on perfectly well giving her lectures on optometry and teaching her students the practice of their profession — and she had no experience of, and knew nothing about, hypnosis. Much better to put the evidence I had provided in a drawer and forget about it. So I imagine that that is exactly what happened. Of course I do not suggest for a moment that hypnosis could completely revolutionize the optometry profession — but I would very much have liked to find out!

Similar changes occur in connection with another characteristic of MPD: allergies. The papers on MPD refer often to strong allergies in one personality which are absent in an *alter.* Allergies to such things as citrus juices, cats, smoke, appear to be mentioned often. Generally speaking, allergic reactions can be controlled by hypnosis and this is often mentioned in the literature. When hypnotized volunteers are touched by leaves from a poisonous tree which they have been told is harmless this leads to no rashes. Whereas when the reverse is done — they are touched by leaves from a harmless tree and are told that it is poisonous — rashes appear between ten minutes and one hour later. Clearly dermatitis can be produced by a harmless substance if it is *believed* that it is dangerous, and vice versa. It is well known that warts can be cured by hypnosis. Equally they can be cured by the subject's *belief* that some procedure or other can do so.

It is almost always the case that one or several of the personalities of a given patient will be that of a child and the differences in responses to drugs among the sub-personalities are often like those ordinarily found when the same drug at the same dose is given to a child rather than an adult. And someone going from one extreme emotional state to another undergoes major biological changes like those seen in MPD patients; these changes are not easy to catch in other disorders but in MPD patients they can sometimes switch a number of times in an hour. I read of one patient who had a blood pressure of

150/110 in one personality and one of only 90/60 when another took over.

Patients' belief states and 'operant conditioning' (beliefs of the hypnotist, for example) are very important physiological variables. A well known case is that of Dr Mason and the congenital ichthyosis subject. When the doctor discovered that this very disfiguring 'crocodile skin' condition was congenital (and therefore impossible to cure) he was unable to help the patient whereas before he 'learned' that knowledge, he had succeeded in drastically reducing it.[16] Dr Mason evidently provided another example of the Experimenter Effect, so well known to parapsychologists.

It appears that MPD patients offer a unique window on how the mind and body interact. It seems clear to me — and the reader should remember that I am an engineer, not a doctor — that the possibilities here still unexplored are enormous.

The need for a new paradigm

The evidence above suggests that the normal scientific paradigm of realism, in which a human being is no more than an electrochemical machine, is inadequate to describe the type of events recounted. Some other experiences I have had in recent years seem also to need consideration of a different paradigm from realism as they appear very clearly not to fit into it. I suggest to the reader that such experiences do fit a paradigm of idealism.

Above, for instance, I described the immediate and distinct changes in visual acuity on a change in personality — in one case ranging from the need for strong concave lenses in one personality to perfect vision in the other. There are also, I am reliably informed, distinct and immediate changes in blood analysis between personalities. The electrochemical machine representation of a human being hardly seems adequate to understand how these changes could take place if the change is merely of its 'occupant' or its operative 'software' — the physical body remaining the same. The reader will remember that there is no scientific way of proving that there is anything solid 'out there' at all, physical and independent of ourselves. If, as I am suggesting, the world is like a set of 'concretized thought forms,' then changes in thought could indeed produce such radical changes in 'physical' parameters. Why the general appearance of the body should be much the same I have no idea.

The second MPD topic I described above relates to allergies which sometimes occur in one personality but not in another. Hypnosis is sometimes very successful in removing some allergies, which also indicates that the physical machine model of a human being is perhaps not helpful at times. Another fact which also militates against the physical model is that age regression under hypnosis has been used to show that a subject age-regressed to a period before the onset of epilepsy completely removes the epilepsy. The physical machine model again does not appear to be so helpful as an idealist model.

CHAPTER 13

Paranormal Healing

Over the years I have carried out many open-minded experiments with paranormal healers — or should I rather say, with those who claimed paranormal healing abilities. As a result, one of the important things I have learned has been that such healers sometimes have successful results but their explanation of the theory behind what they have done leaves a great deal to be desired.

Having no medical training I am not competent to make pronouncements on diagnoses or 'cures.' However, because of my psychical research experience I have been able to learn a great deal that the medics would not have learned. I propose to start as usual by describing personal experiences. We shall then have the raw material for consideration of theories.

Before we consider unusual methods of healing it is important to note certain preliminary matters. The first is that some 70 per cent or so of illnesses that patients consult their general practitioners about are 'psychogenic,' that is, they are produced by the mind.[17] In other words, a large majority of sick people have nothing physically wrong with them at all. So why do so many feel ill? It is surely because human beings are a psychosomatic unity of mind, emotions and body and most people do not know how to live. Few people these days take religion seriously: it has just about been destroyed by materialistic science. They feel helpless in an alien universe, far from safe and secure. Science and engineering have given most of us comfortable lives and insecure helpless minds filled with stress. Probably most diseases are the results of this — the struggles to 'get on' and keep up. Audiences of doctors do not disagree when I make that point. If headaches, stomach pains, arthritis and ulcers are treated clinically only the physical side, the symptoms, is being treated. The prime cause is probably a mental one. The patients really need wise philosophical advice on how to live their lives — a little reassurance that somebody cares. But how can a harried GP, with perhaps only five minutes or so for each patient, provide this? He has barely time to reach for the prescription pad to write down the chemicals that will suppress the symptoms. The former source of wise guidance, the church, has been destroyed by science and science has put nothing in its place.

The milder psychogenic complaints can be cured by a bottle of coloured water and a strong suggestion. The more serious ones need a complete change in life style, to reduce stress and give tranquillity and balance — combined, of course, with a balanced diet, fresh air and exercise.

This hardly needs to be mentioned but is certainly a necessary pre-liminary to a consideration of unorthodox healing. Most diseases being psychogenic in origin will probably get better anyway, whatever is done, including nothing.

Unorthodox healers tend to have more time to talk to their patients and give friendly advice; that advice is very likely to be accepted, par-ticularly if paranormal sources are claimed for it. All this TLC (tender loving care) can lead to a more tranquil mind and body and natural healing, whether or not the healer's claims are true.

Psychic healing

I was once invited to observe at close quarters the well-known healer Harry Edwards, a Spiritualist, perform his healings during a demonstra-tion in the Royal Festival Hall in London. Edwards believed that a dis-carnate doctor helped him and was doing the actual healing through him. A seat was provided for me in the front row of a few seats placed on the stage within a metre or so of where he was working. His fellow healers, the Burtons, were doing their stuff at the other end of the large stage.

How well I remember that Saturday afternoon! As I waited for Harry Edwards' first patient to come up I noticed mounting the few steps at the other end of the stage a patient with an enormous goitre. Clearly against the light of a window I could see the large grapefruit-like projection at the front of her neck. She sat down on the chair near the Burtons and he appeared to me to be just gently stroking her neck, no doubt also with the mental intention to help her and the probable belief that discarnate healers were present and doing the real work. She may well have believed the same. A few minutes later I watched her descending the steps again back to the audience and her goitre appeared to have completely disappeared. Her neck looked completely normal to my untutored eye. A doctor sitting near me whispered: 'But there is nowhere he could have pushed it!'

Harry Edwards' own patient somewhat totteringly mounted the steps near him and appeared on the stage. She was bent practically double by arthritis and her hands and fingers showed severe signs of the disease. She had great difficulty in walking and I would describe her progress as painfully hobbling. She sat down in the chair by Harry Edwards (and very near me). I watched carefully. The healer first put one hand in the small of her back and the other on her upper chest and straightened her up. She sat in a way that looked about normal. Then he took one of her hands with its badly bent fingers and started on her index finger. He pulled it out straight and then went on to the others. Each one he pulled out straight in about the time it takes to read this. Then he did the same with the other hand. Her fingers then looked approximately normal and she appeared to be able to move them more or less normally. When he had finished he wished her luck and she walked off the stage looking very little different from normal. I was greatly astonished.

Afterwards I had a chat with Dr Louis Rose, Head of the Psychiatric Department at St Bartholomew's Hospital, London, and a member of the SPR. He told me of an experience he had had which taught him, and then me, a great deal. He said that he had attended an earlier Royal Festival hall demonstration by Harry Edwards and saw similar 'healings.' After Harry Edwards and the Burtons had finished and departed he was still sitting in the front row of the hall thinking about what he had seen. Then an arthritic old lady hobbled into the hall in a great hurry and badly out of breath saying: 'Oh dear! Oh, dear! Am I too late? Have I missed it? British Rail delayed me by two hours.' Dr Rose said to her: 'I am afraid you have. However, I am a healer: would you like me to try?' (He did not explain that he was a distinguished psychiatrist from a famous London hospital.) She said at once: 'Oh yes, please.'

Rose asked her to sit on one of the chairs in the front row of the by now nearly empty hall and did exactly what he had just seen Harry Edwards do. He first put his hands appropriately and straightened up her back. Then he pulled out each of her fingers in turn exactly as he had seen Harry Edwards do. When he had finished the procedure she also appeared to be more or less normal. She thanked him warmly and walked out, much better than when she entered.

Dr Rose said to me that he could never have done that in his hospital wearing a white coat and with everyone calling him doctor. And, remember, he did not believe that he had any discarnate doctor working with him. But he got exactly the same result as the famous healer — at least it appeared so.

When I have told this story I have often been asked whether the healings were permanent. I have no idea: I am not a medical doctor and not competent to pronounce on such matters: it is the task of the medical profession to resolve such things.

A *different kind of healing*

May I now describe a second rather different case involving a very different kind of healer. She worked by herself and was very well-known. I attended her healing session in London by invitation as an applied scientist who studied such things. She hoped that I might be able to throw some scientific light on exactly what occurred; in other words, she told me that she wanted an explanation

Her 'clinic' was full of people but I concentrated my attention on one. He was a young policeman whose ankle had been badly injured by a terrorist bomb planted in London. He had undergone a number of operations on his ankle, which was heavily scarred and he was able to move his foot to left and right by only a very small angle. His foot was up on a settee and he demonstrated to me how much he was able to move it. When the healer put her hands on either side of the ankle, but without actually touching it, the patient experienced (without his own volition) strong and growing movements of his foot, which now moved to left and right through a very much greater angle than before — to his very great discomfort. He winced with the pain and could feel discomfort to the top of his leg. The healer told me that she considered herself a channel for 'forces' unknown to science which came to her from she knew not where and flowed through the patient via her hands. 'It is,' she said 'up to you scientists to find out what it is.' I then suggested that we carry out an experiment, which we did as follows.

First, I said to the patient: 'Let me see if I can do that.' I put my own hands on either side of the injured ankle exactly as I had seen the healer do. There was no result and the patient felt nothing. 'Sorry,' he said, 'you are just not a healer.' I then explained the experiment I proposed to carry out and everyone agreed to participate. I said that I would write down on a large piece of paper the words Healer, Myself and No one, in random order. I covered the paper with these three possibilities in what seemed to me an entirely random order. Then I explained to the patient that I proposed to blindfold him (which I did with a scarf so that he had no possibility whatever of seeing anything) and that I would ask a young nurse who had joined us to help, to point to the next person on the list. That person would walk up to the patient and put their hands on either side of the injured ankle. He was to tell me whether it was the healer, myself or no one, whose hands were near his ankle. He expressed perfect willingness and considered that he would have no difficulty whatever in correctly doing this — except that he doubted whether he could tell the difference between Myself and No one.

So we did the experiment. The nurse pointed to me and I walked up and put my hands on either side of his ankle. She then pointed to the healer, who did the same. This was followed by the nurse's giving a shrug of her shoulders to indicate No one, so I just walked up to the patient with my hands behind me. (The ancient floor creaked audibly when someone walked on it so it was most important that the patient was given no acoustic clues!) Throughout this experiment the patient informed us very positively, when he felt the strong movements of his ankle, that the healer's hands were there. When he felt nothing he said that the hands were either my own or no one's.

I wonder whether, having read of similar experiments earlier in this book, the reader is able to say what the results of the experiment were! In fact, the subject was perfectly clear when he thought that the healer's hands were present and when they were not but there was actually no correlation whatsoever between the position of the healer's hands and the movements of his ankle, with all the discomfort that followed. He sometimes experienced the strong movements when my own hands were there, sometimes when no one's hands were there and he often did not feel the movements when the healer's hands were there.

So what do we deduce from this? First, I asked the healer to step outside with me and I then requested her on no account to tell the subject the results of the experiment. He was clearly benefitting greatly from the healing sessions and I did not want this to cease. However, I suggested to her that she give him 'absent healing' on every evening of the week at a specific time. He would, hopefully, then receive many times the benefit he was formerly having.

I should mention that the patient's doctors at a nearby famous London hospital had expressed no objection whatever to the healer's carrying out her procedures on him because they knew that as she did not propose actually to touch him there could be no effect whatsoever!

The healer appeared to agree with me that her initial belief that she was a channel for mysterious forces unknown to science and that it was the task of scientists like myself to find out what they were, was somewhat astray. She agreed that suggestion appeared to be a very strong and important component of her valuable therapeutic system.

There are a number of loose ends which I have been unable to tie up regarding this method of healing. If, before the patient met the healer, I had placed my hands on either side of his ankle, having no reputation for achieving cures, it was most unlikely that any movements of his limb would have occurred. So what started the whole process? I must confess to complete ignorance. Maybe a strong 'thought form' or belief structure had been created by the healer (see the Philip Experiment in Chapter 8) and this was picked up by the patient's unconscious mind (George). Normal suggestion, perhaps partly the result of his hearing of other cases, would have played a part too. However, one would think that if a 'thought form' were the explanation then George would know whether, in the experiment, the healer was putting her hands there or not. You would not think it to be necessary for the patient to *see* the healer as George's ESP would recognize her presence. Maybe the patient observed at his first visit the effect of her procedures on the other patients and *expected* a similar result for himself.[18]

Here it looks as though we are again in the region of 'belief': if you really deeply believe that something is going to occur then it is quite likely to do so. And the body/mind seems to have its own therapeutic and protection mechanisms in such cases. (Does George really have such medical and physiological knowledge? Hardly!) What a pity it is that properly qualified doctors and psychiatrists/psychologists having open minds do not look carefully at this sort of thing! It certainly looked to me, a layman, as though many patients were receiving considerable benefit from this strange form of healing.

Thinking about all that had occurred afterwards I was reminded of statements I had read concerning the 'raising of kundalini' by appropriate yogic practices. The person in whom 'kundalini is rising' is said to assume naturally certain 'asanas' or yogic postures and it could be that an Indian expert in 'kundalini yoga,' observing this particular healer at work, might well comment that she is in some way quite unknown to anybody in the West, manipulating kundalini. Again, we each have to make up our own minds. We have no Western scientific evidence relevant to any of this. Our Western 'scientific belief system' has little in common with such traditional Indian models of what might be occurring.

The reader will perhaps remember certain remarks near the end of the chapter on hypnosis. Suggestion in a hypnotic trance state is not necessary if the subject deeply believes what the 'hypnotist' is telling him anyway. The 'modification of the normal reality' (if we may so put it) will occur as the result of that belief. Perhaps this is the 'correct' way to understand much of what 'healers' of various kinds are doing. Certainly I have found that if a normal scientist investigates using normal 'objective' methods then the phenomena seem to disappear like the morning mists in sunshine. But if everyone present is convinced of its reality then sometimes remarkable things occur. And sometimes they do not! In other words, it is very similar to 'normal medicine' — except that perhaps successes with normal medicine are probably more frequent. But remember that we have nearly all of us been brought up from our earliest years to believe in normal doctors. So one might expect the score of successes to be considerably higher. Again, the reader will be able to make up their own mind how to regard healing of all kinds when all the evidence is in. In the meantime I can only suggest continuing to consider the facts being presented with an open mind with my reassurance that I will do my best to make sure that they are accurate.

Some experimental investigations

Let us now consider some more experimental work related to healing and belief. Some scientific and very instructive experiments were carried out several years ago on the healing of controlled wounds. A specific circular area of skin of the same depth and diameter on the forearms of volunteers from a university population was removed (under a local anaesthetic). The subjects did not know that the experiment was concerned with healing but knew that it was double blind. They were randomly divided into treatment and non-treatment groups. They each once a day for sixteen days put their arm carrying the controlled wound through a 10-inch diameter hole in a specially modified door. The hole was sealed with a rubber material. In the treatment cases a recognized non-contact therapeutic touch healer put their hands near the wound for five minutes with intention to heal; in other cases nothing was done, to form a control group. The area of the wounds was measured independently, from tracings of the wounds, after eight days and after sixteen days. The result of these experiments was that there was a highly significant difference between the two groups. The wounds treated by the healers were brought back to normal in a shorter time than were those of the control group. It will be appreciated that both suggestion and the placebo effect were eliminated in this experiment.[19]

Is it reasonable to assume here that the patients' Georges (personal unconscious minds) knew that a healer was operating upon them or not, and behaved accordingly? Would it have been more direct and better to use suggestion to each George under hypnosis instead? All subjects are, of course, not equal in regard to their hypnotic susceptibility and it is not possible to measure the degree that a suggestion is accepted by the personal unconscious mind of a subject. These considerations serve only to emphasise the enormous difficulties involved in carrying out instructive experiments in healing. Psychical research is, as I have suggested earlier, orders of magnitude more difficult than research in 'normal science.'

Another experiment with a psychic healer

This case will again illustrate and emphasise the matters brought out so clearly in the experiments just described.

I was invited to visit the 'healing sanctuary' of another healer in London. Always I have found that such people are glad to be investigated by scientists and eager to find out all they can of the principles they are using.

Her room was filled with patients who had come for healing. One old lady suffering from arthritis in one of her knees was on the couch and I was allowed to observe her healing closely. (Psychic healers seem to have particular success with arthritis — which, I understand, is considered very difficult to treat successfully by normal medicine.) The healer put her hands one on each side of the affected knee (in this case actually touching it) and the patient said that she could feel her knee becoming gradually hotter and hotter. Everyone considered that the healer was a channel for some sort of mysterious 'force' being put through her by her spirit guide. (In this case the 'belief structure' of everyone present was Spiritualism.) I then put a thermocouple under one of the healer's hands and as the patient described the increasing heat it indicated no change in temperature. The patient described to me the considerable benefit that she gained from her weekly treatment.

I then asked the healer's and patient's permission to try an experiment. This was agreed and so the healer took a seat against the wall with the other patients and I conducted the following procedure. I wound around the affected knee several turns of coloured wire, the ends of which I attached to the terminals of a decade resistance box. This is a box used in physics or electrical engineering laboratories between the terminals of which are electrical resistors adjustable in value by turning the graduated knobs on the top. The box contains no electric supply and merely alters in resistance when the knobs are adjusted. It is, by itself, quite inert.

I solemnly and carefully turned the knobs and asked the old lady (who, of course, had no idea what I was doing) whether she could feel anything. 'Yes,' she said, 'it is getting hotter and hotter.' She got exactly the same benefit from my inert box — which was doing absolutely nothing except give her a suggestion — which she had previously had from the healer.

Need I reemphasise to the reader that no discarnate healer or mysterious 'forces' were needed in order to understand fully the healer's procedure and success? And I certainly had no belief in any discarnate doctors helping me.

Radionics

There is a method of diagnosis and healing which has been around for many years called radionics. This uses a 'black box' which carries a number of graduated dials on the top, a cylindrical container and a small area of rubber. There are various other features which are not relevant for the moment. The system was developed by Ruth Drown in the United States and by George de la Warr in the UK. The practitioner claims that by using this equipment it is possible to diagnose and treat diseases. I talked to George de la Warr in his laboratory in Oxford many years ago and he let me try using his 'box.'

The patients to be treated do not need to be physically present provided the practitioner has a blood spot, sputum sample or a hair from the patient. The sample is placed in the container and the practitioner asks mental questions such as: 'Is the disease below the waist?' They simultaneously stroke the rubber gently with the finger and if the answer is Yes will feel some resistance to the motion — the finger tends to stick to the rubber. If the answer is No then the practitioner asks 'Is it above the diaphragm?' And so on.

When the disease is finally pinpointed, say to the kidneys, the practitioner will mentally ask: 'What is the percentage efficiency of the kidneys?' A dial on the box graduated from 0 to 100 will then be slowly revolved and when the finger begins to stick to the rubber the practitioner will consider that the dial is pointing to the percentage efficiency of the organ in question. In a similar way the practitioner will determine what remedies and treatments to apply. These are usually homeopathic or herbal remedies (which have no unpleasant side-effects): I know of no radionic practitioner who is also an allopathic practitioner. Some of the radionic practitioners do not use the area of rubber in their diagnosis but hold a pendulum over that area. They have a code in which George tells them, via the automatic muscular system after the style of dowsing (or the Ouija board), whether the answer is Yes or No by the way the pendulum swings — in either a circle or a straight line.

When I tried this equipment a great many years ago in George de la Warr's laboratory I was quite surprised by the results. I put a given sputum sample (on a piece of filter paper) into the container and rubbed the rubber area with my right forefinger, meanwhile asking the mental question: 'Is this patient suffering from hay fever?' (I was earlier told by the practitioner that he was.) My finger did indeed stick to the rubber — there was a distinct resistance to its sliding across. When I asked myself whether it was influenza my finger did not stick. I presume the explanation must have been the production of moisture or a slight electric charge by my George: I have never had the opportunity to determine this.

It is important to note that George does not always give the right answer to unspoken questions, whether his replies or communications are made overt by a Ouija board, a hazel twig, or by the rather different methods used by the radionic practitioner. This we need to test and see.

One particular method of treatment which radionic practitioners sometimes use is as follows. They erect what looks like a little aerial on the top of the box and place the box near a board carrying a number of blood spot samples from their various patients, setting the dials on the box to what they refer to as the appropriate 'rate.' They consider that the blood spots are in sympathetic vibration with the patients and that when the 'radiations' from the aerial treat the blood spots then the patients are being appropriately treated. This is all perhaps somewhat of an over-simplification. I am endeavouring to give the principles on which this equipment is considered by the practitioners to operate, and the general flavour of the method.

A medical colleague and I carried out the following experiment on the black box. We asked a number of radionic practitioners in various parts of the world whether they thought they could, using their method of diagnosis, sort out a random collection of blood spots into male and female. It seemed to us that as practitioners claim to be able to establish quite small details of what is actually wrong with a particular organ of the body then it should be very easy for them to sort out blood spots into male and female, as some of the organs are actually different. All the practitioners were very happy to collaborate and stated that they would have no difficulty whatever in carrying out this task as they solved every day many diagnostic problems of a much more difficult kind.

So my medical colleague produced a number of blood spots from his patients and carefully labelled them with letters; he kept to himself the key (which stated whether they were from male or female patients). These blood spots were sent to another collaborator who placed them in other envelopes, putting his own labelling on these envelopes. He therefore had no idea of the sex of the patient whose blood spot was within each envelope. Then we sent the blood spots to each radionic practitioner in turn, in various parts of the world, and eventually (it took about a year) we assembled all their results. Perhaps you will not be surprised to hear that they had about 50 per cent of them right! (Each had a different 50 per cent.)

So the practitioners achieved only the results to be expected by chance in determining the sex of the patients whose blood spots they used. Does this mean that radionics is of no value? Most certainly it does not. It could well be that the strong belief structure of the practitioner plus the faith and belief of the patient in what is being carried out could indeed be of therapeutic value. The reader should remember also that about 70 per cent of the diseases presented to general practitioners are psychogenic (produced by the mind) and would probably get better anyhow, without treatment.

What of the 'technology' of this system? The black box carries, as has been described, a set of graduated dials, the equipment inside being wired together in a certain way. The radionic practitioners — who are not scientists — use a language to describe the equipment, diagnosis and treatment, which sounds like the language of radio engineering. However, the wiring makes no sense to an electrical engineer like me and there appears to be no radiation of any kind that I know about, from the aerial. Also, I know of no evidence to indicate that a blood spot is in some way in tune with its donor and that this can be used for diagnosis and treatment. This is not of course to say that there is no link between a blood spot and a donor — there probably is. But the link is perhaps a subtle psychic one and the diagnosis and treatment ought perhaps to be looked upon as a sort of updated version of psychometry.[20]

CHAPTER 14

Reincarnation and Karma

A brief note on reincarnation

So much has been written about reincarnation that I do not propose to add much here, especially as I have not carried out research on it myself. However, I feel it necessary to mention some matters that are not generally appreciated in connection with reincarnation claims and to point out one or two facts that seem to follow naturally from some of the evidence we have been considering.

The first thing to say is that age regression under hypnosis seems to lead usually to fiction and fantasy and not to what looks like genuine memories of earlier lives. One can imagine how the personal unconscious mind ('George') looks upon it. The hypnotist tells him to take the subject back and further back in time to before birth and onwards. George is quite amoral and very helpful and obliging and 'he' perhaps says to himself: 'Whatever does he want? Ah, he obviously wants evidence for reincarnation!' So he delves around in the subject's memory store and does what he is so good at when he dramatizes dreams every night. He constructs appropriate past lives from all this material. I would not suggest that this is all that occurs, and that it occurs every time, but the more one experiences what George can and will do, the more likely it appears. It is rare that the characters he produces in such 'research' can be traced.

The best evidence for 'genuine' reincarnation appears to be that produced in such quantity and high quality by Professor Ian Stevenson in his work all over the world with children having appropriate memories. Especially is this true of his best cases where he has been able to trace the family where the child ostensibly lived before death and before the child or the child's family knew of the other family. I am particularly impressed by the presence of birth marks imitating the wounds which the child 'remembers' as leading to the previous death. It must be especially impressive when the

child is taken to the other family they have never met in their present life and they recognize their previous relatives and refer to incidents they shared with them.

I know of no, or very little, impressive evidence of reincarnation
relating to adults. Those — usually psychic — adults who claim to
remember past lives often have great difficulty in tracing the people
they say they were. (There are one or two exceptions — see the
Reading List.) This might be expected, of course, as a majority of us if
we have lived before must have been quite insignificant and it is most
unlikely that we made any mark which would be traceable. Again one
cannot possibly be dogmatic and there is always the odd fact difficult
to account for, but the sum total is quite different from that in the case
of children.[21]

My own temporary view is that perhaps when children die young
they can be reborn to other parents while carrying along with them the
same mind with its memory store (*not* to be considered as the 'software' or other storage in the brain — see the final chapter). However,
the evidence is short. With his customary scientific caution Ian
Stevenson refers to his own outstanding evidence as 'facts suggestive
of reincarnation' and one surely must agree with that, as probably
going as far as is scientifically safe.

The case of the Druze

There are one or two other matters relating to reincarnation that I
should like just briefly to mention. The first I have remembered for
many years after originally hearing it from a distinguished Jewish lady
from Israel. She seemed to me a careful and reliable researcher who
had carried out research on the Druze tribe in the Lebanon. She mentioned that the Druze believe in an immediate reincarnation after death
and said that this occasionally led to surprising results. For example,
one Druze might have been murdered by another Druze who lived in
the same street. The murdered Druze was occasionally reborn (also in
the Druze community) and, on reaching a suitable age, remembered
that the person who had murdered him lived nearby. Accusations
which obviously could not be proved to the satisfaction of a Court of
Law would have been likely to lead to nothing but ill feeling so, she
told us, it was the custom in Druze communities never to refer to memories of a preceding incarnation of that kind.

If Druze people really are immediately reborn after death then it
would appear that the general belief in this is what leads to the rebirth.

So far as I can see the vast majority of Hindus, who also believe in reincarnation, consider that a long time is spent in other spheres between incarnations and this phenomenon of immediate reincarnation appears to be peculiar to the Druze. It can perhaps be taken as evidence slightly increasing the likelihood that we (whatever is meant by we! — presumably a 'higher part' of us, as discussed in the final chapter) choose before our birth the place and family in which we shall be reborn.

A brief note on karma

Until recently I considered that it was hardly possible to do scientific research on the eastern doctrine of *karma* (a Sanskrit word pronounced to rhyme with *cur-ma.*)[22] This is a twin doctrine to reincarnation and is widely believed in by followers of Hinduism and Buddhism who consider that their series of lives are linked together by *karma,* which is a law of cause and effect. Misfortune in the present life is considered to be the result of unkind or unwise activities in former lives. Similarly, good fortune is accounted for by helpfulness to others. It may be seen that the belief in this law leads to the patience in adversity of many Hindus.

Dr Stanislav Grof is a distinguished American psychiatrist who has been carrying our outstanding research for many years into altered states of consciousness. He started originally in eastern Europe using the psychedelic drug lysergic acid diethylamide (LSD), which appears to lead to mystical experiences. When he moved to the United States and LSD became illegal for such work, he changed to what he calls holotropic breathing, which seems to lead to similar results. Those results include wide-ranging experiences involving what appear to be former lives and even including existence in animal, vegetable and mineral forms. This work is mentioned here because it appears to be producing evidence relevant to *karmic* links between lives.[23]

CHAPTER 15

Parapsychology:
the Controlled Laboratory Work

The operation of psychic faculty seems to occur most readily and most often in everyday life where often coincidences can occur which make its operation in any particular case doubtful. If one wants to know with a greater degree of certainty that psychic faculties really do exist apart from normal coincidence or misinterpreted normal factors or deliberate cheating on the part of someone claiming them, then all extraneous factors must be brought under control or eliminated. This can be done only in a laboratory where all the factors considered to be relevant can be determined or, in the case of extraneous factors, excluded altogether. There are certain disadvantages inherent in laboratory work which tend to inhibit the operation of psychic faculties, and these will be mentioned later. However, as a result of many years of good laboratory experimentation certain facts are now known with an excellent degree of confidence. One can 'know' that they are true with the same sort of confidence that one has concerning many more 'normal' facts. (We must always remember that *nothing,* but nothing, is 100 per cent certain — except the tautologies of mathematical proofs.)

This laboratory work — beginning with tests under properly controlled conditions — was started about 1930 by J.B. Rhine at Duke University at the instigation of Professor McDougall, who appointed him. This work started with telepathy, tested by 'card guessing' in which a subject in one laboratory looked at a card and then another subject in another laboratory, signalled to do so by a buzzer, 'guessed' what that card was. As ordinary playing cards were inappropriate in various ways another and more suitable type of card was devised by a researcher in Rhine's laboratory named Zener. So-called Zener cards were simpler and clearer and consisted of five different kinds of card carrying a star, cross, circle, square or wavy lines, a complete pack consisting of 25 cards — five of each. So the Agent (transmitter) would be presented by the first experimenter with one of these and the Percipient (receiver) would guess which it was, the second experimenter recording their guess. Simple statistics would be used to calculate the odds against chance of getting the number 'guessed' correctly in a long run of trials. Clearly the expectation of success by chance would be one in five correct. If the score were not 20 per cent correct then the odds against chance as accounting for this could be readily calculated.

Perhaps it should be added that the above statements assume an equal preference for each of the five cards. It is easy to show by tests that this is not true. In a very large television audience the star is selected more than any of the other symbols. Good experiments today must take account of such psychological factors.

In experiments like this the cards presented would be selected from random number tables rather than by shuffling, and every possible precaution to prevent normal leakage of information about the cards was taken. Most subjects usually get about 20 per cent correct but a very few outstanding subjects sometimes do very much better than that and get a score with odds of many millions to one against chance as accounting for it.

When after an appropriate time Rhine published his first paper the 'normal scientists,' who did not have the open minds which surely should be a characteristic of a good scientist and who considered that they already knew that telepathy was impossible, suggested all sorts of reasons for the normal transmission of information to the Percipient about the card being looked at by the Agent. They suggested such things as a spy looking through a hole in the ceiling and then telling the Agent what the card was. As a result of this perfectly legitimate and valued criticism later experiments used a kind of booth surrounding the Agent on three sides and over the top. The selected card was presented by the experimenter to the Agent by placing it against a suitable hole in the screen between them. Even the first experimenter did not know what it was until after the run of guesses, the cards being placed face down in front of them and selected using random numbers from one to five. Several independent witnesses were arranged to be present so that there was no doubt that all the precautions had been correctly taken. Still the outstanding subjects scored successfully with enormous odds against chance.

These results were so astonishing and appeared to be so fundamentally important that S.G. Soal, a University of London mathematician, decided to repeat them in London. I start with him because he was the first in the UK and he made some new discoveries. Soal worked for several years without apparently any success until he had a brainwave, re-examined his results, and discovered that two of his subjects were scoring correctly with large odds against chance as accounting for it, on the card *next ahead* rather than on the one being looked at at the time. He so demonstrated *precognition.* Sometimes they scored on the card two ahead in this way. Later experiments usually compared the subject's guesses with cards both one and two ahead and one and two behind. It is important to mention that Soal's results were carefully looked at by a statistician member of the SPR many years after his death and it was discovered incontrovertibly that there had been alterations in some of his score sheets which improved the success rate. In addition he claimed to have lost many score sheets on a train during World War 2. In accordance with normal psychical research practice his results are therefore not now taken seriously by other researchers. However, there is no reasonable doubt in my mind that precognition and retrocognition do genuinely take place, as shown by many other independent experimenters, both in the UK and the USA. Also, I knew Soal as an academic colleague for some six months and he seemed a most unusual man — rather peculiar, reticent and withdrawn. I do not myself believe that he cheated at the beginning when he made his discoveries but there seems little doubt that he did later, either consciously or unconsciously. But this latter is my own opinion only and not to be taken as evidence.

Another type of experiment was soon tried in which there was no Agent but the cards were left face down and no one looked at them. The Percipient guessed in the usual way on a signal. This was a test of what is called *pure clairvoyance* and resulted sometimes in equally high correct scores. However, the experimenter determined what the cards had been later when the scores were calculated and the Percipient could have precognized at the time of the experiment the state of the experimenter's mind when the results were evaluated. This is called 'precognitive telepathy.' It is perfectly possible to conduct tests on pure clairvoyance in which the cards or numbers used are *never* in anyone's mind. We had an example earlier when I described experiments I did with a volunteer hypnosis subject having an out-of-body experience and attempting to read numbers at the back of a box. This illustrates one of the difficulties of such tests and why the subject is so much more difficult than is normal science. This will be considered further when we give consideration to the view, strongly indicated by quantum mechanics, that the existence of the physical world depends on human perception of it in order to exist. It may be that perception/consciousness can never be eliminated and that the human mind and the physical universe are, as one famous physicist said, like the two sides of a single coin — neither can exist without the other.

A new phenomenon was soon discovered. It was often found that after successfully scoring for a while the results fell off to those expected by pure chance. This was called the *decline effect* and may have been due to boredom. The reader will appreciate the enormous tedium of sitting and looking at and guessing thousands of cards in this way. Card guessing seems now to have given way to more interesting and stimulating ways of testing ESP. We shall now deal with some of these. (The decline effect still rears its ugly head occasionally.) However, before we leave this foray into the earlier laboratory work we must briefly sketch the work of Rhine on *psychokinesis*.

Rhine in the early days of the laboratory work did not restrict himself to telepathy. Claims had been made that it was possible to move objects by direct mental action. Tables appeared to have been levitated in spiritualist seances without force being applied underneath (we have earlier described Batcheldor's experiments).but because such activity usually occurred in the dark no scientist was confident that no normal forces had been applied. Rhine therefore started a programme on the direct action by the mind on physical objects: that is on *psychokinesis* (PK). Gamblers had been claiming for a long time that they could directly mentally influence the fall of dice. Rhine therefore started his laboratory work on this and arranged to throw dice automatically and randomly from a tilting basket onto a table, a subject trying to 'will' the dice to show certain predetermined numbers. This seemed even more unlikely to the normal scientists than telepathy. However, again Rhine got positive results which, with some subjects, showed large odds against chance expectation as accounting for them. He carried on this work for some three years before he felt sufficiently confident to publish the results.

It is interesting that some scientists suggested, when they were sure that the experiments were valid, that the standard statistics used (and of course widely used in normal science and engineering) might in fact be wrong. This led to a pronouncement by the American Mathematical Association saying that they were not qualified to pronounce on the experiments but that there was nothing wrong with the statistics that had been used to evaluate them.

We shall now consider much more recent work in which, with the aid of modern electronics and computers, telepathy, clairvoyance, precognition and psychokinesis have been established, in my view, without much reasonable doubt. We shall consider first the work of Charles Honorton and then the work of Robert Jahn. We shall also mention the enormously important 'meta-analysis,' which enables the results of many experiments to be combined to make the equivalent of one very large experiment.

Ganzfeld experiments

Reduction of the impacts of sensory information and the paying of attention to internal states have been thought for many years to increase ESP. Positive results have been found using hypnosis, meditation and sleep. Mesmer claimed to demonstrate 'mental suggestion' to a distant subject and meditation has many times been shown to increase ESP. However, one of the most successful methods began with work on telepathy in dreams in Maimonides Hospital in New York in the 1960s. In this an experimenter looked at a picture and the sleeping subject was awakened when showing REM sleep (rapid eye movement — dreaming sleep) and asked to describe their dream. More often than would be expected by chance, it coincided with the picture being looked at by the experimenter. Later, vivid and emotive film clips were used with even greater success. This led to the enormously successful Ganzfeld (German for whole field) work. In this a subject lies down on a comfortable surface and has halved ping pong balls placed over their eyes onto which a red light is shone. They thus see a uniform visual field. At the same time unstructured sound ('white noise' — like the 'hissing' of the sea) is played into their ears via headphones. This situation, in which the patterned — information bearing — sensory stimulation is reduced to a very low value, has proved very successful in demonstrating telepathy. An experimenter looks at one of say five pictures or one of five film clips while the subject 'in the Ganzfeld' describes images and other impressions which come to them. They are later shown all five and attempt to pick out that one which most closely matches their impressions. Today all this can be and often is done automatically using a computer, in which case the experiment is described as an 'automated Ganzfeld' experiment. Many university laboratories all over the world have had great success with this experiment and obtained very large odds against chance as accounting for their results. When many experiments are combined using the generally accepted meta-analysis, astronomical odds against chance are found. Any reasonable person who fully understands this would be likely to claim that telepathy has been demonstrated so that we can be as certain that it exists as we can be of anything else normally known. Charles Honorton's is the best known name associated with this experiment. Honorton died at a tragically early age when working at Edinburgh University.

Princeton Engineering Anomalies Research

Another well-known team producing outstanding results is that led by Robert Jahn (Emeritus Dean of Science and Engineering) at Princeton University. Their work relates to what they refer to as human/machine anomalies, usually referred to as psychokinesis (PK), the direct influence of the mind alone on a physical system, no 'known force' being involved; and remote perception, usually referred to as clairvoyance, or general extrasensory perception (GESP), or the acquisition of information concerning an object or contemporary physical event, the known senses not being involved; and precognition: a form of extrasensory perception in which the target is some future event that cannot be deduced from normally known data in the present.

Jahn devised an experiment using a source of electronic white noise (non-technical readers can skip the small amount of technical information here without any loss of understanding) typically a commercial micro-electronic noise diode unit. Circuitry then transformed this noise into a regularly spaced string of random alternating binary pulses, + or -, which are then counted, displayed and recorded. At this point in the data processing the output consists of a sequence of binary (+ or -) pulses, regularly spaced. The actual sign of each pulse is randomly determined on the basis of the white noise output of the diode source. Thus the sequence of the pulses randomly alternates between plus and minus with equal probability of 0.5, regardless of the sign of the preceding pulse. This Random Event Generator produces the output series by sampling the noise pattern at preset regular intervals: when the sample is greater than the mean, a + is produced and when less a -. The non-technical reader can think of it as a very rapid coin tossing machine producing heads and tails in a completely random fashion. It is adjustable so that the number of tosses in a trial can be chosen and also the rate at which they are produced. It can be set to count only heads or only tails or only those alternating regularly as head, tail, head, tail, etc. The latter eliminates any possibility of bias in the noise pattern and is the one normally used. To become technical again for a moment, frequency of count distribution is plotted and, as any engineer or scientist would expect and understand, a truly random Gaussian distribution is obtained for the unattended device. This is called the base line.

The results obtained in experiments with this device cannot be attributed to any plausible uncontrolled physical effects. The random noise source is specially designed to be insensitive to such external factors and, in addition to its intrinsic shielding, is contained in a well-shielded container which is maintained at a very nearly constant temperature regardless of the environment. Thorough and extensive calibrations have been carried out under varying conditions of temperature, humidity and attendance and show no detectable sensitivity to such extraneous physical variables. Most importantly, the primary experimental correlate to be described is the difference between the operator's high and low intentions; these are run under identical physical conditions, the only variable being the prerecorded intention of the human operator.

The subject or operator (all are ordinary volunteers) sits in front of the apparatus and endeavours, by any purely *mental* strategy they like, to influence the stream of pulses. In some experiments they try to produce higher counts, in others lower, and in others to ignore them. This tripartite arrangement is always used to eliminate any possibility of 'drift' in the equipment. One subject, when trying to increase the rate of count, shifted the distribution in the positive direction while, when trying to reduce it, shifted it in the opposite direction, and the difference in the two was about 0.5 per cent.

A perhaps more illuminating and understandable way of plotting these results is to use a 'cumulative deviation' graph. Here, when the equipment is running freely with no human subject mentally trying to influence it, the number of 'heads' coming up is about equal to the number of 'tails' with what is called a 'stochastic variation' (roughly meaning 'random,' within certain limits) about a mean. The curve wanders about the horizontal line, sometimes being above it and sometimes below. When the subject tries to increase the number of 'heads' then the curve, having the same stochastic variation, gradually moves further and further away from the horizontal axis showing an ever increasing deviation from the mean. The same result is obtained in the opposite direction when the subject tries to reduce the number of counts. The greater the number of trials the greater the deviation from the chance mean. In their 1987 book *Margins of Reality,* Jahn and Dunne give the results of 33 different operators who produced a total of 250,000 trials. Since then and up to seven or eight years ago the data base had increased to 2.5 million trials with 91 operators with continually consistent correlations with intention that remained highly significant. (The probability that they occurred by chance is less than one in 100,000.) A majority of this large group did not achieve significant results but their results overall show clearly departure from chance while the base line remains close to the theoretical mean. Interesting variations between operators showed up which are discussed in their book.

It is significant that several other noise sources were used with no appreciable difference in the results. For the technical it is interesting to note that when a pseudorandom source was used, with all else the same, the results were very similar.

Jahn and his team tried to get further information on PK by using a quite different kind of apparatus not involving electronics — a Galton's desk (which used to be a feature of many schools' physics labs.) which they called a Random Mechanical Cascade. This was some three metres high by about two metres wide and was mounted on a wall facing a couch. In operation 9000 light spheres 1.9 cm in diameter trickled down from an entrance funnel in the middle of the top, bounced on an array of horizontal pegs as they descended and eventually fell into bins at the bottom forming, as is well known, a roughly Gaussian distribution. That is, in simple terms, many more fell into the bins near the middle than in those near the edges giving roughly the well-known bell shape already mentioned above in connection with the other experiment. A counter at each bin entrance observed the arrival of each sphere and a graph was drawn on the computer screen.

Using all the obvious precautions, extensive calibrations were accumulated to provide background statistical data. The operator, sitting some 2.5 metres away, attempts mentally to distort the distribution of the spheres towards the right of the apparatus (called PK+) or towards the left (PK-) or, by doing nothing, to generate base lines. Again, efforts are interspersed in sets of three runs (taking about 12 minutes each) to provide tripolar strings of data. Here the mechanical features are too complicated to predict theoretically, so the statistical treatment of the data is based on comparisons of the means of the PK+ and PK- distributions, with the local base lines of the same experimental set-up.

In this experiment both temperature and humidity are observed and correlations with these variables removed in the course of the data analysis. Sensitivity to the position and movements of the operator or other people in the vicinity is found to be negligible. As with the other experiment clear correlations between the movement of the spheres and the intentions of the operator are shown. These experiments take much longer than do those described above involving electrical pulses. (The total time for all the spheres to fall in one experiment is about 12 minutes.) The data base is therefore much smaller. However, the total number of series conforming to the intended direction to any degree is considerably higher than chance would predict. Again some quirks specific to particular operators show themselves. For example, one operator was unable to succeed in influencing the falling spheres to move to the right whereas he had no difficulty in moving them to the left. He did not have the same difficulty with the electrical pulses in the other experiment. Different operators had different characteristic 'signatures' (as Jahn calls them) of this general kind. These will form interesting problems for psychologists of the future when perhaps we know a great deal more about the unconscious mind than we do now.

Jahn's team used a number of other kinds of experiment which showed PK, but that is sufficient here for the present.

Experiments in ESP

Let us now turn to the work of Jahn's team in regard to general extrasensory perception. This deals with 'remote perception' (clairvoyance or telepathy or a mixture of the two — there is no way of telling exactly what) and 'precognitive remote perception.' The protocol in one form is as follows. The computer has been provided with a list of 100 geographical targets within some 15 minutes' drive of the locked room where the percipient is first stationed. The agent then goes to the computer and is provided with one of those places, randomly chosen, to which (s)he drives. On arrival the agent then spends 15 minutes or so there recording impressions and taking photographs. At that time the percipient tries to visualize where the agent is, recording impressions arising in their mind and making sketches as necessary.

The realist would say that there could be no relationship whatsoever between the impressions of the agent at the distant, randomly selected, site and the 'guesses' or fleeting images or otherwise of the percipient. However, this is distinctly not so: those perceptions range in their agreement with the perceptions of the agent at the site from photographic precision to total irrelevance. Some elements may be incorrect and others correct, some emphasised and others ignored. Earlier experiments of this kind carried out at Stanford Research Institute used juries to match the 'perceptions' to the sites and awarded scores ranging from 0 for total inaccuracy to say 10 for total accuracy. However, the Princeton statisticians did better than this and developed a statistical way of assessing the amount of information acquired in this process. In its simplest form it is as follows.

A standard set of questions all answerable by Yes or No were assembled that could be applied to any geographical site. For example: Is it indoors (outdoors); dark (light); noisy (quiet); cars present (no cars); water (no water); and so on. The probability of each descriptor had to be weighted as some are more common than others. The most powerful aspect of the Princeton technique is that every perception can be scored against every possible target except the actual one, giving a large array of deliberately mismatched scores providing an empirical chance distribution, and this may be used as a reference distribution for statistical analysis of any single perception or group of perceptions scored against the proper target.

If all the answers given by the percipient were correct the maximum possible score for the target would be produced. The weighted actual total score for all the thirty descriptors is divided by this to give a normalized total score. The statistical merit of this is found by comparing it with the distribution of similarly normalized empirical chance scores calculated from the array of perception/target mismatches. So we have a normalized mean and a standard deviation for this target pool and a binary scoring method. Hence by seeing how many standard deviations we have, say, to the high side of the mean, we can calculate the probability of achieving this score by chance. Enormous odds against chance are often found with some remote viewers.

Certain questions immediately arise in the mind of any scientist/engineer. Does the effect become weaker or less accurate with distance? And what if we vary the interval between perception effort and target visit? Many experiments have been carried out with distances varying from a few hundred metres to thousands of kilometres. Distance makes no difference: the effect does not seem to obey something like the inverse square law of physical radiation. Time also makes no difference and that includes both *positive* and *negative* times: in other words, the degree of accuracy is not affected whether the target is visited before or after the perception effort has been made. Expressing that again differently, *acquiring the perceptions from the percipient and then going to the computer and randomly choosing the site to which the agent then goes makes no difference to the accuracy of the score.* So now nearly all the Princeton tests are done precognitively, and the experiment is called Precognitive Remote Perception.

What are we to make of all this? Can we rely on these data? The first fact to consider is that these results are not unique. Other laboratories have, over the years, obtained similar results. However, in my opinion the Princeton experiments were impeccable and confirm, in a very satisfactory manner, the earlier results from other laboratories.

I felt that these experiments were so important and so significant that I went myself specially to Princeton to examine them, received a warm welcome and inspected everything I wished. And all my questions were satisfactorily answered. There is no doubt whatever in my mind of their truth and great significance.

I would have thought that if they considered this evidence carefully and with an open mind few good scientists would disagree that it makes nonsense of a simple philosophy of naïve realism. Even if one suggested tentatively that the brain or body perhaps produces a new kind of field, it could hardly make sense of precognition. Causation is basic to realism. Jahn suggests that the similar effects on the statistical distributions of the electric pulses (increased or reduced counts) and of the falling spheres (moved to the left or to the right) rather drives one away from ideas of the mind, as it were, exerting 'force' on the targets. He suggests that it is more helpful to consider the mind to be 'inserting information' into those physical systems. He finds 'quantum mechanical metaphor' helpful in thinking about these matters. There are other ways of modelling these facts, also related to quantum mechanics, and we shall be considering them in other chapters. For the reader who would like many more helpful details and thoughts they are to be found in the excellent book by Jahn and Dunne. I am enormously indebted to Robert Jahn and Brenda Dunne for permission both to inspect at first hand and to describe their work.

So is 'normal science' obsolete?

As the reader will know by now, I am an engineer. Classical realism is the basis of our normal Western science and engineering. In my normal work as a professional engineer I use Newton's laws of motion and

Maxwell's equations of electromagnetism. So if realism has considerable doubts cast upon it as a valid all-embracing philosophy by this kind of evidence what happens to the 'normal science' on which engineering is based?

Other than opening up vistas of possibilities which may never have been formerly considered, the effects on our daily work (with the possible exception of those engineers involved in very low energy switching) will not be great. We shall go on using the rules of the mental models that others just like ourselves have devised to pattern their experiences, and we shall go on using them until they are shown to be inadequate. But we may no longer consider them to be 'laws of nature.' We find that Newton's laws are still useful (including for 'space shots' etc.) even though we know that Einstein's quite different model is needed under certain conditions. We shall perhaps realize, as suggested earlier, that human beings are indeed mental model-building creatures, and we shall go on using our models just so long as they continue to be useful and give us the 'right answers.' But we shall surely not confuse our mental models, patterning and ordering our mental experiences (which is all we can ever have) with truth or reality. We shall surely look with interest on all the other excellent scientific work on psychical research published during the last 120 years or so and perhaps not properly examined because the claims were thought to be impossible. And some of the traditional literature of the East, which has long referred to the effects of the mind on the somewhat illusory 'matter' of the physical world, the communication of thoughts from one person to another, and many other matters of equal interest, might be given more than a cursory glance. We might, many of us, perhaps call ourselves philosophical pragmatists rather then classical realists.

That is perhaps a sufficient foray into the very best of the Western laboratory work in psychical research and shows as clearly as it can be shown, that the mind alone has important effects on the physical world and that what we *believe* is perhaps sometimes as important as the 'physical facts.' The Experimenter Effect and the Sheep/Goat Effect reinforce this further and are dealt with in other chapters.

CHAPTER 16

Limited (Normal) Science and Pseudo-Science

Normal science

Few people have many doubts that what I call 'normal science' has been of enormous value to mankind. As a result of its application by professional engineers and others most people in the Western world have a high material standard of living, food and shelter, and health care that enables most to live to a ripe old age. Where scientific knowledge is not applied as a result of ignorance or lack of material resources the difference in all these factors is marked.

The contrast with the situation some hundreds of years ago is also marked. Galileo, Newton and other Europeans started modern science some 400 years ago in which 'facts' were discovered not by reading Aristotle (or others) but by directly referring to nature — the 'natural world.' Observations were made, hypotheses — explanations, which appeared to fit them — were devised and then these were confirmed by directly referring back to nature: by doing experiments in which tests were made and attempts made to falsify the hypotheses (not to 'prove' them — one can never prove anything except a tautology). If a hypothesis correctly predicted the results of experiments then it assumed the status of a theory. If it appeared never to break down then it became looked upon as a universal law of nature. We have today a vast collection of so-called laws which enable many things which earlier generations would have looked upon as miracles to be achieved.

All this is well known. However, it is sadly limited — of enormous value, but limited. Let us now again briefly summarize what has been said earlier as to why. Scientific facts — the data with which a scientist works — are the experiences of normal rational people. In other words, they are purely mental. They are usually interpreted in terms of a mental model patterning and ordering them which is the paradigm; and the normal overall or meta-paradigm in the West is based on the philosophy of realism: it is all 'out there' in physical space and independent of the perceiver. The words used to describe those scientific facts are almost always based on this fundamental paradigm. The human being is looked upon as an electromechanical/chemical machine with five (and only five) input channels to a little computer in the head. Everything that can be known is obtained in this way. Many psychologists are still behaviourists who look upon a human being — very consistently, considering the model they have of a human being — as a 'black box,' and the 'outputs' from it — the words and actions — are dependent entirely on the inputs. To speak of thoughts and emotions is believed by such people to be silly and pointless, since every 'output' depends only on prior 'inputs,' 'conditioned reflexes.'

By and large, this model is the one which is taught in schools and universities over most of our Western culture. I say 'by and large' because more and more people are realizing that the so-called scientific model of reality is limited and explains only a small proportion of the experiences of human beings. However, the teaching which is carried out in Universities and medical schools is still broadly based on the realism model. This is bound to be the situation because the leading members of the scientific community — university professors, editors of important scientific journals and the like — are those scientists who have been most successful in applying the paradigm and have written scientific papers describing their contributions, those papers being refereed by other similar successful scientists. Any scientist who writes a paper which is unorthodox — not based on the usual paradigm — has great difficulty in getting his work published and read at all. I am able rather proudly to say that this does not seem to apply to my own professional body. Provided the evidence is good enough and a paper is rational, logical and well written, then the absence of a generally accepted 'explanation' does not seem to stand in the way of publication in the Journals of the Institution of Electrical Engineers, which has published several papers by me on the paranormal. Jahn at Princeton has similarly had a long paper published in his fairly early days, I remember, by the American Institute of Electrical and Electronics Engineers. Engineers are pragmatists. If it is true and 'works' then that is acceptable.

Another major difficulty in this system which stands in the way of anything unorthodox being published and read is the enormous defence reaction of those orthodox scientists — the Establishment —

to facts which contradict their views of how the universe works. I have often been astonished at the power of this reaction in those I may have previously considered good open-minded scientists who know that the science of the day is never the last word because science is a living, growing thing. When presented with experiences which clearly do not agree with the ways they believe the universe works they appear to become blind and deaf to facts and, having exhausted all 'normal scientific' explanations, resort to blustering, anger and eventual withdrawal from the dissonant experiences. A number of such experiences have been earlier described, most in connection with the paranormal — all of which is of course impossible according to the normal realist paradigm. Examples daily increase in number. Well-qualified academic normal scientists are also normal human beings and well equipped with prejudice and preconception.

Information has recently been appearing — but rarely in the orthodox scientific journals — showing that the standards of the scientific work of most of the university researchers in the area of the paranormal (so-called parapsychology) is at a much higher standard than is that of the 'normal scientists.' There is plenty of evidence showing that the beliefs and expectations of the researcher affect the results of their experiments: much more often than many scientists realize. Single- and double-blind experiments are clearly necessary to eliminate this. Every parapsychologist knows this but few normal scientists appear to do so. The latter like to think — despite the evidence to the contrary — that they are completely unbiased, but this is clearly not so. These effects are evident in medical experiments (and usually in those cases the need for blind conditions is appreciated) but certainly they occur in other areas of science too.

When a good scientist has an experience, or has described to them something which is ostensibly paranormal, the first thing they do is to look for an explanation in terms of the science they already think they know. And sometimes the result of that is further measurements and an extension to their normal science. All this is, of course, perfectly satisfactory. I remember well an example of that which I met some years ago. I was informed that when a sensitive voltmeter was clipped to a leaf of a plant and there were locally held thoughts of harming the plant the voltmeter would show signs of severe disturbance, indicating that the plant had picked up in some way the malevolent thoughts directed towards it. Taking such a matter seriously would surely gravely disturb the equilibrium of almost any normal scientist!

However, I had been asked by a distinguished scientific friend, to provide some laboratory space for a visitor to carry out this experiment and to show me the result, so I collaborated. I arranged to borrow an appropriate plant from a well-known botanical research institution and was eventually asked to come and witness the experiment. The visitor told me that he was entertaining thoughts of burning the plant and pointed to the voltmeter, which was oscillating violently. However, I had glanced at the voltmeter on my arrival and it had seemed to me to be doing very much the same then. So I rubbed one of my shoes across the floor and the voltmeter went really wild. I pointed out to him that this was just one of the effects of electrostatic charge and suggested that he repeat the experiment in the screened and earthed enclosure elsewhere in the laboratory. He did this and after a week had returned crestfallen to his native country.

Often, claimed paranormal effects are the results of misunderstood normal causes and the misunderstanding is compounded by measuring some parameter which has not been measured before in that connection, sometimes with very sensitive instruments. I remember an example of this in connection with a well-known psychic mentioned earlier. This was in connection with the haemolysis of blood samples. (Haemolysis is the disintegration of red blood cells, with the release of haemoglobin.) Adding salt water to raw blood samples is known to damage the cells and cause haemolysis. The psychic considered that he was able to protect the cells in some way by psychic power. Most of those in the investigating team attended the university clinic and blood samples were obtained from them for the tests, which were, of course, to be analysed statistically. Briefly, from the results it looked as though it was true that the psychic could surround the sample under test with a protective healing field which reduced the damage. However, careful thought later showed that the elapsed time between the parts of the experiment was a very important factor. The haemolysis of the samples took a time which varied with the time which had elapsed since the sample had been taken. Haematologists normally take all their tests of a sample at one time and were not aware of this characteristic of blood. So the tests for paranormality showed up a new (and useless) fact about blood which was not in the textbooks. There was nothing paranormal about this.

Pseudo-science

Many people interested in the paranormal who have not had a scientific training become involved in what they think is science but is in fact nothing of the kind. They often protest that scientists will not take them seriously. A few examples of this will be useful to consider.

The commonest examples of pseudo-science I have met have appeared in connection with claimed paranormal healing. There has been mention of some of them in Chapter 13. There are many others. The commonest example is the 'mysterious forces as yet unknown to science' which give a therapeutic result which is clearly that of 'suggestion,' i.e. the result of belief. The result would probably be enhanced if it were done just by suggestion under hypnosis without the unnecessary complication of such matters as 'discarnate doctors' or 'mysterious forces.' However, the healers who do this sort of thing, whether in trance or out of it, usually know nothing about suggestion under hypnosis but they do have a strong belief in their 'guiding medic' and would protest with a vehemence equal to that of the most normal scientist presented with the paranormal if it were suggested to them that their practice could be better explained in terms of suggestion and belief. Nevertheless, such healers do a great deal of good in that, as pointed out earlier, they can give the time for the TLC which an orthodox doctor rarely has the time to give. And if the methods of the healer are to the taste of the healee and the result is as desired — who should complain? But it would not help for such healers to ask to be investigated by scientists — unless they really do want to know!.

Another area in which there is much pseudo-science is that of the so-called Kirlian photography. Let us describe briefly and consider the commonest form in which it is found. Here a high voltage very high frequency electric supply source is connected between a metal plate and the body of a subject — usually to a finger or fingers. On the metal plate is placed a sheet of insulating material and a Polaroid colour film. The subject's finger is placed on the Polaroid film. An electrical discharge takes place between the subject's finger and the metal plate. The result of this discharge on the Polaroid film is a Kirlian photograph. This appears as a dark round central patch where the ball of the finger had rested, surrounded by a coloured nimbus. The latter, because it bears a superficial resemblance to the psychic's view of the 'psychic aura,' is said to be a photograph of this aura, and as the aura is supposed by some psychics to have characteristics dependent on the physical and psychic/spiritual health of its owner, is so interpreted. The colours of the pictures actually depend on the chemicals of the skin and the ways in which the electric current flows between the finger and the plate below, through the three emulsions of the film.

It is common sense that if some factor is to be studied by carrying out an experiment, then all the possible variables except the one to be studied must be kept constant or otherwise controlled, so that the effects of their variation are zero or can be allowed for. In the case of Kirlian photography the pictures obtained (they are not strictly photographs as no lens is used and no image so obtained) depend on a number of variables. These include the pressure of the finger on the film, the radii of the curvatures on the finger, the chemicals on the finger, the ambient temperature, air pressure and humidity, the waveform of the high voltage, its frequency and the time it is applied, the chemicals on the film, the consistency of the film and others. (There are something like forty different variables I was told many years ago by an internationally-known expert when I visited him in New York.) In the common use of Kirlian photography by non-scientists for diagnostic purposes none of these variables is controlled. The result is that two pictures cannot be compared after altering one variable because every variable is likely to have changed and there will probably be variations in them all.

I well remember a lecture by a user of Kirlian photography in which he showed two pictures. One showed two finger impressions side by side and separated which, he informed us, were of two strangers. The other showed two finger impressions the same distance apart but the coloured nimbuses in this case merged with each other. He told us that they were of an engaged couple and showed their 'psychic auras' merging.. I said to him that I assumed these were not the only pictures he took. He told us that he had 30 or 40. On being asked why he showed us those two he explained, 'Because they showed the effect best.' All the scientists present looked at each other meaningfully. Most of the non-scientists thought that what he had done was a sensible thing to do!

An American researcher, Leonard Konikiewich, made some Kirlian pictures in which he controlled the temperature and humidity by taking the pictures in a humidity chamber He also washed the fingers in distilled water to remove extraneous chemicals and kept the subjects in white gloves for a time to allow the body's own chemicals to reestablish themselves on the skin. After an appropriate time he took the pictures by removing the gloves and controlling the pressure of the fingers. He used an oscillator producing a reliable and consistent sine wave voltage supply (and not the usual random voltage produced by a Tesla coil) and he controlled the time of application of the voltage. With all these precautions he was able to diagnose with a good degree of accuracy from a random population both cystic fibrosis sufferers and cystic fibrosis carriers. However, I understand that doctors are able to do that with better accuracy and less trouble using other methods.

Communications from 'discarnate scientists'

A number of times I have been sent communications ostensibly from such 'surviving scientists' as Sir Oliver Lodge and Sir William Crookes. The control personality in charge of the Spiritualist circle has specified me as the scientist for whom the communications are intended. Interested scientists often say to me that if the great scientists of the past survive, then surely their scientific knowledge must be much greater now and why do they not give us some help with current scientific problems? Many Spiritualist groups try to get scientific information. Sadly it is always gobbledygook looking like science to the non-scientist. It looks as though the concepts to be obtained from any discarnate scientists who are considered to be present need the corresponding material in the medium's memory store before they can be expressed. (This has been discussed, with examples, earlier — see Chapter 11.) The personal unconscious mind (the ever-helpful and obliging 'George') is very good at producing scientific-looking writing for the eager non-scientist. Mediums who are also scientists and who would have the appropriate facts and concepts in their memory stores ready for George to use are somewhat rare! (This assumes, of course, that the evidence for survival is accepted.) We shall have more to say about this in the final chapter (on 'theory') — in which a model of a human being is suggested which appears to fit the facts of experience we have.

Much pseudo-science is bandied about by non-scientists in connection with all aspects of the paranormal. The commonest pseudo science is the misuse of scientific terms. This amounts to expressing ideas which are not understood in terms of other (scientific) ideas which are also not understood. The commonest misused terms are 'vibrations,' 'energy' and 'fields.' Entities from 'higher planes' are said to have to lower their vibrations (whatever that may mean) before they can communicate with us. I used to attend many seances and conduct small experiments while we were waiting for the medium. On one occasion I was quietly asking the two psychics who happened to be sitting beside me in the circle to describe the aura of a lady opposite.[24] The lady on my right gave me a description differing in several apparently important respects from that of the lady on my left. I asked her how she accounted for the difference between them. She explained that she 'worked on a much higher vibration' than the lady on the other side of me. One assumes that 'a much higher vibration' must be better in some way than the lower vibration! But it is not clear in what respects — she probably meant that she was more 'spiritual' than the other lady!

'Energy' is a widely used term and usually appears to mean vitality. When a healer applies healing to a sick subject they are said to transfer energy, usually by moving their hands across the patient or perhaps holding their hands on the part of the patient's body where the pain is. Reiki is a form of healing using this method. This appears to be akin to the Eastern idea of transferring *prana*. The *vitality globules* of *prana* are believed by some to come from the sun and to be sorted out in the so-called *chakras,* which are supposed to be ten in number in some systems and seven in another (or seven major chakras and three minor ones) and are 'vortices of energy in the subtle body.' This 'force' or 'energy' was called 'animal magnetism' by Mesmer and has appeared in various cultures. Very powerful effects can be produced on those who *believe* in this, ranging from healing to unconsciousness. I have not been able to obtain any reliable (normal) evidence for their existence but belief in them does seem sometimes to lead to useful results. (Sometimes Mesmer's patients lay almost unconscious on the floor of his salon.)

Another application of pseudo-science is shown by those who measure the extent of the 'aura' by 'feeling' it with their hands or detecting the edge of it with a pendulum. As the aura is easily shown not to be in physical space (described here in an earlier chapter) this would appear to be clearly an example of self-deception and thoroughly pseudo. 'Blind' experiments, where the position of the subject whose aura is being detected by the hands or the pendulum is not known to the person detecting their aura, lead to erratic results. (Also described earlier.)

The phenomena based on the Drown or de la Warr 'black box' have already been described in Chapter 13 and useful results are much more cogently attributed to belief than to the 'mysterious forces' the practitioners speak about. The enormously important place of belief in this whole subject cannot be overstated and has been referred to earlier on various occasions.

CHAPTER 17

The Case for Idealism

It is my hope that the reader will by now be reasonably convinced by
the evidence of the earlier pages that many paranormal phenomena
exist, are by no means uncommon, and need an explanation. The commonest question I am asked by 'media people' is: 'Well, how do you
explain that?' They expect an explanation of paranormal phenomena in
terms of normal science — which is a contradiction in terms. Or they
expect me to say that it is all impossible and cannot be as described —
as some of the scientists say who know next to nothing about it. Let us
then briefly review some of the material we have considered earlier.

I have heard these same normal scientists say that if the paranormal
were true it would invalidate the whole of science. That is as foolish as
to say that paranormal phenomena are impossible and never occur.
They believe this because, it appears, they do not clearly understand
what science is. For them science is the process of describing a world
observed only through the five senses. For a realist what else is there?
But we have nothing except mental experiences. Many scientists might
have to agree that there is no way of proving conclusively that there is
anything at all 'out there' (outside the body) by way of a 'real world'
because in their model all the signals from the five senses end at cortices in the brain, the computer in the head. What occurs then to give
the impressions of a world out there is a mystery in terms of their realism model. Who, or what, is appreciating that world is a mystery too.
The more thoughtful might argue that the sheer consistency of the normal world, which always appears to be much the same for us all, shows
that there is a permanent 'something' out there even though in principle we can never know exactly what it is. The scientist I have called
somewhat pejoratively a naïve realist is the one who does not appreciate any of this and considers that the external world is exactly as it
appears to him. Karl Popper and John Eccles called what is 'out there'
World No. 1 and the world we think we know, which they called World
No. 2, is only in our minds. The reader may recall that I have earlier
suggested that there is no World No.1.

My suggestion is that the 'reality' is one of thought images or, as they are sometimes called, thought forms. We are here very close to the views of some of the world's greatest philosophers such as Plato and Kant. We are also, it seems to me, agreeing fairly closely with some of the greatest of the quantum physicists. Usually those normal scientists are not physicists (two I immediately think of are biologists) and know nothing about quantum mechanics and the view, based on good evidence, that nothing exists if it is not perceived. In my view the Copenhagen interpretation of quantum mechanics firmly supports the paranormal even if some physicists prefer not to look too closely at the view that the universe and the observer are two sides of a single coin. Nonetheless they do not hesitate to use the mathematics — and always get the correct answers.

Now let us remind ourselves of the powerful evidence of the paranormal (most of which the old philosophers did not have when they were working out their systems of philosophy). The facts of the paranormal are so valuable in trying to understand human experiences that they have led me to consider seriously an idealism philosophy. We have set out earlier phenomena which occur apparently only when we *believe* that they will — and by 'believe' I really mean 'know.' That eleven-year-old girl who bent the heavy steel spoon I brought myself and under my eagle eye by gently rubbing it between finger and thumb was surely able to do so because, having as she thought seen Uri Geller do it, she *knew* that it was possible. Her slightly older brother, closely observed by Arthur Koestler, was unable to do it on that occasion. Perhaps it was always less likely for him because he had been subjected to rather more of the mental conditioning that we call education and was rather nearer to our Western 'scientific' norm of realism, in which it is impossible. It will be remembered that Geller himself bent Arthur C. Clarke's Yale key upwards from a flat rigid surface by gently rubbing it on top (described earlier), Clarke's finger being firmly on it the whole time and the operation being under the close and experienced eyes of Clarke himself, of Arthur Koestler and of myself. Geller from long experience knew that he could probably produce this result in that way. (How and under what conditions he first did this many years ago would make an interesting story.) I remember that Geller originally would not say whether his 'spoon bending' was a trick or genuine because it added to the entertainment value (he was a paid entertainer) if normal realist viewers (practically everyone) tried to see how he was doing it. However, when he was interviewed by Professor

Anthony Clare in the TV series called 'In the Psychiatrist's Chair' he stated quite unequivocally that he was genuine and that it was not a magician's trick. Needless to say, this is not 'proof.' A majority of magicians and many others will still prefer to say that what he appears to do is impossible: it *must* be a trick and can be easily duplicated by a competent magician. They have, of course, not studied the evidence presented in earlier chapters. (I agree that it can sometimes be quite well imitated by a competent magician.)

There is plenty of other evidence for the paranormal produced in scientific laboratories. That especially important work presented so impeccably by Professor Robert Jahn at Princeton University was earlier described in some detail.

Further powerful evidence was given (and also described in detail earlier) by the psychiatrist Batcheldor, who found that a 'temporary suspension of disbelief,' produced by what was really a trick, was sometimes sufficient to cause a table to levitate paranormally in the dark, the table being fitted with instrumentation so that it was possible to tell afterwards when no normal force had been exerted upwards.

The so-called Philip phenomena produced by George and Iris Owen and their group in Toronto and described in Chapter 8 must also be considered. It will be remembered that the group devised a character Philip, imagined all sorts of detail of his lurid and fictitious life and when he and his background were very clear in their minds, attempted to 'communicate' with him just as the Spiritualists do. They had excellent 'communications' via raps on the table, which gave answers to questions and which agreed with the facts they had imagined about him and his life. Questions to him about other matters of this historical period of which the sitters were ignorant often received wrong answers, it was found when later checked. Clearly 'George' was up to his usual obliging tricks. However, it will be remembered, when they told Philip that they had only made him up and would send him away if he did not communicate more positively the communications almost faded away and they had to imagine him again strongly and 'believe in his existence' before the phenomena started again. Their (temporary) belief in him was essential before the 'real' physical phenomena, including movements of a table around the room and into the air, as well as raps, would take place.

More and powerful relevant evidence is provided by the two 'effects' which have been verified and re-verified in many laboratories: the Experimenter Effect and the Sheep/Goat Effect. It will be remembered that an experiment carried out with a group of subjects by an experimenter who believes that psi is perfectly possible is more likely to produce results showing the presence of psi than would be the case with another experimenter carrying out exactly the same experiment with exactly the same subjects who believes that it is impossible. The only difference between the two experiments is a matter of belief. Obviously there will be other slight differences in the manner of the experimenter ('body language,' tone of voice, etc.) which might strengthen the positive results for the subjects, as these are likely to strengthen the beliefs of the subjects in psi. But for the 'realist' who considers psi impossible anyhow this would make no difference. The Sheep/Goat Effect is a similar but reverse situation in which there are two groups of subjects who carry out the same experiment with the same experimenter. The results are more likely to show the presence of psi for the group of subjects who believe that psi may be possible than for another group who consider it to be impossible. Again, the only difference between the two experiments is a matter of belief, in the latter case of the subjects rather than of the experimenter.

I often think about why I never seem to have any problems with finding psi in lots of areas whereas friends of mine who also consider it to be possible appear not to have had so much success. This may be because of my personal history: having been exposed to so much Theosophical literature when I was young and scientifically naïve I have had for many years a 'model' in my mind permitting it to occur. Even though many experiments have sometimes failed to confirm this model and sometimes have shown it to be false, nevertheless deep down in my personal unconscious mind must be a basic belief that it is certainly true and one day someone will find a model that fits it. I am here suggesting that that model may be a completely different fundamental paradigm — idealism rather than realism. But before we look carefully at the implications of the facts briefly summarized again above, we must also look further at how belief is an important factor in our normal realism-based experience of the world.

The reader will remember the experiment described earlier in which I caused, normally but in a way not immediately obvious to the whole of the audience, the levitation of a bowl of flowers. Except for my colleague the professor of physics, who was a naïve realist and already 'knew' that levitation by mind alone was impossible, every member of the audience observed the levitation and interpreted it according to their own model of the universe — for most, realism. One lady 'understood' the levitation in terms of 'ectoplasm' and she saw other features which were not there. The physicist stated unequivocally and authoritatively that he observed no movement of the bowl of flowers. The other members of the audience (having had a normal Western education) looked for strings or rods (the 'normal' explanation) and as there clearly were none were completely mystified.

The reader will also remember the reaction of another colleague of mine, a computer engineer, when invited to witness a paranormal movement of the pointer of a voltmeter produced by Matthew Manning. This academic, another naïve realist, did observe the phenomenon, was unable to discover a 'normal' reason for it, stated angrily that nevertheless there *must* be a normal reason, and rushed rapidly from the laboratory and the unhappy state of cognitive dissonance in which he found himself. Two other more open-minded academics also present — it will be remembered — accepted that the phenomenon had occurred and that they could not understand how — in terms of their 'normal science,' of course.

Let us now turn to a different aspect of consciousness and consider the facts of experience provided by lucid dreaming. The reader may remember my experiment in which I found my body in a lucid dream almost exactly the same as during normal daily life yet I was able to levitate it by the use of my imagination. I mentioned at that time why certain Tibetans practised lucid dreaming in order to have full consciousness for all of the 24 hours a day so that they would discover for themselves that our 'normal life' is also a dream (as Gurdjieff taught) — that things are not at all as they seem.

Another piece of evidence favouring idealism — or, at least, not contradicting it — comes from the placebo effect. In many instances if the patient *believes* that they are taking a curative drug when actually it is just sugar then the effect is for a fair proportion of people much the same. This amounts to the physical alteration of the body by a belief. The somewhat similar phenomena of stigmata were mentioned earlier — clear modifications to the physical body by a strong belief and the use of the imagination.

The relevance of hypnosis was discussed in some detail earlier. The importance of hypnosis, it will be remembered, is that it is possible by hypnosis to change an unconsciously held belief, the hypnosis keeping out of the picture the conscious rational critical mind, which normally 'keeps guard' and prevents this happening. However, for a young person the belief can sometimes be changed immediately by a statement from an 'authority figure.' In the example earlier described a medical friend, in order to demonstrate to another sceptical medic, informed a young patient in the hospital who had a greenstick fracture of an arm, that a gas he asked him to breathe for a short time would take away all pain. The gas was actually oxygen. The sceptical doctor was able to manipulate the fractured bones (producing a loud crack while doing so), with no pain whatever experienced by the patient, who watched what he was doing with interest and pointed out that the crack had come from his arm.

Many examples illustrative of the points being made concerning the possibility of unusual and 'impossible' occurrences in the physical world when the mental state concerning them is different are provided by mediumship. Perhaps the most important and producing the most astonishment in the minds of normal experiencers of them were provided by famous mediums, in particular those of D.D. Home were described. That famous medium, producing his phenomena thousands of times before famous observers, often including well-known and distinguished scientists and never in the whole of his life discovered in fraud, handled red hot coals and also rubbed his face in the coals of an open fire, without being burned. His levitations of both himself and of heavy tables, sometimes carrying several weighty men, are legendary. D.D. Home believed that these feats were carried out by 'spirits.' Maybe, if this is in some way 'true,' it was the knowledge of the 'spirits' that made the phenomena possible. However, the point at issue is that they certainly occurred and were genuinely paranormal.

The many paranormal occurrences which are reported in other parts of the world in aboriginal and other non-Western contexts are outside the scope of this book, which surely shows that there is ample evidence to be found in the Western world where Western science is the normal approach to understanding 'reality.'

The final bit of evidence should surely come from our best modern Western science — quantum mechanics. I have suggested several times that those I consider our greatest scientists appeared to be idealists. Niels Bohr and his colleagues in their Copenhagen meetings certainly appeared to me to be numbered amongst them when they suggested that the physical universe depends for its meaning and reality on our observations of it. Before we observe it (or perhaps it would be more generally acceptable to say before the observation by particular experiments of the particles of which it is considered to be composed) it is a possibility only. Consciousness and the universe, the perceiver and the perceived, are two sides of a single coin; consciousness is a singular for which there is no plural, have both been stated by Western scientists. It is part of our consensus trance, or 'waking dream,' that we are all separate consciousnesses. It is a 'tangled hierarchy' that leads to this confusion, explained so well by Amit Goswami. It has become clear to me over the years that my ordinary daily self is little if anything more than a collection of memories and elaborations of memories of this very illusory physical world. If any of us meditates we find little more arising within us than these (at least in the earlier stages). It is the association of this somewhat illusory daily self with the unitary consciousness that leads to 'self consciousness.'

One of the leading researchers in altered states of consciousness in the United States is John C. Lilly, who did much of the earliest research in sensory deprivation (and also excellent research on the consciousness of dolphins). He put himself into a tank containing salt water in which he would float in darkness and silence for many hours; sometimes he had also taken LSD. His experiences were fascinating and relevant and are described in his book *The Center of the Cyclone.* I mention this book because it is instructive and helpful to us to read what he discovered about consciousness in his outstanding and possibly unique pioneering research. He found that there was a central point of darkness and silence from which he could programme any kind of universe he wished — or could imagine. He says this: 'In the province of the mind, what one believes to be true either is true or becomes true within certain limits, to be found experientially and experimentally. These beliefs are limits to be transcended.' In my experience, some of which we considered above, this certainly appears to be true, both in the lucid dreaming state and in the normal physical world. The thoughtful reader will appreciate this complementary view from a researcher into a quite different aspect of consciousness from the paranormal. (Much more supporting detail will be found in his book.)

John Lilly wrote the introduction to a book by Ralph Strauch about consciousness looked at, again, from quite a different point of view. He says: 'The world you think of as "out there" is not separate and external at all, but is instead your *reality illusion.*' Strauch also is a Western scientist who has discovered that the normal picture of a 'world out there' independent of ourselves yet capable of being accurately described by science is, as he puts it, fundamentally wrong. Again, the reader who would like Strauch's full thesis will find his book very stimulating.[25]

May I hope that in this short summary chapter I have convinced the reader that looking upon the world as a great thought rather than a great machine (as Sir James Jeans suggested so many years ago) is worth serious consideration as providing a model which 'explains' paranormal as well as normal experiences in a very satisfactory way and would be immensely fruitful to investigate. But it is important to realize that the impact on our daily lives if this is accepted will not be great. The so-called 'laws' of the normally experienced physical world — Newton's laws of motion, Maxwell's equations of electromagnetism and the rest — will still apply in predicting with good accuracy the results of our normal actions which we experience in our normal way in this illusory physical world. One is then a 'pragmatist.'

It is perhaps worthy of passing note that all the great Teachers of antiquity in the Eastern world told us from their own experience that mind is the only reality and 'magical' feats have often been described relating to them. The numerous 'miracles' of the Bible should also not be forgotten and indicated that another World Teacher, revered here in the West, understood the mind basis of our experience of the world, including our bodies. Of course we have no reliable witnesses of such matters as the raising of Lazarus, but the facts of this present book might be sited as evidence that such things are perfectly possible.

Those enormously strong psychological defences of 'normal realism' which I have earlier mentioned must, however, never be forgotten. A reader whom I have now convinced of the possible value of idealism in understanding not only the paranormal but also the normal may well find that (s)he has switched back tomorrow! If that is the case then major problems of understanding such facts as how metal can be bent by mind power will remain! Or there will be renewed doubts that it ever genuinely occurs. Repeated first-hand experience of at least one but preferably of several paranormal phenomena may well be needed to establish a new view! And this experience may not be easy to obtain. I have myself travelled many thousands of kilometres seeking these experiences and have many times been disappointed. But the occasional genuine experience was worth the trouble!

There is a final thought that has occurred to me and may have occurred to the reader. In the East there is a widespread belief in the existence of such things as acupuncture points and meridians, chakras, prana and kundalini. Perhaps, in view of the evidence cited above, these things do 'exist' — so many generations have believed that they did, and have used them — whether or not we can detect them by the normal Western scientific means. If that is so then we have an 'explanation' for the phenomena of Reiki, of therapeutic touch and the like. In the chapter on hypnosis we have something to say on hypnosis, mesmerism and 'animal magnetism,' and the advanced psychic phenomena which appear to have been possible and to have occurred as a result of the beliefs of researchers (especially of their personal unconscious minds — 'George') in this.

CHAPTER 18

A Different Model

The chapter coming up is perhaps the most controversial in this book!
The reason is as follows. I shall be suggesting again, as I did in Chapter
17, that the reader consider a philosophical basis for all our experiences which is quite different from the one which is the foundation of
just about all our western culture. The latter is realism; the one I invite
you to consider is idealism. The reason I think it worth considering, it
will be remembered, is because realism has proved quite incapable of
dealing with the paranormal. If our philosophy is incapable of providing a rational basis for experiences which a large part of the population
share, then perhaps alternatives should be considered. Obviously an
adequate philosophy must provide a basis for not only paranormal
experience but also for all our normal experience. I have found only
one alternative which seems acceptable to me: monistic idealism.
There is certainly no way of showing that it is not true and — to me at
least — it makes sense of much that I do not at present understand (or
should I rather say, which at present I cannot model). It also appears to
be in agreement with at least some interpretations of quantum physics.

In effect classical monistic idealism suggests that there is nothing
else but mind. The objects of the physical world, which appear to be
all about us and independent of our consciousness, are actually nothing of the kind. Consciousness and the world are interdependent. Had
some of the great philosophers and quantum physicists studied and
experienced the paranormal and had been familiar with the vast
amount of modern data which seem to be in favour of idealism then
perhaps many might have become idealists.

Several times earlier I have suggested that when a different philosophy or interpretation of well-evidenced experiences is put forward
our 'defence reactions' immediately come into play to try to persuade
us that what we have for so long considered true is still adequate and
that there is no need to contemplate an alternative with the feared possibility that much of our life and work may be seriously undermined, a
fear particularly relevant for normal scientists. We must keep a wary

eye open for this tendency and take care that we maintain an open mind and give proper consideration to something new, remembering that it must be appropriately supported by good and acceptable evidence. I am not suggesting that we consider altering our views for no sound reason!

Two facts of which to remind ourselves at this point are: it cannot be proved that there is anything 'out there'; secondly, that consciousness is unitary.

The model now to be put forward for consideration attempts to include all this. When it has been sketched we shall be able to see how well it fits the facts of experience. We remember that scientific facts are no more and no less than the mental experiences of normal rational people.

The model shown in the diagram is based on, and is an elaboration of, the model put forward by Roberto Assagioli in his book *Psychosynthesis*. Assagioli was a friend of both C.G. Jung and H.P. Blavatsky (the founder of the modern version of Theosophy). When I attended a week's introductory course on Psychosynthesis some years ago, the opening talks about what it was, and with what it dealt, seemed strangely familiar to me. It was then that I realized that Assagioli had created a modern psychology/psychotherapy based on the Theosophy I had read and studied in my earlier years. Jung had also studied Theosophy and related it to his psychiatry while extending and modernizing it in certain respects. Both these distinguished pioneers have been often mentioned in earlier chapters.

The diagram given opposite is only just a start and has in it 'dark areas' which we (or rather, I) know little about — except that they clearly exist — and which might be given more detail later when greater experience is available.

We have to imagine that a human being is represented by an ovoid in the infinite plenum of consciousness (Jung's Collective Unconscious) separating off, as it were, an individual human being from the rest of consciousness by a permeable membrane. The 'separation' is a virtual temporary separation. The model, pictured in the diagram as an ellipsoid rather like a symmetrical egg, is not to be considered secondary to our normal way of looking at our consciousness (in the western world as a sort of software of the cerebral computer) but is to be considered as a more fundamental model in its own right — a quite different way of representing consciousness. George, as we shall see, is not to be considered as working in some way through the brain but as

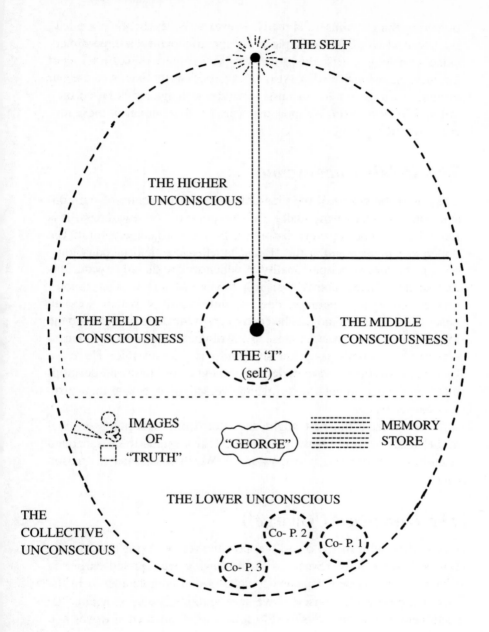

THE SELF

THE HIGHER
UNCONSCIOUS

THE FIELD OF
CONSCIOUSNESS

THE "I"
(self)

THE MIDDLE
CONSCIOUSNESS

IMAGES
OF
"TRUTH"

"GEORGE"

MEMORY
STORE

THE LOWER UNCONSCIOUS

THE
COLLECTIVE
UNCONSCIOUS

Co- P. 2

Co- P. 1

Co- P. 3

REPRESENTATION OF A HUMAN BEING
(AND OF THE UNIVERSE)

operating things 'himself' directly. However, necessarily we are having to use a two-dimensional piece of paper to represent a three-dimensional ellipsoid because this is the way we normally think (in terms of a three-dimensional world). Also we are necessarily having to use our normal language for the discussion, and this language is based on a philosophy of realism. We must take care not to let either of these limitations lead us astray.

The Middle Unconscious

The dot in the centre of the diagram is the 'I,' the centre of our consciousness — the normal daily self, the point of self-awareness. It is like a lighted cinema screen before pictures are projected upon it. The dotted circle surrounding the 'I' and labelled the field of consciousness, is the part of our personality of which we are directly aware. It is there that we have, quoting Assagioli, the incessant flow of sensations, images, thoughts, feelings, desires and impulses which we can observe, analyse and judge. The centre part of the diagram, labelled the Middle Unconscious, contains 'psychological elements similar to those of the waking consciousness and easily accessible. There we have the assimilation of experiences and the elaboration and development of ordinary mental and imaginative activities' before their birth into consciousness.

Now we have the first slight deviation from Assagioli's original model in that I have shown the Middle Unconscious to be separated from the outer ovoid by a narrow space. We shall see later the reason for this.

The Lower Self ('George')

Below the centre of the ovoid we have the region Assagioli calls the Lower Unconscious. (Some of the following was quoted earlier in Chapter 4, but is here repeated for clarity and completeness.) In the Lower (Personal) Unconscious we have, quoting Assagioli again, 'the intelligent co-ordination of bodily functions; fundamental drives and primitive urges, many complexes charged with intense emotion; dreams and imaginings of an inferior kind, lower uncontrolled parapsychological processes; various pathological manifestations; phobias, obsessions, compulsive urges, paranoid delusions.' All the other contents of the Lower Unconscious shown in the diagram I have added and

Assagioli is not responsible for them. Here we begin to deviate from Assagioli into what has sometimes been called the Lower Self — the part of us I have called George. I call this 'personal unconscious' George because it is a part of us which seems to have a certain autonomy and is very obliging but not highly intelligent. As explained earlier, I got the name from two sources: first, it is what aircraft pilots call their automatic pilot as it seems to have much in common with it, running many of our bodily operations and activities when we are not paying attention to them. As we shall see, George also produces our impressions of a physical body. In a real sense, according to the model, he 'creates' the physical body and the physical world which appears to be all around us. It is George who drives the car home from the station when our conscious thoughts are on other matters. George acts as though he is a separate part of us. When a hypnotist, by producing a state of deep relaxation, has effectively removed the conscious critical rational mind (the 'I') from the scene he can talk directly to George and George will take instructions and carry them out if he can. George can signal to a hypnotist quite independently of the conscious mind and tell the hypnotist whether he is able to carry out a certain instruction and when he has done it. These signals are often made by slight finger movements, the hypnotist telling George which finger to move for Yes and which for No. He does not seem capable of spelling out long sentences.

George then is the part of us which is in charge of the body but he has many other functions too. One of them is to keep the memory store in order. This is shown in diagrammatic form. When a memory is needed by the conscious mind George tries to find it (and usually succeeds) and send it up into the conscious mind. Sometimes George becomes confused. For example he might associate a loud bang with being dropped (as a baby) because these two events occurred in juxtaposition soon after birth and forever after he causes the body to experience a sense of fear and trepidation, with all the associated biochemical changes, whenever a loud bang occurs nearby. The conscious rational 'I' can see no reason for this but it occurs nevertheless. George in this sort of way gets phobias, obsessions and delusions.

George uses all this material in the memory store to construct our dreams at night so that a psychiatrist who is trying to cure some unfortunate complex is very interested in the patient's dreams for the clues they may give as to the cause, i.e. what occurred to give George this particular problem and which may have been long forgotten. It is interesting to note that George produces the sort of dreams that appear most meaningful to the psychiatrist, no matter to which school the psychiatrist belongs, i.e. no matter what model he uses for representing the patient. This collaboration of other 'parts of us' with a therapist is also referred to in the chapter on multiple personality disorder. The reader is aware that I am not a psychiatrist. However, I have had on my courses on scientific approaches to the paranormal many psychiatrists and they have not expressed any substantial disagreement with my non-technical descriptions of the functions of George.

George is the psychic and intuitive side of us. Down there in the unconscious he is in touch with vast concepts and archetypal objects. Past, present and future appear to become an 'eternal now' deeper down in the collective unconscious. So George is able occasionally to incorporate into our dreams matters which are in the future so far as our daily consciousness is concerned. Psychic people will have in this model a crack or opening, from George through the horizontal dotted line which represents a permeable membrane, going to the 'I.' Just to the left of George in the diagram is shown a representation of what I have called 'images of truth.' These are the 'facts' mentioned earlier and given to us throughout our life by 'authority figures' and accepted without question as Truth. This has been considered several times in earlier chapters together with the evidence for it. The evidence in Chapter 6 on hypnotism is especially relevant. It will be remembered that the understanding that most psychic people have of their psychism is also based on the statements of authority figures, usually from the spiritualist movement, so that they will have 'images of truth' related to that, influencing George when he produces their psychic experiences. Alcoholism or drug addiction appear to have the effects of breaking down these permeable membranes so that the 'I' is exposed to unconscious material from the collective unconscious which it is not fitted to handle.

George does his best to maintain the integrity of the self. If a child is sexually abused or beaten then George attempts to keep these out of consciousness as being too disturbing. He 'suppresses' the memories. This can cause a great deal of trouble later and a psychiatrist often tries to bring back the memories later in life when they can be dealt with by the more mature 'grown up' personality, with the psychiatrist's help. In very extreme cases George appears to cut off, partially or wholly, that part of the memory store containing the disturbing memories and so forms a new and separate personality. We earlier considered several cases of multiple personality in Chapter 12. The treatment — reintegration to form a whole personality — commonly involves hypnosis, which is the usual very effective way the psychiatrist can use of talking to George. The diagram also shows the different co-personalities we assume during our normal lives and are briefly considered later.

The Higher Unconscious

The upper part of the ovoid is called by Assagioli the Higher Unconscious and here, he explains, are the 'higher intuitions and inspirations, artistic, philosophical and scientific; ethical imperatives — urges to humanitarian and heroic action.' Here is 'the source of higher feelings: altruistic love; genius; states of contemplation, illumination and ecstasy. Here latent are higher psychic functions and spiritual energies.'

At the top of the ovoid is the Self (sometimes called the Higher Self, the Superconscious or Transpersonal Self). There are various ways of looking at this, such as the Christ Within (St Paul), inseparable from the Father. The reappearance of the conscious self or ego when we awaken after sleep or faint, or after the effects of an anaesthetic or narcotic, or after a state of hypnosis is due, it is suggested by some writers, to the existence of a permanent true Self beyond and above it. Assagioli shows the Self to be joined to the self by a fine line. I have opened this out to a narrow tube through which the light of the Self can be occasionally glimpsed by the daily self. The meditation method taught by the Brahma Kumaris involves envisaging a point of light in the head just behind the nose and this might be looked upon as the lower end of this tube to the Self with the 'light of God' shining through it. When that day arrives — if Jung is right — when the membranes have dissolved so that the unconscious is made conscious and the spiritually developed human being is eventually one with God, the Source, the Logos, the tube will have enlarged to an infinite extent. These thoughts seemed to me to make a lot of sense and to justify the inclusion of that tube in the diagram.

The Self seems to be the wiser higher part of us mentioned in the case discussed in Chapter 12 when it appeared to help the psychiatrist do his work of reintegrating the split personalities and, according to him, was never wrong. It appeared to be able to see the likely future as well as the present and past (because, in the diagram, it is 'one' with the source of all life and consciousness — the collective

unconscious). In the other case mentioned in Chapter 12, the pre-
diction of the long queue at the petrol station was probably just the
normal psychic functioning of George, who is not quite so limited as
regards time and space as the normal conscious daily self — the 'I.'
Chapter 2 on the near death experience also mentions one of a number of cases where the patient having the NDE was able to see visitors at considerable distances away entering the hospital and
separated by walls and doors from their body. As the level of consciousness moves down the diagram into the normally 'unconscious'
parts (they are not really unconscious, it is that the conscious self,
the I, is not normally aware of them) then the normal physical limitations of time and the immediately surrounding space are gradually
removed until, in the depths of the Collective Unconscious they disappear and the point of consciousness is the Eternal Now. This is the
mystical experience.

All around the permeable ovoid in the diagram is therefore what
Jung called the Collective Unconscious. This is also, in this diagram
and as mentioned earlier, the Infinite Plenum of all Possibilities of
the Maharishi. It is also the Region of Non-Locality of quantum
physics and the Eternal Now of the mystics, just mentioned. It is the
First Person of the Christian Trinity, the Father. (The Christ Within,
the Self, is shown on the edge of the ovoid to indicate that the Son
is inseparable from the Father. The Kahunas, the ancient priests of
Polynesia, called this the Aumakua, the Older, Parental, Utterly
Trustworthy Spirit.)

On those rare occasions when a normal human being has the mystical experience they describe how all is One, the source of the
Good, the True and the Beautiful. It is a state of the All, and they
appear to be in an infinite bliss, and experience vast joy and light,
and sometimes refer to it as God. This is surely hardly consciousness at all: the experiencer is overwhelmed by a vast 'information
overload' of goodness, truth and beauty. Perhaps (we are necessarily
speculating now) somehow we shall have evolved one day to the
point when we can be fully conscious in that state. I have met in my
lifetime only one person who was usually in that state. He was a
dear old Bishop in the Liberal Catholic Church. He told me that
when he lost it — which occurred only occasionally — he could get
back to it by uniting himself with the flames of a fire. I am told that
several spiritual teachers in India are in that state whenever they
wish it — but I have never discussed this subject with one of them.

Before we reach that elevated spiritual state the present moment of time and the immediate surroundings of space provide sufficient information input for most of us to deal with, while remaining fully conscious.

Beliefs of the Huna people

Here I must gratefully acknowledge ideas from another author, Max Freedom Long, who wrote *The Secret Science Behind Miracles,* about the ancient Huna religion of Polynesia, one or two aspects of which were briefly mentioned above. Long explains that he received from the 82-year-old Dr William Tufts Brigham, who was the Curator of the Bishop Library in Honolulu, a great deal of relevant data, the results of forty years of research. Some of these ideas I have included in the diagram. Huna went underground, Long explains, when the missionaries arrived in 1820. Huna means secret, and the priests were the Keepers of the Secret — the Kahunas. This religion had only one Rule, to live so that you did no harm to any living creature. It had what the missionaries thought was a most curious idea: that there were three 'selves' living in each human body: the Middle Self or ordinary daily self — the 'I' in the diagram — which they called the Uhane; the Lower Self, which I have called George and which they called the Unihipili; and the High Self or Self, in the diagram which they called the Aumakua. (It seemed clear that the Kahunas knew about the 'subconscious' many years before Freud.) They spoke of the 'grand company of the Aumakua' as they were not to be thought of as separate. I imagine that Assagioli put his Self on the edge of the ovoid to indicate, as I suggested, that it both shared in the unity of the Collective Unconscious but also gave life to all within the ovoid as the 'Father in Heaven,' to use the Christian terminology ('separated off,' as it were, in the form of the Christ Within).

Using 'George' as a model

Now let us consider in more detail some of the contents I have added to the Lower Unconscious, which I have been calling the Personal Unconscious. First we have the memory store, which I have shown diagrammatically like a computer store. Even memories consciously forgotten will still be there and in principle accessible. Then I have shown the Personal Unconscious Self, which I have been calling George: the part of us which the hypnotist addresses with his simple instructions, having first removed from the scene, so far as possible, the conscious, critical, analytical self. Although George can cause us (the 'I') a great deal of trouble, it should be said from the outset that if we learn to work with George and trust him/her we can greatly enrich and enlarge our life in many ways. He is, remember, our automatic pilot, working to our benefit down there in the unconscious in many ways while the conscious mind is engaged on quite other matters.

The Huna philosophy looked upon George (the Unihipili) as having the psychic faculties. I have given George in my scheme a number of vital jobs. One of them is to find the memories, when they are called for by the 'I,' and push them up into consciousness.

George is the part of us which suffers from the 'various phobias, obsessions, compulsive urges, paranoid delusions' to which Assagioli refers. George believes anything stated by an 'authority figure' and also is subjected to statements made by authority figures before the 'I,' the conscious rational critical analytical mind, is 'old enough' and has sufficient experience to be critical and analytical. George can also associate experiences which came together at a young age, and when s/he experiences one, expects the other, which can lead to considerable difficulties. As all these are going on in the personal unconscious mind they are not amenable to analysis by the conscious mind and sometimes need a psychiatrist to discover them and understand and correct them.

When we looked at this earlier it was pointed out that at birth a baby has experiences in its mind which 'do not make sense.' The parents teach it words and concepts, point to objects and name them and gradually the baby builds a representation in its mind of a 'world out there,' separate from itself, in terms of which its mental experiences (and remember that there is never anything else) 'make sense.' So gradually George assembles from the statements of these authority figures a set of what are called in the diagram 'images of truth' and he makes sure that the 'world out there' conforms. At school and college he elaborates these along the lines of our Western science-based culture given by more authority figures. By the time the critical rational mind has developed, the major parts of experience have been formed along these lines. As we shall see in more detail later, these 'thought forms' that we observe and mistake for a 'world out there' are, to a large degree, shared by others. This is not a philosophy based on solipsism.

These facts clearly apply not only to the external world but to religious and political beliefs in the same way. Few people often use their rational critical mind to analyse what views they have in order to see whether they are congruent with other views. Most people born in the West are Christians, real or nominal, or have ideas about life and death generally based on this religion. However, as science creates an ever better (more useful) model of the world, religious belief tends to wane. However, it rarely switches to the religious beliefs common in an Eastern country, for example. Much the same applies to political views in general. Most people appear to have political views similar to those of their parents although the ever-present television seems in time to weaken and possibly change them.

The chapter on hypnosis illustrated cogently how George can be simply told that your opinion (on art, in the example given) is different from what it has been for years and it will *immediately* change. George will devise convincing arguments for the new opinion. In the hypnotic trance state the hypnotist is the 'authority figure' and anything he says is accepted without question, just as was the case when we were much younger and had little conscious critical faculty.

Another of George's jobs is to dramatize our dreams while we are asleep; and he does this from material he can find in the memory store — and sometimes from material perhaps lying in the future so far as normal daily consciousness is concerned and which has floated in from the collective unconscious. All this material from dreams is sometimes of great help to a psychotherapist in giving clues to the cause of, and how to help in regard to, those psychological difficulties, neurotic and psychotic, which were mentioned above. George (the 'automatic pilot') also looks after the mechanics of doing anything we have learned to do, such as riding a bicycle or driving a car, so that the conscious mind can consider other matters needing its different abilities.

In the case of a psychic we must imagine an aperture in the membrane separating George from the personal unconscious so that he can push up additional material when called for, in the way now to be considered.

A successful sitting with a medium

Using this model of the mind we can remind ourselves what occurs when a client has a sitting with a medium. Assuming there to be rapport between the two we can imagine the permeable ovoid of the medium and that of the sitter coming into juxtaposition so that the medium is presented with the memory store of the sitter. The medium's George then can be imagined, having been trained to do this, to push up into the conscious mind of the medium, in the form of visual impressions and voices (some of which are necessarily symbolic), material related to deceased relatives and friends with whom the sitter wishes to get into touch. The medium's George is well used to doing this sort of thing because s/he does it with the medium's dreams every night. The medium will have no idea that this insertion into her conscious mind of visual and auditory material is going on, and considers that the hallucinatory visions and voices are from deceased communicators coming from the next world in their astral bodies to communicate with the sitter. Mediums have usually had their psychic experiences of this kind 'explained' to them by 'authority figures' — spiritualists who have the usual spiritualist philosophy. It is certainly cogent. Of course this explanation, which clearly applies to many normal sittings, is not always complete. As discussed earlier, the evidence for survival is extremely good and so one cannot always say for certain whence the material is originating. It may well be occasionally put into the medium's unconscious mind by a genuine communicator (from the vaguer parts of the diagram lower down) — but, I think, not so frequently as is often thought. As suggested much earlier, many perfectly 'satisfactory' seances are, I feel sure, held without any entities from 'the next world' coming into it at all. And that applies equally to cases where the medium is apparently normally conscious, where she is in trance with a 'control personality' apparently speaking, and in physical seances. All the evidence has been given in earlier chapters.

Co-personalities

The diagram shows in the Lower Unconscious various 'co-personalities' (Co-P.1, Co-P.2 , etc.) which can occasionally take over from the 'normal' personality under certain circumstances. This is all quite normal. The somewhat stuffy headmaster, for example, is a quite different personality from the one crawling on hands and knees on the carpet playing with his grandchildren. The peppery sergeant major barking out orders on the parade ground is a quite different person from the meek little man receiving orders from his wife in the supermarket. Each co-personality is well aware of the others and shares the same memory store. But co-personalities of a different kind can be constructed and the control personality of a medium is perhaps a case in point. The reader will remember when I described earlier (Chapter 7) how, in my view, control personalities were built up in at least one spiritualist development circle. All these normal co-personalities are quite different from the pathological split-off co-personalities formed in cases of childhood abuse and the like and which require skilled psychiatric treatment to produce a reintegrated 'normal' personality.

'Images of Truth'

There is a most important part of the diagram where I have sketched what I call 'images of truth.' These are representations of the models and ideas of our culture, normally given to the growing child by those first authority figures the parents, and later by other authority figures such as school teachers and college lecturers. There is also something I have called a 'printed circuit board' (p.c.b.) which is present at birth. From all these images of truth in this model George constructs the ego's experiences of the 'physical world.' He does this in just the same way that he constructs the 'next world' of dreaming sleep, experienced several times during each night. The 'printed circuit board' I have had to include in the model in effect because I find it impossible to explain in a reasonable way every experience we human beings have had from our birth. Someone (I have forgotten who) once said: 'There is no "absolute outside ourselves" truth,' and this is effectively built into the diagram in the form of the 'images of truth.' 'Outside ourselves' are only 'all possibilities.' It is important to understand clearly how our images of truth got into us. (The reader might like to refer to the description of the hypnosis demonstration by Dr Black and Dr Stafford Clark in Chapter 6.)

One of the quite complicated images of truth represented with the others is the physical body, which is experienced by the ego. I would guess that a great deal of this is in the 'printed circuit board.'

The changes in perception which can be readily brought about by a hypnotist are easy to appreciate. Having removed from the picture the rational critical mind, the hypnotist has merely to tell naïve believing George that something or other is different and, when back to 'normal consciousness,' the 'I' perceives it as different because George has made it different, having been told that it is so by another authority figure, the hypnotist — and this without the conscious critical eye of the ego to stop the hypnotist's 'suggestion' passing uncensored to George. In a similar way the normal (non-lucid) dream is accepted as 'reality.' The lucid dream is quite different because the experienced critical ego is also present. However, the ego in a first lucid dream is unable to bring about many things which greater experience of lucid dreaming will later allow.

Possibilities of removal of headaches and other inconveniences by simple suggestion become obviously possible, remembering that the physical body is created by George from another image of truth.

Hypnosis

A short review of hypnosis in the light of the model might be useful. The hypnotist can easily communicate directly with George, completely bypassing the conscious mind, and find out whether George considers that he is able to bring about some result at which the hypnotist is aiming. The questions put to George must not be complicated — bearing in mind what has already been said about George's intellectual limitations, and simple Yes's and No's are often perfectly sufficient. This can be done by setting up a code and, for example, asking George to move the right little finger if the answer to a question is Yes and the left little finger if the answer is No. The question may be: Are you able to bring about this situation ? If the answer is No then further questions can be used to find out why, so that the difficulty can be corrected. (This technique is used in Neurolinguistic Programming.) An experienced hypnotist can easily tell if the answers to his questions are genuinely coming from George by the slight trembling of the designated finger. If the movements are too definite and clear then an overobliging conscious mind is probably responsible. The conscious mind is quite out of the picture in a good and effective hypnotic state.

Many of these things can also sometimes be brought about by simple autosuggestion without the presence of another person using hypnosis. There are various techniques which will bring the body into a very deeply relaxed state and then the critical analytical mind is more or less in abeyance. The conscious mind can then give George certain simple instructions which may well be very effective when the ego is back in the 'normal' state of consciousness. A reminder of how to do this may be useful. Three components of such instructions are necessary. The first is a short instruction in very simple words (because George is not the bright and intellectual part of you) repeated clearly several times (and devised carefully before you start on the relaxation); the second is a clear imaginative picture of what things will be like when the change has been brought about; and the third is the feeling of great joy that you will have at that time. That strong feeling of joy is the emotional charge, the 'energy' that George needs to bring about the desired change. If you want to cure yourself of, say, smoking, then this set of instructions, always after the attainment of the deepest state of relaxation you can achieve, should be followed every day for some weeks. That initial short instruction to George should be along the lines of a gradual reduction in the number of cigarettes per day until the number has declined to zero. (The time needed obviously depends on various individual factors.) You will find that the more practice you have the better you will become at achieving deep relaxation and the deeper the relaxation the more effective the procedure. A regular practiser of meditation will find it particularly easy — in fact it is most unlikely that a regular meditator would be a smoker anyhow! That is all that is needed. If it sounds too simple try it and see! But it will all be to no avail if the subject does not really want to give up smoking before starting, but is merely being pressured by someone else worried about their health. This method of giving George instructions might be used with advantage by subjects suffering from insomnia or headaches. Successful cures were described earlier.

Near death experiences

Before considering another major subject which illustrates how this model can be used to 'explain' a major psychiatric problem (that of Multiple Personality Disorder — MPD) let us look at a smaller illustration which fits it well. The reader will perhaps remember that Popper and Eccles have a model which they put forward to explain how we know the physical world, suggesting that there is a world 'out there' — World Number 1 — which is the cause of the world we know (which, they agree, is nowhere but in our mind). The world we know when we are normally wide awake and conscious they call World Number 2 — our ordinary daily world. I have already argued that there is no World Number 1 but only World Number 2. The evidence? When a subject has a near death experience or NDE (see Chapter 2) then they seem to be floating above their physical body and observing the normal physical world. They 'see' the doctors and nurses working on their clinically dead (or near-clinically dead) physical body, they 'hear' what they are saying to each other, and often they tell us (afterwards) that they knew what the doctors and nurses were thinking before they actually said anything. It will be remembered that Dr Michael Sabom, an American cardiologist, listened to descriptions of all this from a number of NDE subjects, made a record of these descriptions, and then looked up the patients' medical files to see what actually occurred. He found that the patients' descriptions, sometimes including quite unusual activities not normally to be expected, were accurate. I suggest that what they were experiencing was the normal physical world (Number 2 in the Popper/Eccles scheme) and therefore that it was not surprising that it was the same. However, the conditions and limitations of the normal daily consciousness were not present and so some of the NDE subjects had also a wide-ranging clairvoyance, with the ability to observe people coming into the hospital and hear what they were saying too. George was able to push up this information also into the conscious mind in the altered state of the NDE. When I first read of Dr Sabom's research I felt it to be so important that it should be repeated by others. Sadly, Dr Sabom tells me, as yet it has not — so far as he knows. We must hope that repetitions in other hospitals will not be long delayed.

Multiple personality disorder

Now let us turn to MPD. We had an example in my own experience described in Chapter 12. We must imagine that extremely unpleasant experiences such as childhood abuse all go necessarily into the memory store but are too painful to face and are, as it were, walled off — suppressed, as the psychiatrist would say. In the case of MPD we must imagine that another co-personality having that set of memories is set up. That co-personality is not always known to the 'normal' daily personality but sometimes spontaneously takes over and temporarily replaces the normal personality. There are several excellent illustrative cases in the literature, which were mentioned. *The Three Faces of Eve,* one well-known book describes one famous case and another is told in Dr Morton Prince's book on the Sally Beauchamp case, *The Dissociation of a Personality.* In some of these cases different personalities have a quite separate memory store; in others, parts of the memory store may be shared. Using the model to 'understand' these cases we must imagine lines drawn connecting certain co-personalities with particular parts of the memory store and they are the parts used when that particular co-personality becomes the 'I.'

Prayer

We have not yet considered why I have the Middle Unconscious separated from the outer ovoid by a small space. We here go back to the Huna system. The Kahunas said that prayers were directed to the Aumakua (who had enormous 'paranormal' powers) but they had to go via the personal unconscious mind, George, the Unihipili. As one particular job George had to send on these prayers — via the spaces in the diagram at the sides of the Middle Unconscious so that they bypassed it. However, he would not do this if he was not completely free of guilt and so could look up trustingly and lovingly to the 'Father in Heaven.' So the Kahuna (the priest) would tell the petitioner, who perhaps wanted an instantaneous healing, that he must first free the Unihipili from all guilt feelings. For example, if there was for some reason bad blood between him and a neighbour then he must first put relations right between them and do whatever was needed to accomplish this. When all relationships had been set right and the Unihipili completely freed of guilt, then he would transmit the 'prayer clusters' to the Aumakua. (This reminds one of the Catholic practice of penance so that forgiveness might be obtained. There seem to be excellent psychological reasons for this practice.)

Karma and reincarnation

Many thoughtful people look upon life in the physical world as periods in a sort of school in which nascent souls have a series of lives on earth all linked together by karma, a law of cause and effect, through which lessons are learned — in which pain follows acts of selfishness and joy follows unselfishness. It seems to me that the happenings of life cannot be fully explained without those Eastern doctrines of karma and reincarnation.

In Christianity they appear to have been commonly misunderstood. Surely when Jesus said: 'God is not mocked, what a man sows he shall also reap,' He was referring to karma. When He was asked whether John the Baptist was Saul returned, He did not reply to the effect that human beings do not reincarnate; He took it as a sensible question. Does this not perhaps mean that there was at that time a general acceptance of reincarnation?

When evolution under this system has led to spiritual perfection then, to quote Jung, the unconscious will be made conscious (which Jung suggested may be the purpose of life). In this case the ovoid will have dissolved away, with all its subsidiary divisions, and there will be complete conscious unity with, I imagine (or rather, cannot imagine!), the source of all life and consciousness and the formerly apparently separate 'I' is no more. But we have here left science and are in the region of speculation.

Implications for personal life

There are certain clear corollaries of this model. The first is the possibility of changing oneself in any direction that is wished. It is merely to think regularly and imagine clearly the sort of person one would like to become. Then George will gradually build up a changing set of images of truth and life will necessarily change in appropriate ways. Many meditators regularly meditate on an ideal such as Christ or the Buddha, and the corresponding changes will take place in them. 'As a man thinks in his heart, so is he.'

Less exalted goals can also be approached by use of this model. George can be used to help. If one has a clear picture of some goal which it is desired to reach and it is held in the mind clearly and unwaveringly then George will help to reach it. Remember that George has the psychic powers. If you do this you will find such things occurring as wandering into a bookshop, walking over 'at random' to a shelf, and finding there an excellent book on just what you needed to know or do next! Most people have goals which waver and vary every day and have futures as unsatisfactory as one might expect. But if a goal is held clearly and unwaveringly then who knows what is possible! Many books on achieving success in life have been written from all sorts of standpoints — religious or psychological. Using this model at least makes clear the mechanism and the whole business becomes more straightforward.

George can help to his maximum ability only if he is consistently trusted. (This is quite difficult to do in the presence of the rational intelligent conscious mind!) I did some experiments some years ago concerning finding car parking spaces. When driving around a crowded car park it is obviously impossible to find a space by the use of the intellect. So one is thrown back on using psychism — George. George is ready to help if s/he knows clearly what to do and the conscious mind does not interfere. It is necessary to let George do the steering without the use of one's normal reason and logic. In other words, do not go where reason says but just let your 'automatic pilot' decide. I have been astonished at the results of doing this — but you will find it very difficult to *prove* that success was not just coincidence! (Women seem to be better, in my experience, at finding car park spaces than men. But I have no statistics to prove that statement!)

There are four things to remember if you wish George to take some action for you. The first is to allow the body to become very relaxed as this makes the conscious mind very relaxed too. The second is to give the instruction in the form of a very short and clear sentence. The third is to *imagine* clearly doing what is desired successfully. The fourth — this gives him the necessary drive or 'energy' actually to do all this — the fourth is to *feel* (emotion) the joy and delight you will have when it begins to occur successfully. It is a good idea to repeat this procedure several times, perhaps on successive days. Then you can just forget it — leave it to George. Trust him! I assure you that this really does work. George can even 'alter the physical world' for you (see almost any hypnosis demonstration) — but that is another story.

George has been compared to a heat-seeking missile — he steers us towards our goals, but only when they are clear and consistent, perhaps as a result of meditating regularly on them, and he has been given the necessary energy.

The deeper one goes down into the model the more distant one becomes from the normal time and space of the physical world, which are part of the 'experience' produced by George. Passing through the permeable membrane into the Collective Unconscious' puts one into the mystical experience where time and space cease to exist and one is in the Eternal Now. Some relevant material is to be found in Chapter 10 concerning Eileen Garrett and her control 'personalities.' A temporary dissolution of the ovoid is one way of looking at the mystical experience. There all is one. This is certainly what I consider one of the darker regions of the diagram

I hope that this model of a human being, which has gestated for many years in my mind, will be clear and can be used to 'understand' many of the experiences and phenomena described earlier. The more experience I had of the paranormal and the more psychics and mystics I talked to (only a few of the latter!) the clearer and firmer it became. Of late years I have found thinking along the lines of the model to be of great value.

I am aware that changing one's fundamental view of one's self is asking rather a lot of most of us! We can only do our best to understand this mysterious complicated fascinating world in which we find ourselves! I think that part of our job here is to try to understand why; to try to solve the numerous problems that surround us in life. A model such as that briefly sketched might be a help to stimulate the intuition. For most of us it is probably all we have. Eventually we shall transcend it. Bon voyage!

Endnotes

1. Clearly it is a gross over-simplification to think that a psychic, when experiencing an OBE, has moved, in a rather literal way, away from the physical body and is not using the brain. We shall of course be considering this important matter on later occasions.

2. The shaman informed me afterwards that the temple with the WOM was in the shamanic Upper World and not in the Lower World. The Middle and Upper Worlds are entered only via the Lower World.

3. As an aside may I mention that little girl is now a graduate with a first-class honours degree and is doing a Ph.D. I tried to ask her fairly recently — not having seen her since that occasion when she paranormally bent my spoon — whether she could still do it. She refused even to discuss it with me. She is surely trying to avoid her cognitive dissonance by suppressing it. I strongly suspect that she can no longer do it because of the considerable conditioning she has now had along the lines of 'normal science,' in which it is impossible. This conditioning we call 'education.'

4. The only member of that audience who knew how I had produced that levitation was my friend Professor Eric Laithwaite, who was also researching magnetic levitation. Sadly he died in 1998.

5. I have gathered that all physicists do not have exactly the same interpretation of quantum mechanics. I could hardly believe it when I discovered that Niels Bohr was a rabid realist!

6. Professor of Physiology at the Sorbonne and later Nobel Laureate, who did valuable investigation of the physical phenomena of the Italian medium Eusapia Palladino.

7. Readers who would like all the details of the safeguards will find them in the SPR Proceedings paper. So far as we were able to ensure it, the films were untouched by anyone but Kodak and ourselves.

8. The controversy was partly because Raymond 'communicated' that deceased comrades were drinking whisky and smoking cigars in his 'afterlife.' Many people thought that this was ridiculous: I suppose they thought that dead soldiers should have been playing harps and singing hymns. However, in a thought world — if that is a helpful way to look at it — one can do whatever one wishes. We shall have more to say on this later.

9. The same applies, as I discovered (and describe in Chapter 3) to Matthew Manning and Ingo Swann.

10. This has often surprised me too. So few subjects are ever asked by investigators what exactly they are doing with their minds. The resulting papers are full of statistics, completely omitting the really interesting part — how the subjects themselves consider successful results are obtained.

11. I am sure that I no more understand this than does the reader: the only way to understand ASCs is to experience them for oneself! I have never met another psychic who talked in these terms — or indeed was able to do so. The 'eternal now' is usually referred to only by mystics.

12. It is interesting that the same allusion turned up in material which appeared to have Myers again associated with it in the Scole phenomena (see Chapter 8).

13. He did, however, alter the very brief chapter on MPD in his book as a result of the information he got from the case. He also suggested — as he was himself somewhat at a loss — that the Society for Psychical Research might be consulted, and affirmed that this body was 'scientific.'

14. The Spiritualists, it will be remembered from Chapter 7, consider such a control personality to be someone who died and is now in the next world. Evidence for their previous existence is usually impossible to discover.

15. He gave me a copy of the tape for the record and for safe keeping, which I have extensively used in preparing this account.

16. I recently read that a number of other hypnotists have also had success with this disease.

17. I have asked several audiences of doctors what their estimate of that figure is and they usually agree that 70 per cent is not far wrong.

18. When I attended, she was surrounded by other patients making all sorts of 'therapeutic movements' on her carpet: some of them with spinal problems were arching their backs like cats stretching, to their great benefit. When the contortions ceased she merely put her hands near again and they restarted. No one ever seemed to be harmed by what occurred and none of it was the result of their own volition. The other patients confirmed this to me. We are clearly in deep water.

19. See Daniel P. Wirth, 'Unorthodox Healing: The Effect of Noncontact Therapeutic Touch on the Healing Rate of Full Thickness Dermal Wounds,' *Proceedings of the Parapsychological Assoc. 32nd Annual Convention,* San Diego August 1989, pp.251–68.

20. As an aside I should mention that I was told of an experiment in which all the wiring between the components was surreptitiously removed from the inside of the box — but the practitioner was not informed. He noticed no problems when he next used the box. Whether or not this story is apocryphal I do not know, but certainly this would be exactly the result I should have expected. What mattered was his belief in the box.

21. I have been informed of a practice of painting a mark on a deceased grandparent and noting an identical mark on new grandchildren. My informant believed that it was quite widely evidenced. I have not myself had experience of that.

22. There is also a Sanskrit word *kama,* pronounced to rhyme with car-ma. I was once given a short lesson on Sanskrit pronunciation by a Hindu Ph.D. student of mine.

23. The interested reader is referred to the books of Stanislav Grof, amongst which I found *The Adventure of Self-Discovery* particularly relevant. See Reading List.

24 One well-known book has a table giving the meanings of the colours of the aura and this would clearly be nonsense if they did not appear the same to all psychics.

25. See Reading List for Ralph Strauch's *The Reality Illusion.*

Reading List

My grateful acknowledgments for permission to quote from the following sources: to Lisette Coly, Parapsychological Foundation, New York, for material from E.J. Garrett, *My Life as a Search for the Meaning of Mediumship*, Rider, 1939 (see Chapter 10), and also from I. Progoff, *The Image of an Oracle*, Helix/Garrett Publications, 1964 (see Chapter 10). For material from Gladys Osborne Leonard, *My Life in Two Worlds*, Cassell & Co. 1931 (see Chapter 9), every attempt has been made to find the copyright holder, and this and any other omissions will be corrected where possible in future editions.

Chapter 1

Kuhn, T.S. *The Structure of Scientific Revolutions*, Univ. of Chicago Press, 1962.
Ellison, Arthur J. *The Reality of the Paranormal*, Harrap, London; Dodd, Meade, New York 1988.

Chapter 2

Fenwick P. and E. *The Truth and the Light*, Hodder Headline, 1995.
Moody, R.A. Jnr. *Life after Life*, Bantam/Mockingbird, 1975.
—, *Reflections on Life after Life*, Bantam/Mockingbird, 1977.
Ring, K. *Life at Death*, Coward, McCann & Geoghegan, NY 1980.
—, *Heading Towards Omega*, Quill/William Morrow, NY 1984.
Grey, M. *Return from Death*, an exploration of the near death experience, Arkana/Routledge & Kegan Paul, 1985.
Sabom, M. *Light & Death*, Zondervan/Harper Collins, 1998.

Chapter 3

Muldoon S.J. & Carrington, H. *The Projection of the Astral Body*, Rider, 1929; & later editions.
Jinarajadasa C. *First Principles of Theosophy*, Theosophical Publishing House, 1921; & later editions.
Popper K.R. & Eccles J.C. *The Self and Its Brain*, Springer Verlag 1977; & later editions.
Edmunds, S. *Hypnotism and the Supernormal*, Aquarian Press, 1961.
Monroe, R. *Journeys Out of the Body*, Doubleday, 1971.
Schnabel, J. *Remote Viewers: the secret history of America's psychic spies*, Bantam Doubleday Dell, 1997.
Morehouse, D. *Psychic Warrior*, Michael Joseph, 1996.

Chapter 4

Dunne, J.W. *An Experiment with Time*, Macmillan, NY 1927.
Assagioli, R. *Psychosynthesis*, Turnstone Press, 1965.

Fontana, D. *Dreamlife. Understanding and using your dreams*, Element, 1990.

LaBerge, S. *Lucid Dreaming*, J.P. Tarcher, 1985.

LaBerge, S. & Rheingold, H. *Exploring the World of Lucid Dreaming*, Ballantine/ Random House, 1990.

Fenwick, P. & E. *The Hidden Door, understanding and controlling your dreams*, Hodder Headline, 1998.

Chapter 5

Leaning, F.E. *An Introductory Study of Hypnagogic Phenomena*, Proc. SPR, Vol. XXXV, Part XCIV, May, 1925, Society for Psychical Research, London.

Nicholson, S. (ed.) *Shamanism*, Theosophical Publishing House, 1987.

Walsh, R. *Spirit of Shamanism*, J.P. Tarcher 1990.

Harner, M. *The Way of the Sharman*, Harper, 1980; & later editions.

Chapter 6

Waxman, D. *Hypnosis: a guide for patients and practitioners*, George Allen and Unwin, 1981.

Heap, M. & Dryden, W. *Hypnotherapy: a handbook*, Open University Press, 1991.

Elman, D. *Hypnotherapy, Westwood Publishing*, 1983. (Originally: *Findings in Hypnosis*, 1964).

Hartland, J. *Medical and Dental Hypnosis*, Tindall, 1989.

Watkins, J. *Hypnotherapeutive Techniques*, Vols. 1 & 2, Irvington Publishers, NY 1987.

Erickson, Milton, & Rossi, Ernest *Hypnotherapy: an exploratory casebook*, Irvington Publishers, NY 1979.

Chapter 7

Saltmarsh, H.F. *Evidence of Personal Survival from cross correspondences*, Bell & Sons, 1938.

Cummins, G. *Swan on a Black Sea*, Routledge & Kegan Paul, 1965.

Ellison, A.J. *The Reality of the Paranormal* (see Chapter 1 above).

Chapter 8

Keen, M., Ellison, A.J. & Fontana, D. *The Scole Report*, Proc. SPR, Vol.58, Part 220, Nov. 1999.

Soal, S.G. *A Report on Some Communications Received Through Mrs Blanche Cooper*, Proc. SPR, Vol. XXXV, Part XCVI, Dec. 1925.

Owen, I. *Conjuring Up Philip, an adventure in psychokinesis*, Fitzhenry and Whiteside, 1976.

Crawford, W.J. *The Reality of Psychic Phenomena, raps, levitations, etc.*, Watkins, 1916.

—, *Experiments in Psychical Science, levitation, 'contact' and the 'direct voice,'* Watkins, 1919.

Chapter 9

Leonard, G.O. *My Life in Two Worlds*, Cassell, 1931.
Neech, W.F. *Death is Her Life*, Spiritualist Press, 1957 (Lilian Bailey's biography).
Roberts, E. *Living in Two Worlds*, Regency Press, 1984.
Twigg, E. with Brod, R. H. *Ena Twigg, medium*, Star/W.H.Allen, 1974.
Burton, J. *Heyday of a Wizard: Daniel Home the medium*, Harrap, 1948.
Inglis, B. *Natural and Supernatural, a history of the paranormal*, Hodder & Stoughton, 1977.

Chapter 10

Garrett, E.J, *My Life as a Search for the Meaning of Mediumship*, Rider, 1939.
Progoff, I. *The Image of an Oracle*, Helix/Garrett Publications, 1964.

Chapter 11

Lodge, O. *Raymond, or Life and Death*, Methuen, 1916 & later editions.
Beard, P. *Survival of Death, for and against*, Hodder & Stoughton, 1966.
An interesting book for additional reading:
Gibbes, E.B. *The Road to Immortality*, being a description of the After-life purporting to be communicated by the late F.W.H. Myers through Geraldine Cummins, with evidence of the survival of human personality, Ivor Nicholson & Watson, 1932.
For readers who would like to read the original papers from which many of the quotations or items paraphrased in this chapter have been taken, most will be found in Proceedings of the SPR Vols. 21, 38 and 43.

Chapter 12

Prince, Morton, *The Dissociation of a Personality, the hunt for the real Miss Beauchamp*, Oxford University Press, 1978. Originally Longmans Green, 1905.
Thigpen, C.H. & Clecky, H.M. *The Three Faces of Eve*, Secker & Warburg, 1957.

Chapter 13

Barbanell, M. *Harry Edwards and His Healing*, Spiritualist Press, 1953.
Wirth, D.P. 'Unorthodox Healing: the Effect of Noncontact Therapeutic Touch on the Healing Rate of Full Thickness Dermal Wounds,' Research in Parapsychology 1989, Henkel L.A. & Palmer J. (eds.) Scarecrow Press 1990.
Edmunds, H. Tudor (ed.) *Psychism and the Unconscious Mind*, Theosophical Publishing House, 1968.

Chapter 14

Stevenson, I. *Children Who Remember Previous Lives: a question of reincarnation*, University Press of Virginia, 1987.
Grof, Stanislav, *The Adventure of Self-Discovery*, State University of New York Press, 1988.

Chapter 15

Rhine, J.B. *Extra-sensory Perception*, Faber & Faber, 1935.
Jahn, R.G. & Dunne, B.J. *Margins of Reality, the role of consciousness in the physical world*, Harcourt Brace Jovanovich, 1987.
A reliable book strongly recommended to the scientific reader is:
Radin, D.I. *The Conscious Universe*, the scientific truth of psychic phenomena, HarperEdge, 1997.

Chapter 17

Goswami, A. et al. *The Self-Aware Universe: how consciousness creates the material world*, Simon & Schuster, 1993.
Lilly, J.C. *The Center of the Cyclone, an autobiography of inner space*, Bantam, 1972 & later editions.
Strauch, R. *The Reality Illusion, how we create the world we experience*, Theosophical Publishing House, 1983.
Pearce, J.C. *The Crack in the Cosmic Egg: challenging constructs of mind and reality*, Lyrebird Press, 1973.

Chapter 18

Assagioli, R. *Psychosynthesis* (see Chapter 4 above).
Long, M.F. *The Secret Science Behind Miracles*, DeVorss, 1948; & later editions.
Sabom, M. *Recollections of Death, a medical investigation*, Corgi/Transworld, 1982.

Further reliable books written by non-scientists

Haynes, R. *The Hidden Springs: an enquiry into extra-sensory perception*, Hollis & Carter, 1961.
Heywood, R. *The Sixth Sense: an inquiry into extra-sensory perception*, Chatto & Windus, 1959.

A valuable (but difficult) book, one of several by a scientist/mathematician who had first-hand experience from his earliest years of all states ranging from the out-of-body experience to complete mystical union:
Whiteman, J.H.M. *The Mystical Life*, Faber & Faber, 1961.

Index

Sir George Trevelyan
and the new spiritual awakening

Frances Farrer

The first biography of Sir George Trevelyan,
the grandfather of the movement for
spiritual regeneration in Britain.

Sir George Trevelyan espoused alternative values long before the phrase became as popular as it is today. After hearing a lecture by a pupil of Rudolf Steiner, Trevelyan declared 'The agnosticism of thirty-six years faded like morning mist. The spiritual world-view was clear to me in its glory and wonder.'

During his lifetime he explored beliefs in angels, the calming effects of crystals and the power of ley lines, alongside organic farming and communal living. In 1971 he set up the Wrekin Trust to promote spiritual education and knowledge, and in 1982 he was awarded the Right Livelihood award (the 'alternative Nobel Prize') for his contribution towards healing the planet.

He inspired and encouraged the emerging synthesis between science and spirituality, putting his faith for the future of society in the transforming power of spiritual awakening. He taught extensively, inspiring communities, universities and spiritual groups worldwide. He died in the year 1996 at the age of ninety.

Frances Farrer is a writer, journalist and broadcaster. She has written for most national broadsheets and has been published widely on educational subjects as well as on children's fiction.

Floris Books

Thinking Beyond the Brain

a wider science of consciousness

Edited by David Lorimer

... a very exciting book. Breathe
... deserves both close and wide attention. Universalist
... essential reading. Christian Parapsychologist

Consciousness is the cutting-edge topic in scientific circles, its precise nature holding huge implications for the future of science itself.

With so many recent advances in brain studies, questions of mind and consciousness have become of critical importance for scientists and theorists alike. Are we 'nothing but a pack of neurons' that will reveal their secrets in the laboratory? Or do our conscious mind and self-awareness stem from some dimension beyond material investigation? How, too, are we to account for 'parapsychological' phenomena in which consciousness seems to defy space and time boundaries?

These recent contributions to the debate, selected from the annual 'Beyond the Brain' conferences, show that it is time for radical rethink of our theories and methods in investigating phenomena of the human mind.

Contributors include: Willis Harman, Peter Fenwick, Brian Josephson, Kenneth Ring, David Fontana, Erlendur Haraldsson, John Beloff, Michael Grosso, Charles Tart, Stanislav Grof, Andrew Powell, Marilyn Schlitz, Roger Woolger, Mark Woodhouse, Ravi Ravindra, Anne Baring.

David Lorimer is the former director of the Scientific and Medical Network, an international group of academics and professionals dedicated to an open-minded exploration of boundaries in science.

Floris Books

The Spirit of Science

from experiment to experience

Edited by David Lorimer

The huge technical successes of modern science have obscured a deeper understanding of its place in human knowledge and in our value systems. For many, science belongs in a separate 'compartment' from normal human experience, confined to the world of the laboratory. This can give rise to a dark, impersonal and inhuman image of science.

In this collection, distinguished scientists and thinkers from a wide range of disciplines examine the relationship of scientific knowledge and practice to the wider dimension of human life and awareness. For some this appears as a dialogue between science and spirituality, for others an investigation into consciousness and the intelligent heart of the cosmos. Whether in physics, cosmology or biology, these essays explore the very nature of knowledge itself and the continuing role of human creativity, emphasising the need for crossing disciplinary boundaries in our search for understanding.

The contributions are based on papers given over twenty years at the annual *Mystics and Scientists* conferences in England, and this collection brings together some of the most remarkable and far-seeing thinkers of our time.

David Lorimer is the former director of the Scientific and Medical Network, an international group of academics and professionals dedicated to an open-minded exploration of boundaries in science.

Floris Books